DREAM ENCOUNTERS

Seeing Your Destiny from God's Perspective

Barbie L. Breathitt

Breath of the Spirit Ministries, Inc.
P.O. Box 820653
North Richland Hills, Texas 76182–0653
www.BarbieBreathitt.com
www.BarbieBreathittEnterprises.com
www.MyOnar.com

Barbie Breathitt Enterprises, LLC
P.O. Box 822044
North Richland Hills, Texas 76182–2044

ISBN:978-1-60383-256

Published by:
Barbie Breathitt Enterprises, LLC.
P. O. Box 822044
North Richland Hills, Texas 76182-2044
www.BarbieBreathittEnterprises.com

Printed in the United States of America and the United Kingdom

Endorsements

"I am impressed with the revelation God has imparted to Barbie Breathitt to unlock our dreams."

Sid Roth
Host, It's Supernatural! Television
www.SidRoth.org

I met Barbie a number of years ago and was very impressed by her contagious passion for the Lord and her pure, steadfast, immoveable faith. She regularly encounters God in dreams and is a seasoned teacher on the subject. *Dream Encounters, Seeing Your Destiny from God's Perspective* is a must read. It is well written and Barbie makes it all seem so ... easy. It makes me want to go dream right now!

Patricia King
President, XPmedia.com

Barbie Breathitt has done a phenomenal job of communicating God's heart for understanding dreams, visions, and supernatural experiences. Her book, *Dream Encounters, Seeing Your Destiny from God's Perspective*, has been needed for decades. It is the best and most accurate book I have read about dreams. This book will help people understand more clearly how God speaks and help them use it to expand the Kingdom through dream outreach events.

Doug Addison
InLight Connection
www.dougaddison.com

I have observed Barbie in many aspects of life, and can attest to you it is through her spiritual maturity of obeying God, by her submitting to her accountability, through her vigilant study, and demonstrated ministry application, she offers the Family of God a "must have" dream ministry reference book. Now is the time to acquire this necessary ministry. We must embrace the sound biblically–based foundation that Barbie so carefully– through many years of "in–the–trenches" stewardship of her life's calling– offers to so many people, concentrated between the covers of this dream ministry handbook. If you want to understand the cutting edge, dream ministry tools of revelation knowledge for the Kingdom, you could not find a better source of a reference manual that is foundationally sound as a "how–to" textbook on dream ministry. In context with God's plan and will, it is with great respect and honor I recommend to you this new book, ***Dream Encounters– Seeing Your Destiny from God's Perspective***, by Barbie Breathitt.

Always a Voice for God,
John Mark & Sandy Pool,
Founders–Prophetic Ministries
Author–"Path of A Prophet–Understanding the Journey"
Word to the World Ministries
www.w2wmin.org

"A sign of the Last Days is that dreams and visions will be restored as a heavenly communications language to mankind as the Holy Spirit is poured out on all flesh. In this period of time, not only will dreams abound, but the Spirit of wisdom, and revelation will be profoundly released. Barbie Breathitt rests under such an anointing. She is one of the top revelatory interpreters of our day. I have benefited greatly from reading "***Dream Encounters,***" and so will you!"

James W. Goll
Encounters Network
Author of The Seer, The Lost Art of Intercession,
The Coming Israel Awakening, and many more.

"A Christ-centered, mature, yet exciting and captivating approach to understanding the world of dreams is now here. Barbie Breathitt has provided the believer with accurate and safe insights to help you understand how God speaks to you in the night and additionally what He is specifically saying to you."
Don Nori, Sr.
Founder/CEO, Destiny Image Media Engineers
Destinyimage.com
donnorisr.com
dfn@destinyimage.com

4

Foreword

Since I was a child, I knew I could "know things" that were not readily understandable. I knew that there was a realm of seeing that was available to me that was not concrete. I knew that there was a world dimension beyond my daily routine of life. Because of having godly influences in my life, I came to embrace the God of the creation around me, the One who came to us as Man in the form of Messiah, the One who left His Spirit to make my spirit alive so I could perceive the layers of revelatory knowledge that make life filled with abundance. All I had to do was to learn how to communicate with the One who knit me together in my mother's womb. When I could not "get it" from a book, an instructor, the hurts of life, the trauma of man, or my or others' experiences, I would dream. If I meditated on what was being communicated deep within me, I could understand why I did things, why things happened, or even what was going to happen. *Then He said, "Hear now My words: if there is a prophet among you, I, the* LORD, *make Myself known to him in a vision; I speak to him in a dream"* (Numbers 12:6 NKJV).

We all dream. Even if a person is an island unto himself, he or she dreams. But to know the One who is allowing you to dream causes your dream to create significance in your existence. One of the primary ways that God has always used to communicate with His people is through dreams and visions, yet they are often misunderstood, dismissed, or ignored. We find in the Bible over 50 references for messages being sent by God through dreams and visions to both the righteous and the unrighteous alike. The Lord used dreams and visions to guide, to warn, to direct, to help—to communicate His heart. God has not stopped communicating to humanity by these means. There have been many books written from many perspectives on the dream world, but this book, *Dream Encounters, Seeing Your Destiny from God's Perspective,* by Barbie Breathitt, exceeds them all.

Miss Breathitt is a person who seeks to present herself as the one God made her to portray. She is unique and lovely. She carries a glow of righteousness in her eyes. When I first met Barbie, I enjoyed the level of communication that she presented. She had tapped into a dimension of

5

revelation that needed to be heard. She would come to gatherings and bring individuals that she had trained to assist others to better understand what God was attempting to communicate to them. Not only was she a wonderful minister of supernatural truth, but she had disciplined herself to learn a different language—not Spanish, Latin, German, Finnish, or Swahili, but a language beyond those spoken on earth. She had allowed the Spirit of God to teach her His dream language. Therefore, she was no longer held captive to communicate by using the linguistic earth forms, but she had tapped into Heaven's realm. She was not "spooky," but very practical in assisting individuals to better understand their destiny. Most importantly, she carried the fragrance of God in a dark world and brought truth and light to individual searching souls.

Dreams, which are formed in the subconscious mind of a man or woman, based on images and symbols which are unique to that individual are a mirror reflection of what has been imprinted on our soul. The mind's eye is always searching to better understand what we were destined to become. Through the world of dream revelation, we are allowed to see into a dimension depending on our own background, experience, and current life circumstances. Dreams can communicate to us truth—the needed information that our conscious mind could not understand during our waking hours.

A dream is a release of revelation (whether natural or spiritual) that comes at a time when your body is at peace and you are settled. Sometimes this is the only way God can communicate with us because our soul is quiet enough for Him to speak deeply into our spirit man. A dream is like a snapshot of something you are able to relate to in picture form. Ecclesiastes 5:3 tells us that a dream comes when there are many cares. They can either be a subconscious response to the circumstances of our lives, or the Holy Spirit communicating to us.

In my book, *When God Speaks*, I wrote the following: "In the ancient eastern world dreams were treated as reality. Israel was forbidden to use many of the same type of divining practices as Egypt and other neighboring countries and peoples. However, God would visit them in the night to communicate His will and way to them. Dreams were the world of the divine or the demonic. They often revealed the future. Dreams could be filled with revelation that would cause the dreamer to make the right decision for his/her future. For instance, I once had a dream because I was in prayer over a trip to Israel. Bobbye Byerly and I were going to be leading prayer for a meeting that would reconcile Arab Christian leaders and Messianic leaders. Dr. C. Peter Wagner was going to be facilitating this meeting. There was much warfare surrounding this meeting. I became very anxious and called Bobbye and told her we should pray and fast for three days before going. Bobbye agreed immediately. In the second day of the fast I fell asleep and had the following dream:

Barbara Wentroble, a well-known prophetess, was in the dream and asked me a question. 'So, you are going to Israel. There are two ways. Which way are you taking?' I told her the way we were going. In the dream it was as if I was showing her a map and we were wandering through the Arab desert to get to Israel. She then said, 'You may go that way, but if you do, you will experience much warfare. There is a better way for you to take.' I said, 'Oh, what is that way?' She replied, 'Go straight to Israel and meet with the leadership you know. Then, have your meeting with everyone else.' I woke up and knew I had revelation that God had spoken to me to give me direction for Dr. Wagner as he proceeded in pulling together this meeting. I encouraged him to first have a meeting with the leaders of Israel that we knew. Then we could have the overall meeting and reconciliation time. This proved to be straight revelation from God and really affected the overall outcome of our mission."

I have not read a book that is as comprehensive, enlightening, and practical as *Dream Encounters*. Both Old Testament and New Testament covenants are filled with dreams that direct God's plan of fulfillment for His people. There are *simple message dreams* like the ones Joseph had in Matthew 1–2 which caused him to understand what was happening with Mary and then Herod. There was really no need for interpretation; the dreams interpreted themselves. There are *simple symbolic dreams*. These are dreams filled with symbols but where the symbolism is clear enough that the dreamer and others can understand it without any complicated interpretation. For instance, when Joseph had his dream in Genesis 37, he fully understood it and so did his brothers (to the point that they wanted to kill him!) even though it had symbols of the sun, moon, and stars. Then there are *complex symbolic dreams*. This third type of dream needs interpretative skill from someone who has unusual ability in the gift of interpretation or someone who knows how to seek God to find revelation. We find this in the life of Joseph in prison as well as when he interprets Pharaoh's dream. In Daniel 2 and 4, we find good examples of this type of dream. In Daniel 8, we see a dream where Daniel actually had to seek divine interpretation.

The way Barbie analyzes and presents God's revelatory communication patterns, symbols, and expressions will help anyone better understand the One who loves them, made them, and longs to communicate to them for His pleasure and their fulfillment.

This book, *Dream Encounters, Seeing Your Destiny from God's Perspective,* will become a timeless piece and treasure to help generations better communicate with a God who knows and has the best in mind for the earth. You will not only read this book, but use this book as a nightstand companion. This is a must for all libraries. I would suggest you have two copies—one to be used in your study, and a second copy ready when your first one eventually falls apart from use. Or, go ahead and buy three so that when you are at a dinner party, club meeting, or business engagement and one of your associates or acquaintants says, "I had this dream last night," you can say, "I have a book that can help you."

History will reveal that *Dream Encounters* led many to come to the saving grace of God who loved them enough to communicate with them when they rested their weary head from life's trials.

Dr. Chuck D. Pierce
President, Global Spheres, Inc.
President, Glory of Zion International
Watchman, Global Harvest Ministries

DEDICATION

To my loving father, Douglas H. Breathitt
March 2, 1930– August 17, 1999

He was a man of impeccable moral character and godly wisdom. He was a beloved husband, father, and honest attorney who spent his life helping his family and working for the betterment of his friends and those who benefited from his spirit of counsel.

And to the next generation of dreamers who desperately seek to fulfill their own dreams as their unique destiny is written in the chronicles of time.

Table of Contents

ACKNOWLEDGEMENTS

Dream Encounters, Seeing Your Destiny from God's Perspective is a book that could not stay locked inside for much longer. The writing of this work required many hours of painstaking detail work and labor. But it has been a labor of love. And to all those who made it possible for this labor to come forth and be birthed I give a heartfelt thank-you.

The first group of people who come to mind are the Partners of Breath of the Spirit. Without their constant prayers and encouragement my ability to write this book may have been completely thwarted.

The next group of people I honor are the mentors and beloved pastors who have poured words of encouragement into my life. Their constant expectation of something great being wrought in my life gave me the inspiration to continue undaunted in the face of constant hindrances and obstacles. I wish to mention by name just a few: Dr. Chuck Pierce, who on many occasions has spoken into my life; Patricia King who encouraged me at a crucial time in my life to step up to the calling God has placed on my life, and my own Pastor, Dr. Jack Deere and his lovely wife Leesa of Wellspring Church, who have been close friends, a constant bulwark, honest censurers and fervent supporters of my endeavors.

Amanda Pitt spent countless hours going over these pages of script with a fine tooth, culling, cutting, and adding an amazing touch of class to make this presentable to the public.

Linda Madden endeavors to keep me looking presentable from a chair in her salon in Fort Worth, Texas. Only she knows the true color of my hair.

Without a doubt, my greatest support comes from my family who has stood by me through thick and thin. They have stood beside me and cheered me on during times of both triumph and trial. They endured the many hours of separation as I studied and prepared this manuscript and only complained a little.

Finally, my greatest thanks are to my God who has never failed me. He continues to bring me to the place of my destiny. I am not perfect but my God who sees all and knows all has chosen me to carry his banner of love. His gift to me is an understanding of dreams and the ability to both interpret and to encourage others to gain this gift.

It is my desire to spread this understanding to as many people as possible so that the Kingdom of God will both prosper and expand throughout the world, and to bring as many people to the saving knowledge of Jesus as is ordained by God.

INTRODUCTION

The society in which we live is hectic, overworked, overindulged, and exceedingly navel-centric. We are so active and eager for the next experience that we have to read and write articles telling our generation the benefits of sleep. This book calls to all who are weary and tired from the constant ambush on our limited time to stop the rush and relax long enough to sleep, dream, and hear from God.

Of all the many activities our society is called to surrender to, dreams are too far toward the bottom. Perhaps, if we paused long enough to discover the continuous flow of inspiration found during the night hours, we could arise from our slumber better prepared to meet the challenges of our frantic days. *Dream Encounters* invites the reader to delve into the untapped mysteries of our sleeping road map.

People living in the East have long paid close attention to their night parables. They know how to interpret what is played on their mind's eye while they sleep. The West however, is so lost to the idea of the importance of dreams that many of us deny we even dream at all. Rest assured, if you did not dream you would lose your mind. Sleep and dreaming are so vitally important, not only to our mental health, but also to our spiritual life, that we must engage with these locked messages until we find the key to open their door of destiny.

In these few pages you will find the keys to unlock the life changing visions of our REM sleep. You will discover how perfectly sane the inane images are that we experience during the night while slumbering on our cushy pillows, if only interpreted through the correct viewfinder. In your hands lies the "Rosetta Stone" to the dream world of our day. Uniquely inspired, and written to convince the greatest skeptics and educate the most ardent believer, *Dream Encounters* will introduce you to the mysterious world of dreams and dream interpretation. You will be better equipped to discover the meaning hidden in your own dreams and those with whom you come in contact during your busy rampaged life.

Steven A. Breathitt

Chapter One
The Mysterious Benefits and Power of Sleep

What is the purpose of a dream? How does God use dreams in our lives? What dreams should we pay attention to and what dreams should we ignore? How much influence should they possess in our lives? Is it safe to ignore them and how safe is it to act on them? The premise of this book is to explain the depths to which the Lord uses dreams to affect our lives. He uses dreams to wake us up, to give us prophetic insight, and to spur us forward toward our dreams and destiny so that we don't lose sight of them.

In a society where success often looks like busyness and hurried insanity, God sometimes talks to us the only way he can ... when we are asleep. That is when we are quiet enough to hear him. He can reveal our emotions, our pain, future events, and even the secrets of other's lives to us. The puzzles that God uses in dreams are a secret language known to us, God, and to the people we have the dreams about.

Do dreams have restorative power? Can a good dream life make the dreamer live longer, be healthier, happier, and even thinner? In today's society of rush and clamor, everything is tied to speed and production. Whipping around a drive-through or "speed" surfing the internet, we tend to spend less time sleeping and more time searching. While we sleep our soul continually searches for God. We desire to make intimate contact with the all-knowing Creator.

> *"He will not let your foot slip—He who watches over you will not slumber; indeed, He who watches over Israel will neither slumber nor sleep"*
> *(Psalm 121:3–4 NIV).*

Sleep is the time God chooses to give us his perspective, to steer us away from harmful events, and to give us life, vision, direction, provision, and destiny. As our understanding is enlightened we will be able to follow the leading our dreams provide.

A scoffer may seek wisdom and find none, but spiritual knowledge comes easily to one who has an understanding heart. Wisdom rests in the hearts of those who seek to have spiritual understanding of their dreams.

A true dreamer is one who sees the impossible, and knows through God it will become possible. Dreamers are able to see the shadow of things to come as if by moonlight, by joining their faith to believe, the rays of the morning's dawn bring the understanding and visionary clarity.

> *In a dream, in a vision of the night, when deep sleep falls on men as they slumber in their beds, He may speak in their ears and terrify them with warnings, to turn man from wrongdoing and keep him from pride, to preserve his soul from the pit, his life from perishing by the sword (Job 33:15–18 NIV).*

A fantastic, almost nightmarish, and horrific dream sequence is recorded in *Genesis 15:12–13* when Abram the patriarch was cast into the dream realm by hearing the voice of the Lord as a deep sleep fell over him.

> *As the sun was setting, Abram fell into a deep sleep, and a thick and dreadful darkness came over him. Then the LORD said to him, "Know for certain that your descendants will be strangers in a country not their own, and they will be enslaved and mistreated four hundred years" (NIV).*

God spoke to Abram in the night seasons so that Abram would listen and hear God's voice while in a peaceful state. Dreams unlock the deepest depths of knowledge and understanding as we peacefully rest in God's embrace. Dreams allow our hearts to express our inner beliefs in a grand way.

Abram's descendant Jacob experienced a desert sleep, which allowed him to see a heavenly stairway that joined the gateway of heaven to an entrance point on earth. The Lord's angelic messengers were ascending and descending upon the ladder delivering the Lord's prophetic declarations and visions to Jacob as he slept.

Genesis 28:10–17 is an account of this heavenly event:

> *Jacob left Beersheba and set out for Haran. When he reached a certain place, he stopped for the night because the sun had set. Taking one of the stones*

there, he put it under his head and lay down to sleep. He had a dream in which he saw a stairway resting on the earth, with its top reaching to heaven, and the angels of God were ascending and descending on it. There above it stood the LORD, and he said: "I am the LORD, the God of your father Abraham and the God of Isaac. I will give you and your descendants the land on which you are lying. Your descendants will be like the dust of the earth, and you will spread out to the west and to the east, to the north and to the south. All peoples on earth will be blessed through you and your offspring. I am with you and will watch over you wherever you go, and I will bring you back to this land. I will not leave you until I have done what I have promised you" (NIV).

When Jacob awoke from his sleep, he thought, "Surely the LORD is in this place, and I was not aware of it." He was afraid and said, "How awesome is this place! This is none other than the house of God; this is the gate of heaven" (NIV).

Jacob was able to feel and sense the powerful presence of the glory realm that was deposited in the natural realms of earth. He presented a memorial offering in honor of God's visitation. Jacob left that place with an assurance that God was with him, and was watching over him to direct his path as he journeyed through life. To know the path to our future and destiny we only have to embrace the dreams God gives. Out of the obscure will rise the clear, out of the dark chaos will rise the light of a new day dawning, and out of a dream will rise our destiny. God-given dreams of destiny and success will empower us to conquer our mistakes and nightmares of the past.

Dreams are God's night parables that direct our path and speak to our daily needs in life. These dream events and awesome promises came while the dreamers, both Abram and Jacob, were sleeping.

It is the same for us today. The questions we have about the future are answered in our dreams today. The time we spend sleeping has many diverse and varied benefits. Sleep allows the physical body to rest, repair itself, and improve our health. It also gives us the vision for tomorrow.

Life would be so much smaller if we were not able to dream. So dream largely and see God's hand move to bring increase, largeness, sufficiency, and a grand future to pass. The quality and length of our lives is related to the quality and quantity of our sleep patterns and dreams. The lack of proper sleep cycles is directly related to an increase in high blood pressure, heart disease, high cholesterol, migraines, diabetes, and weight gain. "Anything that disturbs the quality and quantity of sleep can have long-term consequences for both body and mind," says Gerard T. Lombardo, MD, director of the Sleep Disorders Center at New York Methodist Hospital in Brooklyn. (*Reader's Digest*, "The Magic Power of Sleep," October 2007). Without receiving the proper amount of sleep we will not be able to receive or recall the dreams that we have at night.

Hormones become imbalanced due to anxiety and stress, which leads to a decrease in the proper function of the immune system, stomach problems, metabolic changes, and other physical ailments. These conditions appear more frequently in people with insomnia or sleep apnea who only sleep an average of four to five hours a night.

Sleep deprivation for prolonged periods causes forgetfulness. It also affects our cognitive reasoning, our concentration, our moral judgments and memory skills as well as our physical performance. This accelerates the aging process. No wonder our physical appearance changes with the lack of sleep. As we grow older, the levels of growth hormones drop drastically, causing variations in our moods, muscle mass, skin tone, and energy levels. Sleep disorders cause disruptions in the normal patterns of brain waves, heartbeats, and respiratory system which affect our dream cycles. Depression is also prevalent in people who are not able to maintain healthy sleep patterns. Getting the proper amount of sleep is a good way to keep our hormone levels in balance and maintain a youthful appearance.

It is essential that we learn to still our racing minds by releasing stress and calming ourselves. Instead of ruminating or mulling over problems and concerns of the day, make it a habit to compile a list of thoughts, worries, and concerns on a pad of paper kept near the bed. Whisper a simple prayer. Ask God for the needed answers and then allow his peace to take over. We should believe that we will receive God's divine intervention and answers and enjoy peaceful, deep sleep.

Proverbs 3:24 When you lie down, you will not be afraid; Yes, you will lie down and your sleep will be sweet.

We can trust God to supply the needed answers by formulating dreams that bring needed insight as we slumber. Our dreams are God's answers to the questions we hide within. Once our dreams are embraced we have the courage to give them expression.

> *1 Peter 5:5–7* tells us *"God resists the proud,* [those who try to deal with their problems on their own without asking for his assistance or Divine intervention] *but gives grace to the humble* [to those who ask]." *Therefore humble yourselves under the mighty hand of God, that He may exalt you* (raise you above the problem so you don't remain beneath it) *in due time, casting all your care upon Him, for He cares for you."*

As we learn to bring our cares and concerns to God, he will deliver us from the weights that try to bury us. There is a biochemical nature to dreams in that we all carry the capacity to dream. Dreaming by day *and* by night allows the Holy Spirit to fill in the missing pieces of the puzzle with the wisdom God sends in answer to our prayers. Our souls desire spiritual growth and fulfillment. Dreams unlock and release the creativity that is held captive within the soul. We must dream to maintain a healthy life, both spiritually and physically.

The body's need to rest, relax, and rejuvenate is an essential part of remaining healthy and prosperous.

> *3 John 2 says "Beloved, I pray that you may prosper in all things and be in health, just as your soul prospers."*

The link between our ability to enter into a deep, restful, good night's sleep in order to receive and then to understand the messages of our dreams is an important part of maintaining the health of our physical and spiritual bodies. In this way, dreaming is as much a physical event as it is a spiritual one. We must cherish the dreams we are given and guard them with determination. If we allow them to be stolen, or fall to the floor by ignoring them, they will be trampled underfoot and their benefit will be lost.

Chapter Two
The Realm of the Spirit

Our Image Center, God's Wide-Screen TV

In a dream, a vision of the night, when sound sleep falls on men, while they slumber in their beds, then He opens the ears of men, and seals their instruction, That He may turn man aside {from his} conduct, And keep man from pride; He keeps back his soul from the pit, And his life from passing over into the river of death (Job 33:15–18 NAS).

It is a scientifically proven fact that everyone dreams every night when we enter a stage of sleep called Rapid Eye Movement (REM). But have you ever had a dream that made you wonder if there was more to it than a physiological experience? Maybe you asked yourself if it had a hidden or profound meaning. If so, you are not alone. Biblical history agrees that God has spoken to mankind through dreams since the beginning of time. Our dream life is like a highway on which messages are carried to the mind's eye and then to the spirit. These messages may come from a variety of sources: from the body, from the soul, from evil influences in the demonic realm, or from God through messengers of the angelic realm. As the Holy Spirit hovers over mankind, he embraces us during the night season, and gifts us with dreams that call us to pursue him with all our hearts.

Trust in the Lord with all your heart, and lean not on your own understanding; in all your ways acknowledge Him, And He shall direct your paths (Proverbs 3:5–6).

The mysteries he seals within our spirits create urgency within us to seek after him for the key to unlock the revelation he has deposited.

And those who know Your name will put their trust in You; For You Lord, have not forsaken those who seek You (Psalm 9:10).

When the message is from God, REM sleep is an opportunity for him to bypass the rational thinking of our logic and deposit messages through the mind's eye, or what we refer to as the image center. The *mind's eye* can be defined as: the human ability for visual perception, imagination, visualization, and memory. In other words, the mind's eye is one's ability to see things with the mind. Because many dreams are symbolic mysteries, God's guidance is necessary to uncover their hidden meanings. God intended that we get to know him better through this process of discovering the meaning of our dreams. Our image center is a vehicle that the Holy Spirit can access if we are open to him. The Holy Spirit will give us dreams in the night or streams of thought during the day to bring revelation and direction to our lives.

Repeat the following simple exercise to activate your image center.

Close your eyes and begin to visualize yourself in your bedroom. Now quickly envision your kitchen. Move to your car, and finally arrive at a beautiful beach where the sun is setting. The sky is painted with a multi-colored sunset as you walk barefoot in the sand. The waves are rippling over your feet and the wind is gently blowing in your hair. Your mind's eye allows you to speed through time and space.

Visualization creates awareness that incorporates all five senses. Many people use this technique to relieve stress by reflecting on positive memories.

Through activating the image center we can travel at the speed of thought and transition through time from setting to setting. In prayer, this technique enables us to visualize friends, family members, or situations that God wants to bring to our attention. When we surrender our image center to the Holy Spirit he is able to lead and guide us into truth through a series of impressions, which give us his insight on a situation. We can develop our understanding of the images projected onto the screens of our hearts by allowing the Holy Spirit in his still, small voice to teach us how to interpret, sense the urgency of, and understand the symbolism of what we see. This process may occur as a simple interruption in our thoughts, during times of intentional reflection, while daydreaming, or during sleeping hours.

Think back on an experience of not seeing someone for a while, and the thought of that person comes to mind out of the blue one day. Then a short time later, the phone rings and it is that person on the line. This is an example of how natural use of the image center can become supernatural. When faith is used to activate this process, God begins to show us things we would not naturally know during the course of our everyday lives. He often shows us pictures and impressions that pass across the mind's eye. By communicating in this way, God works to strengthen his relationship with us. He takes us on a journey of supernatural guidance through the Holy Spirit, and teaches us to discern between good and evil influences. Whether specific dreams are to reveal hidden issues, to inspire us to greatness, to keep us out of harm's way, or to provide insight into the world around us, God leads us through a revelatory cycle of dreaming to build a transitional bridge. This connection is where our dreams become the link between his infinite wisdom and our finite thinking. It is God's desire to draw us by the Holy Spirit to a place of acknowledgement that this bridge is a point of crossing from the limited realm of our plans to his limitless realm.

The Music of Our Spiritual DNA

For you formed my inward parts; You wove me in my mother's womb. I will give thanks to You, for I am fearfully and wonderfully made; Wonderful are Your works, And my soul knows it very well. My frame was not hidden from You, When I was made in secret, {And} skillfully wrought in the depths of the earth; Your eyes have seen my unformed substance; And in Your book were all written The days that were ordained {for me,} When as yet there was not one of them
(Psalm 139:13–16 NASU).

God places a piece of himself into every person who is born. *Genesis 1:27* states
So God created man in His own image; in the image of God He created him; male and female He created them.

Just like with physical DNA, God has written the formula on our spiritual DNA of what we have the potential to become in this life. Our spiritual DNA has been designed for God's purposes. He reveals sin and error in our dreams and gives us the choice to replace them with power, anointing, revelation, and the ability to overcome. It is an individual choice to receive this revelation and apply it to our lives. However, when it comes to our spiritual DNA (our destiny) we each get to choose what forces will influence our destiny the most—self, darkness, or God's light. It is up to the individual to not only recognize God's spiritual DNA in our lives, but to activate our destiny for godly purposes rather than for evil or self-fulfilling purposes. Before I moved to Texas, God revealed a powerful truth to me about spiritual DNA. I had a spiritual encounter in a dream in which I was visited by someone who said that he had been sent to change my spiritual DNA and he was going to give me a blood transfusion for my next spiritual assignment.

The interpretation of the dream revealed that it was given to prepare me for a change in location. Different geographic regions and states require a shift in our thinking, body metabolism, and even the sound frequency we will release to come into harmony with the new assignments God is giving us. Like musical instruments, we have to be fine tuned and polished in order to harmonize with the new seasons God has for us. We must resonate with a new sound for a new season and assignment, otherwise we will be off-key and the favor of man will not be extended to us.

> *Deep calls unto deep at the noise of Your waterfalls; all Your waves and billows have gone over me. The LORD will command His loving kindness in the daytime, and in the night His song shall be with me—A prayer to the God of my life (Psalm 42:7–8).*

This Scripture depicts the truth that the deep places of God call out to the deep places of himself that he put within each of us. He is calling for us to be reconnected and united with him—which is the purpose for which we were created. Although the concept of deep calling to deep between God and us is difficult to understand, quantum physics shows a similar scientific perspective of how different forms of matter give off unique vibrations.

All matter is made up of elements, elements are made up of atoms, and atoms are made up of electrons, protons, and neutrons.

There are twelve major subatomic particles known to man. They consist of six uncharged particles called leptons, and six charged particles called quarks. Physicists have also identified five particles that carry an invisible power force, known as bosons. All these particles are associated with light and exist in the invisible realm. The evasive Higgs boson, better known as the "God particle," has a subatomic mass between 115 and 160 giga-electron volts. This particle is lighter than an atom of gold, but a little heavier than an atom of silver. The God particle boson is believed to be the force that holds everything in the universe together.

> *In the beginning was the Word, and the Word was with God, and the Word was God. He was in the beginning with God.* All things were made through Him, and without Him nothing was made that was made. *In Him was life, and the life was the light of men. And the light shines in the darkness, and the darkness did not comprehend it* (John 1:1–5 NKJV). *Emphasis author's.*

> *Yet for us there is one God, the Father, of whom are all things, and we for Him; and one Lord Jesus Christ, through whom are all things, and through whom we live (1 Corinthians 8:6 NKJV).*

> *And to make all see what is the fellowship of the mystery, which from the beginning of the ages has been hidden in God who created all things through Jesus Christ; (Ephesians 3:9 NKJV).*

> *For by Him all things were created that are in heaven and that are on earth, visible and invisible, whether thrones or dominions or principalities or powers. All things were created through Him and for Him. And He is before all things, and in Him all things consist (Colossians 1:16–17 NKJV).*

When I learned of the invisible boson God particle, its mass being around that of silver and gold atoms, as well as its power to hold things together, I was reminded of the Scripture passage where the man crippled from birth was healed.

Then Peter said, "Silver and gold I do not have, but what I do have I give you: In the name of Jesus Christ of Nazareth, rise up and walk." And he took him by the right hand and lifted him up, and immediately his feet and ankle bones received strength. So he, leaping up, stood and walked and entered the temple with them—walking, leaping, and praising God. And all the people saw him walking and praising God (Acts 3:6–9 NKJV).

Could it be that Peter and John's healing declaration tapped into the faith realm, and the invisible power of the God particle gave strength to a crippled man's bones?

Just like matter, people also give off a vibration or sound. Each one is unique. We each sing a new song and dream our own dream of destiny. God's treasures are hidden in dreams in the darkness of night and we must aggressively pursue their secrets to discover them. Is it possible that a better understanding of our dreams and quantum physics could enable us to do the greater works—for example, walk on water *Matthew 14: 25–31, Mark 6:48–52*; walk through walls *John 20:19, John 20:26, Matthew 28:1–7, Mark 16:1–8, Luke 24:1–9*; be transported *Acts 8: 36–40, John 6: 20–21, 1Kings 18:7–16, Ezekiel 3:14–15, Ezekiel 37: 1–2*; and be translated *2 Corinthians 12:2–5, Revelation 4:1–2*; even appear *Matthew 24:30–31, Acts 26:16, 2 Corinthians 5:10, Hebrews 9:24–28, Matthew 27:50–53*; and disappear *John 10:39, Luke 4:28–30?*

Einstein's formula $E = mc^2$ when applied to the spiritual light realm works at a higher spiritual level than when simply applied to the natural realm … because we are called to be a light in dark places.

Search me, O God, and know my heart; Try me, and know my anxieties; And see if there is any wicked way in me, And lead me in the way everlasting (Psalm 139:23–24).

The dreams we dream become the strategic roadmaps God gives to point us in the right direction to align us with destiny. Dreams contain power that will enable us to see what we were created to become. When we turn to the Lord we see him as he is because the veils of limitation are taken away.

Understanding the Spirit Realm

But whenever a person turns to the Lord, the veil is taken away. Now the Lord is the Spirit, and where the Spirit of the Lord is, there is liberty. But we all, with unveiled face, beholding as in a mirror the glory of the Lord, are being transformed into the same image from glory to glory, just as from the Lord, the Spirit (2 Corinthians 3:16–18 NASU).

There is no time or distance in the Spirit realm. It is not confined to time as we know it in our day-to-day lives. God created time and space for us, as the Bible states one day with the Lord is as a thousand years and a thousand years is as one day. The Holy Spirit can cause us to transcend time and space barriers of the past, present, and future in our dreams by imparting glimpses of the spiritual realm as we sleep. The Spirit of the Lord enters our dreams to remove the veils from our faces so we will be able to see him in his transcendent glory. When we see him we will be like him. He is transforming us from one realm of glory into a higher realm of glory as he reveals himself to us. Science has proven that light can travel seven times around the world in one second; however our thoughts travel even faster. As God's messengers, angels travel at the speed of thought. Angels enter our dreams through the doors of our hearts to bring messages from God's eternal realm.

The heart is deceitful above all things, And desperately wicked; who can know it? I, the Lord, search the heart, I test the mind, Even to give every man according to his ways, According to the fruit of his doings (Jeremiah 17:9–10).

We must activate and train the human spirit to open the door of our hearts by inviting the Holy Spirit to search, test, and teach us; for it is out of the abundance of the heart that our life flows. The Spirit of God will show us glimpses of our nature and our responses to our natural life situations through a spiritual window.

The Bible tells us *He who covers his sin will not prosper, but whoever confesses and forsakes them will have mercy (Proverbs 28:13).*

Here is a prayer that will help us send an invitation for the Holy Spirit to shed light on the circumstances of our lives through spiritual symbolism.

Dear Lord,

Please remove the veils that blind my eyes and give me insight with understanding, the Spirit of wisdom, with revelation knowledge. Let me become a seer of your glory. Anoint my eyes to see, and ears to hear what the Holy Spirit is saying. Through the Spirit of revelation give me access to the heart, mind, and words of Christ where all the mysteries of the Kingdom of heaven are hidden. Immerse me in the Spirit of love. Amen. *Colossians 1:9ff*

God's glory is seen through the eyes of our hearts in the eternal realm of the Spirit. Faith enables us to engage and access spiritual understanding. The prophetic words in a dream interpretation help to frame doorways into our world. Faith is being sure that the things we hope for and dream about can be realized even if we do not see them. God commanded the universe to be formed so that what is seen was brought out of the invisible realm of the Spirit. Hope produces the evidence of faith, and love is the substance or tracks that spiritual gifts run on ... God is love!

Colossians 2:2–3 states:

> *My purpose is that they may be encouraged in heart and united in love, so that they may have the full riches of complete understanding, in order that they may know the mystery of God, namely, Christ, in whom are hidden all the treasures of wisdom and knowledge (NIV).*

Treasures of wisdom and knowledge are hidden in Christ. We are the generation that has been saved for these last times and the end-time revelatory ministry. God has saved his best for last. Just as Jesus had to qualify to move in the fullness of the Spirit, through testing we must qualify to be part of this end-time move of God. We were called, justified, chosen, predestined, and elected to be on the earth at this time.

> *In love he predestined us to be adopted as his sons through Jesus Christ, in accordance with his pleasure and will (Ephesians 1:4–5 NIV).*

30

In him we were also chosen, having been predestined according to the plan of him who works out everything in conformity with the purpose of his will (Ephesians 1:11–12 NIV).

For those God foreknew he also predestined to be conformed to the likeness of his Son, that he might be the firstborn among many brothers. And those he predestined, he also called; those he called, he also justified; those he justified, he also glorified (Romans 8:29–30 NIV).

John 14:3–4 tells us that Jesus has gone to prepare a place for us. He will come back and take us to be with him.

"And if I go and prepare a place for you, I will come back and take you to be with me that you also may be where I am. You know the way to the place where I am going" (NIV).

Jesus tells us that we already know the way to the place in the spirit realm where Jesus is seated. We are able to access that spiritual place in our dreams and through our prayers.

Emanating Light Requires Likeness

Just as the prongs of a lamp are plugged into an outlet, it becomes fully energized by the power source of electricity. Then the light bulb harnesses the power and provides light that goes beyond the vessel to all who see it. As believers, we are similar. God is the power source; the Holy Spirit is the outlet that provides the power. We are the vessel that becomes a conduit of the power when plugged into the Holy Spirit. We fulfill our purpose while at the same time providing light to those around us who were surrounded by darkness. However, others cannot live on our charge alone. They must also "plug in" to the Holy Spirit themselves to become conduits of God's power.

Psalm 18:28 For you will light my lamp; The Lord my God will enlighten my darkness.

The closer we come to God through the Holy Spirit in relationship, the stronger our light shines, which draws people out of darkness. However, our light alone does not reach far enough. That is why we must lead others to the one true power source: God.

> *John 8:12–13 Then Jesus again spoke to them, saying, "I am the Light of the world; he who follows Me will not walk in the darkness, but will have the Light of life" (NASU).*

God loves to reveal secrets to his friends about the deep things he desires to bring about in the earth.

> *For with You is the foundation of life; In Your light we see light (Psalm 36:9).*

God acts upon his Word combined with our obedience as we exercise our faith to believe his plans.

> *Psalm 119:105 Your word is a lamp to my feet And a light to my path. Verse 130: The entrance of Your words gives light; It gives understanding to the simple.*

By walking in God's divine nature we become open to the supernatural realms of dreams and miracles for our lives and the lives of others. In *John 11:40 Jesus said to her, "Did I not say to you that if you would believe you would see the glory of God?"* When we develop our ability to "believe" the things of God with our hearts, and not just our minds, we are able to walk in a spiritual understanding of the mysteries of days to come and what the Bible refers to as the end times, which began two thousand years ago.

Daniel was told that knowledge shall increase.

> *Those who are wise shall shine like the brightness of the firmament, and those who turn many to righteousness like the stars forever and ever. "But you, Daniel, shut up the words, and seal the book until the time of the end; many shall run to and fro, and knowledge shall increase" (Daniel 12:3–4 NKJV).*

This speaks of the natural knowledge of man but more importantly it speaks of the increased knowledge and understanding of the secret and mysterious ways of God. God-given dreams reveal spiritual understanding of truths that have been sealed. This knowledge will enable God's friends to ascend and descend, moving to and fro, with the Spirit of the Lord on an invisible heavenly ladder. Daniel was told to seal up these words until the end time when knowledge of God's ways will increase, and people will be purged and refined with fire.

Many shall be purified, made white, and refined, but the wicked shall do wickedly; and none of the wicked shall understand, but the wise shall understand (Daniel 12:10).

Its no wonder that the process we go through to walk in the ways of God's wisdom are forged by fiery tests and trials that fervently conform us to his glorious image. Those with godly insight will understand the mysteries of Heaven's Kingdom.

The fruit of the righteous is a Tree of Life, [Jesus] and he who wins souls is wise (Proverbs 11:30).

The Bible makes it clear that whoever simply calls upon the name of Jesus will be saved. That does not sound very difficult, does it? Sometimes we try to make salvation more complicated than it should be. We will probably be surprised at all the people who will greet us in heaven, simply because they called out to Jesus as they transitioned from this earthly realm of life into the realms of eternity. Even as they are able to glimpse heaven and hell, if they choose heaven the Lord will snatch them from the fire. However, salvation is only the beginning. After salvation comes a growing relationship with the Creator of the universe that will take the believer on journeys unimagined in this life and the next.

"Things which eye has not seen and ear has not heard, and [which] have not entered the heart of man, all that God has prepared for those who love him" (1 Corinthians 2:9 NAS).

Our relationship with God grows through Jesus under the guidance of the Holy Spirit. As we ask him for discernment, wisdom, and understanding, the Lord will direct and guide our paths using the dreams that he creates for us. Without the understanding of our dreams we remain in unfruitful darkness, but with understanding we can be saved, healed, and delivered. *Proverbs 2:3–12* states:

> *If you cry out for discernment, and lift up your voice for understanding, if you seek her as silver, and search for her as for hidden treasures; then you will understand the fear of the Lord, and find the knowledge of God. For the Lord gives wisdom; from his mouth come knowledge and understanding; He stores up sound wisdom for the upright; He is a shield to those who walk uprightly; He guards the paths of justice, and preserves the way of his saints. Then you will understand righteousness and justice, equity and every good path. When wisdom enters your heart, and knowledge is pleasant to your soul, discretion will preserve you; understanding will keep you, to deliver you from the way of evil ….*

Why dreams and visions?

If Paul knew the way of the Spirit and was translated into the heavenly realms, then we can be too! In *2 Corinthians 12:1–4,* Paul spoke of receiving visions and revelation from the Lord. He said that being caught up into the "third heaven" was an experience; not knowing whether he was in the body or out of the body. He said he experienced "inexpressible things that man is not permitted to tell." He found it difficult to communicate what he saw and experienced in the heavenly realms with his limited vocabulary.

John the Revelator was also invited into the realms of the Spirit when he looked and saw a door standing open in heaven.

> *Revelation 4:1–2 After this I looked, and there before me was a door standing open in heaven. And the voice I had first heard speaking to me like a trumpet said, "Come up here, and I will show you what must take place after this." At once I was in the Spirit, and there before me was a throne in heaven with someone sitting on it"* (NIV).

John was given an invitation to see the future from a heavenly perspective but he had to enter the Spirit realm to access the door. God is not a respecter of persons. The same invitation that was issued to the Apostles Paul and John is being offered to each of us today. So we must learn to navigate the realms of the Spirit in our prayers, dreams, and visions.

I remember a heavenly vision where I was walking around on the golden streets of a city. I was clothed in a simple, very plain, crocker sack-like white robe that was tied at the waist with a rough piece of twisted rope. My robe was clean, simple, and ordinary yet without spot or wrinkle. Those around me in heaven were dressed in beautiful and elegant white floor length gowns that were ornate and glowing with gold embroidery. To my utter surprise I was also wearing a long and full solid gray beard that covered my chest. It was dripping with thick, amber honey like oil.

Let your garments always be white, And let your head lack no oil. Ecclesiastes 9:8

God was imparting the wisdom of the ancient of days into my heart. To be successful in the destiny call he was placing upon me I was not to compare myself to others, but always to remain teachable, focused on the simplicity of the gospel, and to walk in love and humility. Beards also speak of maturity in the things of the spirit. But all I could think was, "Lord when I return and awaken please don't let me wake out of this experience as the original bearded woman."

We must seek God's wisdom and revelation to unlock the hidden mysteries that he wants to communicate to us in today's society. The Spirit of the Lord enters our dreams to remove the veils from our hearts and faces so that we will be able to see him in his transcendent glory. When we see him we will be like him.

2 Corinthians 3:16 But whenever a person turns to the Lord, the veil is taken away (NASU).

We cannot behold him and continue to live in an unchanged

state. As he reveals himself to us, he is transforming us so that we can understand his mysteries.

> *Colossians 1:13–20*
> *For He rescued us from the domain of darkness, and transferred us to the kingdom of His beloved Son, in whom we have redemption, the forgiveness of sins. He is the image of the invisible God, the firstborn of all creation. For by Him all things were created, both in the heavens and on earth, visible and invisible, whether thrones or dominions or rulers or authorities—all things have been created through Him and for Him. He is before all things, and in Him all things hold together. He is also head of the body, the church; and He is the beginning, the firstborn from the dead, so that He Himself will come to have first place in everything. For it was the Father's good pleasure for all the fullness to dwell in Him, and through Him to reconcile all things to Himself, having made peace through the blood of His cross; through Him, I say, whether things on earth or things in heaven (NASU).*

Understanding the secrets hidden in dreams is a key to changing this dark world. Godly wisdom helps us to address the negative interpretations that come from those who walk in spiritual darkness. It is essential today that people learn to tap into the supernatural power of heaven. As the Holy Spirit hovers over mankind and he embraces us while we sleep, he imparts a dream that calls us to pursue him with all of our hearts. The mysteries he seals within our spirits create an urgency to seek after him for the key to unlock the revelation he has implanted.

In *Ephesians 1:17–19,* Paul prays that believers may be enlightened in our understanding in order to have the riches of glory and his power manifest in our lives. This means that every believer must be led by the Spirit of wisdom and revelation (a.k.a. the Holy Spirit) to understand the Father's heart. As our relationship with God deepens through experiencing his activity in our lives from day to day, our knowledge and revelation of him and his perspective on the world also grows. When our eyes are opened to the ways God sees things, we can begin to see our destiny and the world around us from his perspective and point of view. Spiritual understanding or enlightenment is different than natural wisdom. There must be a spiritual presence of God through the Holy

Spirit resting upon our five natural senses of sight, sound, touch, taste, and smell for us to experience the Spirit realm. The presence of the Holy Spirit comes to invite us to meet Jesus at salvation. Then he comes in different measures after salvation when we daily call out in desperation to God for an increased presence of his Holy Spirit and power as needs and opportunities in our lives arise.

Spiritual wisdom directs us regarding the future. In contrast, spiritual knowledge causes us to reflect back on past experiences (both triumphs and failures) through the eyes of God. Biblically, we see this principle at work in *Daniel 5:1–30*, through the life of Daniel. During a drunken feast, King Belshazzar gave orders to bring the holy golden and silver vessels. These sacred vessels had been removed from the temple of God in Jerusalem by his forefather, King Nebuchadnezzar. Belshazzar filled the goblets with wine and gave a toast. His wives, concubines and his nobles proceeded to drink from the sacred cups and praised the gods of gold and silver, bronze and iron, wood and stone. Suddenly, the fingers of a magnificent hand appeared, interrupting their vile celebrations. The hand wrote a message on the plaster wall near the lamp stand in the King's banquet hall. All could plainly see the inscription. We can imagine the immediate change in the atmosphere as the hand of God began to execute his written judgment. Belshazzar's eyes were fixed upon every movement of the hand. As he stood trembling in the presence of one much greater than he, the color in his face drained and his knees began an arrhythmic knocking before they gave way under his weight. His servants scrambled to lift their king from the floor as he summoned the wise men of Babylon, the enchanters, astrologers, and diviners. He said, *"Whoever deciphers this writing and can tell me its meaning will be promoted to the third highest ruler in my kingdom. I will clothe them in purple and adorn them with golden chains."* None of those the world perceived as wise, who studied the dark arts of incantations and witchcraft could read the clear writing on the palace wall. So King Belshazzar was once again stricken with paralyzing fear, and terror gripped his soul.

The queen entered the banquet hall when she heard the fearful cries of the king and his nobles after the writing appeared. Then she reminded the king of Daniel:

Do not let your thoughts alarm you or your face be pale. There is a man in your kingdom in whom is a spirit of the holy gods; and in the days of your father, illumination, insight and wisdom like the wisdom of the gods were found in him. And King Nebuchadnezzar, your father, your father the king, appointed him chief of the magicians, conjurers, Chaldeans {and} diviners. {This was} because an extraordinary spirit, knowledge and insight, interpretation of dreams, explanation of enigmas and solving of difficult problems were found in this Daniel, whom the king named Belteshazzar. Let Daniel now be summoned and he will declare the interpretation (Daniel 5:10–13 NAS).

Daniel was then brought before the King to interpret the message. The Bible says that Daniel was highly educated and was known to have interpreted dreams and their symbols while serving under Belshazzar's [grand]father King Nebuchadnezzar. It states that Daniel's interpretation of the handwriting on the wall was supernatural. He was also skilled in royal protocol and speech before Kings. He honored Belshazzar's kingly position but also delivered great wisdom and counsel as he revealed the reasons behind the writing as well as its meaning in the following interpretation.

O king, the Most High God whom I serve, gave your father Nebuchadnezzar sovereignty, greatness, glory and splendor. But when he refused to acknowledge the true God, his heart became arrogant and hardened with pride. As you know your father was deposed from his royal throne and stripped of his glory. He was driven away from the people in his kingdom and given the simple mind of an animal. The Most High God is sovereign over all the kingdoms of men and sets over them anyone He desires.

King Belshazzar you were fully aware of all this history, yet you have not humbled yourself before the almighty God. Instead you have set yourself up to bring a challenge and offense against the Lord of heaven. You had the sacred goblets from His temple brought so you and your guests could desecrate them by drinking wine and praising the false gods of silver and gold, bronze and iron, of wood and stone which are both deaf and dumb without understanding. You have dishonored the God who holds in His hand your life and all your ways. Therefore He sent the hand to plainly write this inscription.

Although Daniel did literally derive the meaning of each word, he had supernatural insight and revelation which helped him interpret the vision in the context of God's encoded message. The following words were recorded to have been written on the wall of the king's palace: "*MENE, MENE, TEKEL, UPHARSIN.*" Although they are left un-translated in English versions of the Bible, Wikipedia refers to these words as "Aramaic names of measures of currency. According to Wikipedia, Daniel's interpretation was: "*MENE* (literally a monetary toll), God has numbered the days of your kingdom and brought it to an end; *TEKEL* (literally a tokenary weight), you have been weighed on the scales and found wanting; *PARSIN* (literally a division or portion), your kingdom is divided and given to the Persians." The Bible interprets the writing this way: *MENE* God has numbered your kingdom, and finished it; *TEKEL* You have been weighed in the balances, and found wanting; *PERES* Your kingdom has been divided, and given to the Medes and Persians. After Daniel interpreted the writing, Belshazzar was slain by the invading Darius the Mede who became king. The change of thrones is the "historically verifiable defeat of the Babylonian Empire by Persia." Furthermore this incident is the impetus from which we get the age-old cliché "The writing is on the wall."

Redeeming Our Night Life

> *For God may speak in one way, or in another, yet man does not perceive it. In a dream, in a vision of the night, when deep sleep falls upon men, while slumbering on their beds, when He opens the ears of men, and seals their instruction. In order to turn man from his deed, and conceal pride from man, He keeps back his soul from the Pit, and his life from perishing by the sword (Job 33:14–18).*

When we received salvation we were told we had to give up our exciting night lives. But have you ever thought that believers in Jesus Christ should have the most exciting night lives ever? Our nights should be filled with dreams, visions, and visitations of many and varied kinds, inspired by the Holy Spirit. God takes us through a preparation process in our dreams to get us ready to see and experience great spiritual things in our daily lives. Oftentimes we see it in the night seasons so that we can recognize it in broad daylight when we are in the middle of it. *1 John 3:2–3* states that as children of God we will be able to see things that have not yet been made known, and as we see God, we will be like him. We must be totally dependent upon the Holy Spirit for understanding, interpretation, and application of the revelation we receive.

Faith Makes Dreams Come True

God created the principle of conceiving, seeing, conforming, and becoming what we behold. During the goats' breeding season Jacob had a dream in which the angel called his name. He said to him, *"Jacob, look up and see the male goats mating with a flock of white streaked, speckled, and spotted goats. God has seen that Laban has mistreated, stolen wages from, and deceived you. God has devised a strategy for you to gain wealth and prosperity."* So seeing and hearing God's plan in a dream, Jacob took fresh-cut branches from poplar, almond, and plain trees and made white stripes on them by peeling the bark and exposing the white inner wood of the branches. Then Jacob placed the peeled branches in all the watering troughs, so that they would be in the direct visual path of the flocks who were in season when they came to drink. When the stronger animals mated in front of the branches in the watering troughs they bore streaked, speckled, or spotted offspring. These Jacob separated into his herds. If the animals were weak he would not place the carved branches before their eyes to see. So the weaker animals remained in Laban's flocks while all the strong ones were transferred into Jacob's. By following the angel's instructions Jacob grew exceedingly prosperous. He developed vast wealth in large flocks, men, maidservants, camels, and donkeys. The transference of the wealth of the wicked to the righteous came through angelic dream strategies.

To reach our full potential and God-given destiny, we must always set the Lord before our eyes and stay focused on his plans and purposes. We must see ourselves as God sees us, and interpret our dreams according to his nature, his words, and his language to us, not according to what man says or what we believe about ourselves. God has a divine dream plan that enables each of us to reach our destiny in him. Just like our physical DNA, God's heavenly plans, strategies, and blueprints are written on our spirit for us to fulfill. God is holy. He is light, and he is love. Those who worship him must access the Spirit of truth. God reveals himself to us through the Spirit of truth and revelation. The more we come to understand his ways of communication and his revealed nature, the more in love we fall with him.

The following is a series of supernatural events and testimonies that take faith to experience and even more faith to believe, but it is through this type of unrelenting faith that we will see God. I was teaching on dreams using the passage in *Acts 2* one weekend in a Massachusetts hotel. As I came to the part that said, *"blood and fire and vapor of smoke"* the fire alarms began to sound. The terrible noise kept ringing as I attempted to continue the lesson. This phenomenon often happens when a group of believers begin to release faith. Faith is a substance and a power that can be felt and measured. As faith arises so do electrical currents. The currents are detected by computers and appear as fire. The hotel fire alarm system had been triggered by a release of our fiery faith. It wasn't long before the hotel management came through and asked us to please vacate the conference room. They assured us that they were not able to find a fire but that the computer system had indicated the presence of fire at our location. The city fire department responded by sending out several fire trucks. The alarm kept sounding until the group of power-packed believers were outside in the parking lot. I gathered them together and asked them not to reveal to the hotel management that we were the cause of the fire alarm. Once we vacated the building the computer systems returned to normal and no longer detected a fire. But, upon our return to the same conference room, as we picked up where we left off, the fire alarms began to ring out once again. This continued the whole weekend. The magnetic keys that gave us entrance to our assigned hotel rooms were also erased. The hotel management kept apologizing for the inconvenience of us having to always go to the front desk to get new keys issued. They kept saying, "We think there is some type of magnetic disturbance in that conference room but we don't know what it could be."

Anointed believers exude the light and power of God, causing them to succeed and overcome. In comparison, the evil person releases a muted light and a dull sound that calls out to the spirits of darkness to ensnare them, ensuring their continued failure. Faith allows us to transcend natural thinking and carnal reasoning. It's a supernatural gift which enables us to exceed boundaries and limitations which otherwise hinders those who have little faith.

Another example of this tangible supernatural faith occurred while I was waiting to board an airplane. I had just finished a conference and several of the speakers traveled with me to the airport. At the moment we approached the check-in counter the attendant exclaimed that her computer simply crashed. She asked if we would please step to the next computer. When we stepped over to the next window, that computer screen went black as well. She again apologized and requested we move to the third and next available computer for assistance. The third computer also crashed and went to a black screen. Perplexed, we stood and waited for the computers to come back on line. Finally, it dawned on me what was taking place. I asked my friends to take a few steps back away from the counter. As we moved out of the proximity of the computers, they each popped back up in succession and began to work. Eventually, we received our requested seat changes and we boarded the plane. Luckily, we were not seated near any of the engines!

We need to see what God sees in us. God's plans are for us to succeed. He wants his spiritual realms of glory to transfer into this natural realm. In this way God brings his Kingdom purposes to our life. Dreams are one way that God chooses to communicate what he sees in us. A dream is a picture language. Because pictures are easily imprinted on our spirits and minds, we can recall the images back to remembrance. God speaks in a language of signs, symbols, puns, riddles, and mysteries through dreams.

God also speaks to the positives of what we are and what we can become, rather than emphasizing the negatives. For example, God does not speak to our sickness and disease; he speaks to our health. He does not speak to our poverty or lack; he speaks to our wealth and abundance. He does not speak to our failure or mistakes; he speaks to our success. He does not focus on the past; he speaks to the now and to the future.

God speaks the language of hope to encourage each of us to succeed. We do not like to be left in the dark so God brings us into the light. He wants us to know the wonderful plans he has for our futures as much as we want him to reveal them to us.

When we capture a picture of light and God's goodness for our lives in the midst of the dark place of our existence, we have "vision." Vision releases hope. Hope enables us to change. Change releases destiny. Destiny drives us out of the now and propels us into the future. Once we catch a glimpse of who we are in the future we are able to bring it into the reality of today. This is one of the major ways God is able to accelerate good in our lives through dreams and visions. The more we can see and believe, the more we can become. We must see it to be it! God births dreams and visions in us in order to bring revelation, illumination, and inspiration. Revelation is the discovery of truth. Illumination is spiritual or intellectual enlightenment. Inspiration is communicating the understood, discovered truth to others. To inspire means to inhale, or breathe in the Spirit to stimulate the mind, to create or to activate the emotions to a higher level of feeling. To spiritually inspire is to guide, affect, or arouse by the divine influence of the Holy Spirit. Through revelation, illumination, and inspiration, the Spirit of the Lord is calling to the Holy Spirit within us as he leads us into the deep things, secrets, and mysteries of God. The DNA within each of us sings a different song.

> *Psalm 42:7–8* reads: *Deep calls to deep in the roar of your waterfalls; all your waves and breakers have swept over me. By day the* LORD *directs His love, at night His song is with me–a prayer to the God of my life (NIV).*

God created light, time, and space for us. One day with the Lord is as a thousand years and a thousand years is as one day. This is hard for us to understand, but the Bible also says that a nation shall come to God in a day.

> *Isaiah 66:8 Who has heard such a thing? Who has seen such things? Can a land be born in one day? Can a nation be brought forth all at once? (NASU).*

God's higher thoughts, light, and plans enter our dreams to imprint spiritual pictures and blue prints on our image center. God-given dreams are able to make us into world changers by bringing us revelation knowledge from his heart.

Chapter Three
Dreaming and Dream Recall

Everyone Dreams

Now we see but a poor reflection as in a mirror; then we shall see face to face. Now I know in part; then I shall know fully, even as I am fully known (1 Corinthians 13:12 NIV).

I have often said, "Share your dreams with me, and I will not only tell you who you are now, but who you are destined to become." Similar to the powers of our imagination, dreaming is a universal human phenomenon uniting people across barriers of age, gender, racial background, social differences, and historical circumstances. Dreams are our inner man at work revealing our nature to us.

"I never dream!" "I never remember my dreams!" These are two very common fallacies that people assume. Be assured that everyone, regardless of who they are, what they believe, or where they come from, dreams. We dream for about an hour each night. Without dreams, the brain cannot process the massive amounts of information it receives on a daily basis. Mental breakdowns and poor health are the results of lack of sleep and the resulting inability to process information through dreaming. Dreams have many emotional, physical, and spiritual benefits. They bring access to spiritual messages about blessing and they bring insight into God's plans. They bring us vision and guidance in everyday life and circumstances. Dreams free our minds, provide clarity, dispel confusion, and enable us to function with mental lucidity during the day. Dreams release accumulated tension and fear, and they bring release from built up stress by providing a vacation for our minds. Dreams answer questions and bring wisdom to solve difficult problems. They make us aware of how to break bad, perplexing habits, and how to remove hindrances or obstacles that are keeping us from reaching our full potential. Dreams unleash us into creativity and inventiveness. They make us more open, flexible, and attuned to our God-given abilities. In summary, dreams give us the keys to unlock our aspirations, potential, and destiny. They bring healing to our brokenness by helping us to see its root causes. A single dream may have one or many layered messages. A succession of dreams can tell an amazing story as in an adventure movie. Dreams serve as valuable problem solvers. They act as the computer of our subconscious mind that reveals hidden data from the input we receive throughout the day. Other benefits of dreaming include the following:

- Healing, comfort, health, and well-being
- Direction, instruction and clarity
- Prosperity, success, and increase
- Destiny, insight, and wisdom
- Warning
- Correction
- Answers to questions
- Information, revelation, and counsel
- Challenges to the dreamer

Dreams have the ability to take us out of the natural realms of time. They can move us back into the past, help us to deal with the present, or launch us into the future. The past is history, the future is a mystery and the present is a gift. That's why they call it a present. A dream aligns us with the present moment and reveals our true selves. When looking into a dream we are looking into a mirror. When we look into a mirror we see the natural image of ourselves. Just like in a mirror, by looking into our dream life we can see qualities of ourselves represented by characters or symbols in the dream. Spiritually speaking, we are known fully and completely by a loving Creator. We are destined to reflect his image when we come to know him in different dimensions. The closer we draw to him the more of his light we absorb, and the more we are changed because we can see ourselves clearly. We are beings of light because our creator is the Father of Light. We are called to live a life where nothing is hidden from his sight but everything is exposed to his light. Things that are concealed in darkness will only detract from our potential and will eventually cause us to stumble and fall. Dreams bring light to our lives by dispelling the darkness.

God projects pictures and images upon the screens of our hearts. He speaks tenderly with life-giving creative words. If we will embrace these messages with faith and obedience we will be transformed. If we ignore his dream messages we will remain the same. Unchanged people forget who they are called to be. When we do this, we risk never reaching our destiny or full potential. Dreams are a mirror image of the soul and reflect our inner condition by revealing what will transpire if changes do not take place in us. The kind of attitude we have and the emphasis and value we place on dreams will determine the beneficial results we will receive from them. Dreams are like relationships we maintain with friends. If we nurture them and pay attention to them they will grow and develop. If we ignore and neglect them they will dry up, vaporize and disappear. If we listen to them, write them down in a journal and follow their instruction they will become a counselor to us. But if we ignore them they will not flourish.

Historical Dreams and Dreamers

Sleep hath its own world,
A boundary between the things misnamed
Death and existence: Sleep hath its own world,
And a wide realm of wild reality,
And dreams in their development have breath,
And tears, and tortures, and the touch of joy;
They leave a weight upon our waking thoughts,
They take a weight from off waking toils,
They do divide our being

(Ward Hill Lamon, a friend and law partner of Abraham Lincoln)

Recollections of Abraham Lincoln, 1847–1865 (Paperback) by Ward Hill Lamon, <u>Dorothy Lamon Teillard (Editor)</u>, James A. Rawley

History tells of a long line of dreamers, which include the company of presidents, chemists, inventors, sports enthusiasts, and entrepreneurs. The following passages are in-depth stories of how dreams throughout history have brought revelation that has literally shaped our society.

The German born physiologist, Otto Loewi (1873–1961), won

the Nobel Prize for medicine in 1936 for his work on the chemical transmission of nerve impulses. Thirty-three years earlier, Otto received a dream with the idea that the transmission of the nervous impulse was chemical rather than the commonly held belief that it was electrical. The revelation came to Loewi but he did not know how to prove and document it. He pondered the idea for seventeen years when he had the following dream. According to Loewi:

The night before Easter Sunday of that year I awoke, turned on the light, and jotted down a few notes on a tiny slip of paper. Then I fell asleep again. It occurred to me at 6 o'clock in the morning that during the night I had written down something most important, but I was unable to decipher the scrawl. The next night, at 3 o'clock, the idea returned. It was the design of an experiment to determine whether or not the hypothesis of chemical transmission that I had uttered 17 years ago was correct. I got up immediately, went to the laboratory, and performed a single experiment on a frog's heart according to the nocturnal design. (Elliot S. Valenstein, The War of the Soups and the Sparks: The Discovery of Neurotransmitters and the Dispute Over How Nerves Communicate)

For the next ten years Loewi conducted a complicated series of tests to satisfy his critics, his dream-induced experiments became the foundation for the theory of chemical transmission of the nervous impulse and led to a Nobel Prize! Dr. Loewi stated: "Most so-called 'intuitive' discoveries are such associations made in the subconscious." (Otto Loewi, "An Autobiographical Sketch", Perspectives in Biology and Medicine, Autumn, 1960)

In the early 1890s, a woman named Madame C.J. Walker was suffering from a scalp infection that caused severe hair loss. She began experimenting with hair care products and patented medicines to find a cure. She discovered her cure from an answer to prayer that came in the form of a dream. She built an extremely successful cosmetic company that made her a multimillionaire.

Professional golfer Jack Nicklaus found a way to improve his game with a new hold he received in a dream. Nicklaus was having a bad slump in 1964 where his scores were routinely in the high seventies. Suddenly he regained top scores after he reported seeing a new grip designed in a dream.

Wednesday night I had a dream and it was about my golf swing. I was hitting them pretty good in the dream and all at once I realized I wasn't holding the club the way I've actually been holding it lately. I've been having trouble collapsing my right arm taking the club head away from the ball, but I was doing it perfectly in my sleep. So when I came to the course yesterday morning I tried it the way I did in my dream and it worked. I shot a sixty-eight yesterday and a sixty-five today. (Jack Nicklaus, as told to a San Francisco Chronicle reporter, 27 June 1964 The Committee of Sleep, D. Barrett, 2001)

Elias Howe is credited with inventing the sewing machine in 1845. He wanted to create a machine with a needle that would go through a piece of cloth to form garments. The position of the needle and its exact design had him stumped. The prototype of his first needle was horizontal and pointed at both ends, with an eye in the middle. Then one night his answer came to him in a dream.

Elias was taken captive by a group of savage natives and thrown into a large boiling pot. As they celebrated and danced around him their spears made a distinct up and down motion. His eyes were drawn to hole at the tips of the spears. He saw a thread could be strung through the small openings as the natives moved around him.

When he awoke he realized that the dream was the solution to his design problem. By relocating a hole at the tip of the needle, the threads could be caught after it went through the cloth, thus making his machine operable.

Elias made the necessary changes the dream revealed and his new invention worked! (Waldemar Kaempffert, *A Popular History of American Invention, Vol. II*, New York Scribner's Sons, 1924)

Paul McCartney is considered to be one of the most famous songwriters and singers of our day. In 1965, The Guinness Book of

Records claimed that his song "Yesterday" sold the most covers and was performed over seven million times in the 20th century.

The Beatles were filming "Help" in London in 1965. Paul was visiting his family and sleeping in an attic room of their house on Wimpole Street. Paul awoke from a dream one morning with a classical stringed instrument playing the tune of "Yesterday" in his ears.

As McCartney tells it:

I woke up with a lovely tune in my head. I thought, "That's great, I wonder what that is?" There was an upright piano next to me, to the right of the bed by the window. I got out of bed, sat at the piano, found G, found F sharp minor 7th—and that leads you through then to B to E minor, and finally back to E. It all leads forward logically. I liked the melody a lot, but because I'd dreamed it, I couldn't believe I'd written it. I thought, "No, I've never written anything like this before." But I had the tune, which was the most magic thing! (Paul McCartney —Many Years From Now, Barry Miles) (NY, Henry Holt, 1997) (The Committee of Sleep, D. Barrett, 2001 Wikipedia)

Lincoln dreamt only days before his own assassination of great cries coming from the White House's East Wing. Upon investigating, the soldiers on guard told him the weeping was for the President who had been assassinated. Days later, Abraham Lincoln's body was held in state in the East wing so people could pay their final respects.

History records that President Abraham Lincoln recounted the following dream to his wife just a few days prior to his tragic assassination.

About ten days ago, I retired very late. I had been up waiting for important dispatches from the front. I could not have been long in bed when I fell into a slumber, for I was weary. I soon began to dream.

There seemed to be a death-like stillness about me. Then I heard subdued sobs, as if a number of people were weeping. I thought I left my bed and wandered downstairs. There the silence was broken by the same pitiful sobbing, but the mourners were invisible. I went from room to room; no living person was in sight, but the same mournful sounds of distress met me as I passed along. It was light in all the rooms;

every object was familiar to me; but where were all the people who were grieving as if their hearts would break?

I was puzzled and alarmed. What could be the meaning of all this? Determined to find the cause of a state of things so mysterious and so shocking, I kept on until I arrived at the East Room, which I entered. There I met with a sickening surprise. Before me was a catafalque, on which rested a corpse wrapped in funeral vestments. Around it were stationed soldiers who were acting as guards; and there was a throng of people, some gazing mournfully upon the corpse whose face was covered, others weeping pitifully.

"Who is dead in the White House?" I demanded of one of the soldiers "The President" was his answer; "he was killed by an assassin!" Then came a loud burst of grief from the crowd, which awoke me from my dream.

Lincoln realized that his dreams had powerful meanings. He had a recurring dream that always foretold of major events that would soon occur. The night before his assassination he had this same dream. The following morning, President Lincoln was discussing war matters with his cabinet and General Grant. Lincoln said he was expecting good news from General Sherman who was on the front lines. When Grant asked why he thought so, Lincoln responded:

I had a dream last night; and ever since this war began I have had the same dream just before every event of great national importance. It portends some important event that will happen very soon. (*Recollections of Abraham Lincoln, 1847–1885*, Ward Hill Lamon, 1911)

Hindrances to Dreaming and Dream Recall

Dreaming is both a physical and a spiritual event in life. There are factors that can limit or hinder dream recall or impair our ability to dream. Dream impairment and recall issues common to many are:
- Sleeping disorders
- Abnormal sleep cycles
- Jarring wake-up by an alarm clock

- Sleeping in uncomfortable conditions
- Lacking a system to capture our dreams
- Believing negative cultural perceptions of dreaming
- Eating the wrong types of food before going to sleep
- Giving no thought to dreams immediately after waking
- Nightmares or tormenting spirits that enter our dreams
- Experiencing chronic pain or the effects of medication
- Prescription drugs, or recreational drugs, alcohol, sleeping pills, and cigarettes alter the chemical makeup of the body. Medications that treat depression, fear or anxiety may also distort dreams.
- Menstrual cycles and pregnancy cause hormonal changes in the body, which can make dream recall difficult. Sometimes the dreams are nonsensical as the pregnant mother begins to dream the same dream the baby is dreaming.
- Eating heavy, fatty, rich, or spicy foods before bedtime may cause the body to direct the blood flow to the digestive system rather than to the brain during sleep. It is helpful to establish good, healthy habits and take care of the body to ensure a healthy dream life.

Sleep disorders such as sleep apnea, or tossing and turning in bed, sleepwalking, and making frequent trips to the bathroom at night cause interruption of sleep cycles and patterns that prohibit dream recall. There are many great devices that are available to help resolve or lessen these problems.

Various interferences such as waking up suddenly in the morning to an alarm clock will jar the dreamer out of sleep causing the mind to erase details of the dream. Telephones, doorbells, knocking, slammed doors, children playing, family members' voices, or anything that causes sudden awakening may vaporize part of or all of the night's dreams.

Sometimes forgetting a dream is intentional. The dreamer may not want to remember due to fear of the dream's language or message. However, fear of a negative interpretation may cause us to miss out on the true encouraging and hopeful symbolism the Holy Spirit is trying to communicate. Even if the dream means that change is necessary, God is in the business of encouraging his own and he wants to give us hope. Satan wants to discourage us and bring fear into our lives. Likewise dreams from God are ultimately constructive not destructive. Tormenting demons and nightmares can hinder our dreams or wake us and interrupt sleep patterns. It is also important to guard the eye and ear gates so that evil messages do not have ground in our lives to infiltrate our dreams. Statistics indicate the average American will spend thirteen years of their otherwise productive life watching television.

Unforgiveness and bitterness can also hinder one's dream life as tormentors come and invade our dreams. It is important to forgive people quickly and not allow a root of bitterness to spring up in life. God gives us dreams because he loves us and wants to communicate to us 24 hours a day. We sleep one third of our lives and that would be a long time not to be in contact with God. So he invades our sleep and hovers over us causing the void places in our lives to be ordered according to his divine plans. Dreams lead us to the Father's heart. When we are in his presence we are transformed into his image. Dreams are the doorway into the realms of eternity where we can visit our heavenly Father and he comes to visit us.

Removing Hindrances and Remembering Your Dreams

What can we do to remove the hindrances to remembering our dreams? First, we must perceive dreams as valuable and important. In American culture dreams are not held in high regard. In church life we have not been taught to believe that dreams are from God, and in most religious fellowships we are warned against placing any weight or substance on dreams and the messages that they bring. We have not been trained to understand the symbolic language of the Holy Spirit in the dream realm, to discern the source of our dreams and to rightly interpret the ones that are from God. If we do not begin to regard our dreams from God as precious treasures of mystery then he may not continue to speak to us through dreams. Here are some practical things that we can do to improve dream life:

It is important to establish normal sleep cycles. Staying up too late, being too tired and missing sleep disrupts rapid eye movement (REM) dream cycles.

If jarred from sleep in the morning by an alarm clock or sudden loud sounds, dreams have a tendency to disappear. Alarm clocks will jar the dream away from us because dreams come while our minds are at peace and in quiet rest. One way to counteract this effect is to try to wake up gently and immediately reflect on last night's dreams. Upon waking we should listen to our inner voice and ask the Holy Spirit to help us understand and remember the dream(s). Before the rational mind kicks in, it is important to take notes or record the dream and date it. Morning time is a great time to receive the revelation and understanding of dreams, because it is fresh in our memories. Ask the Holy Spirit to bring the dream message to mind and ask God questions to clarify what the symbols mean.

Establish a system of capturing your dreams as they occur. Place a light, pen, and paper by your bed to jot down the outline of the dream. Capture the important facts and details upon waking from the dream. Postponing this important part of the process may result in losing the dream forever.

Another method of capturing the major ideas of dreams is to use a digital recorder to record dreams upon waking. In times of quiet meditation discuss the dream with the Holy Spirit. Write it in a dream journal, pray and actively wait for the Holy Spirit to give the interpretation. Then outline the actions that need to be taken to fulfill it or to derive the intended meaning from the dream. Always date and title dream entries. Typing dreams onto a home computer or online journal creates an ongoing record that can be updated as more revelation and spiritual insight is received. Dreams that remain a mystery or that the dreamer does not yet understand may be submitted to our interactive dream interpretation Web site at www.MyOnar.com. Barbie and a highly trained, very gifted team of individuals who have studied biblical dream interpretation for years will be able to assist you. Their added insights and years of experience can help unlock sealed dreams.

Another tip to uninterrupted sleep is to try to establish a habit of sleeping in a comfortable position. A violent sleeper who tosses to and fro throughout the night may tend to have fragmented dreams due to spurts of waking and sleeping. It helps to calm down and settle into a comfortable place before drifting off to sleep.

Dream Recall Strategies

Dream recall is a technique developed through discipline and practice. Forgetting or ignoring a dream is like walking away from knowledge and divine wisdom that God has imparted. The first three questions the dreamer must ask are:

What were the feelings upon awaking from the dream?

Determine the feelings stimulated by the dream. Emotions will give the dreamer a sense of the issues involved—are they resolved or unresolved? For example, if the dream evokes feelings of being puzzled it may be a message that things in the dreamer's life need to be examined and searched out. If the dream causes feelings of happiness or relief there may have been some issues resolved in the dreamer's life and the dream is a reflection of the change.

Psalm 139:23–24 Search me O God, and know my heart; Try me and know my anxious thoughts; And see if there be any hurtful way in me, And lead me in the everlasting way (NASU).

Psalm 51:10 Create in me a clean heart, O God, And renew a steadfast spirit within me (NASU).

What was the setting?

Although the location of a dream setting may have a literal interpretation, the setting may also define the dreamer's inner life. For example, a hospital in a dream might represent an actual medical facility and a literal illness, or it could symbolize an issue that needs healing in an area of the dreamer's life or relationships. Another interpretation is that hospitals accommodate patients. The meaning may hide a symbolic play on the word "patience" which is needed by the dreamer.

A school setting could symbolize education or preparation, which could be literal or traditional life lessons or spiritual training.

A foreign country setting may symbolize that the dreamer is outside of a comfort zone. Some questions to help reveal the meaning behind a foreign country setting are: How do I feel about this country? Why is this particular country in the dream and not any other country? What is the first thought that comes to mind when I think about this country? These types of questions will help the dreamer identify feelings and the significance of being in the new place.

If this dream was a story, what title would be fitting?

Asking this question will reveal the essence or general theme of the dream. Remember, the symbol vocabulary or meaning attributed to different events, places, or people in a dream is strictly individual, because we each have unique personal histories, attitudes, appreciations, likes, and dislikes.

Dreams are often road maps that help direct our course if we will only learn to read them correctly. Answering the questions above will quickly give the dreamer an overall sense of the issues brought to the surface by the dream. This way, the dream can be broken down into small segments so that the dreamer can take a strategic and structured approach to its interpretation. In this process, the dreamer will identify experiences and analogies in the dream as well as points of similarity between dreaming and waking life.

REM Sleep

REM sleep lasts about 15 minutes during a dreamer's 90 minute sleep cycle. Throughout the night we rotate through several 90 minute cycles which involve rapid eye movement or REM sleep. During REM sleep, as the name suggests, the brain is watching the dream occur. The dreamer's eyes actually shift back and forth almost as if across the movie screen of the soul as the dream unfolds. Oftentimes, women have better dream recall than men due to the differences in brain function. Women have more synapses that connect the two sides or hemispheres of the brain. The right side of the brain deals with the creative, artistic, emotional realm. In general, women are more right brain dominant than men who tend to be left brain dominant, logical, and analytical in nature. Women use the visual memory and inductive reasoning portion of the brain more often. Women remember more details such as the color and design of the clothing worn in dreams.

A good night's sleep is eight hours, and it is essential to have at least six hours of sleep in order for the body to phase through several REM cycles. If we don't get enough sleep or are overly tired it is more difficult to recall dreams because the body is too drained to allow the brain to remember the dreams.

Upon waking, focus in on the images in the dream. Ask the Holy Spirit to reveal the hidden truths and to bring a correct understanding of the dream. Ask the Holy Spirit for wisdom, the right interpretation, and the application of the dream. Write down the title, date, and record the dream in a journal. Record the main facts, setting, colors, feelings, and characters of the dream. Remembering a dream is easiest upon first waking, or in the state of awareness between sleep and awake, if the dreamer is able to do so without fully waking up.

Learning the Language of Our Dreams

Anyone who listens to the word but does not do what it says is like a man who looks at his face in a mirror and, after looking at himself, goes away and immediately forgets what he looks like (James 1:23–24NIV).

During ancient time periods, and across many cultures it was a widespread belief that dreams were divine messages from the invisible realm. Dreams ignite the conscious awareness of our physical, emotional, intellectual, social, and spiritual well-being. Dream symbols come from different areas including our present life, our past memories, and our subconscious and conscious mind. However, unlike the beliefs of those in ancient times, the American culture has a tendency to subdue the importance of dreams. Recalling dreams and understanding them is not an important part of American culture. Dreams are often belittled because in the real world they do not appear to contribute to the ladder of success. Some dreams that are particularly spiritual or revelatory can seem too weird to actually carry any weight of significance. Telling the story can often spark ripples of laughter instead of consideration. If this continues to be our attitude about dreams or if we listen to people who feel that way, the importance of dreams will continue to be lost. It is vital to focus on broadening your views so that we open the door for the Lord to speak to us instead of hindering him. Once we understand that God speaks to all of us in our dreams we will discover the importance of learning and embracing his symbolic language. God created us with the ability to imagine and to magnify. Therefore, whatever we focus on we empower, and what we ignore diminishes.

I will praise the name of God with a song, and will magnify Him with thanksgiving (Psalm 69:30).

If we focus on the negative images in our lives they will seemingly continue to grow until they reach monstrous proportions. They will continue to loom over us and shadow everything we do, think, and say. If we focus on God and the positive visions in our lives by giving thanks, good will be magnified. This brings us to a higher realm, and releases a positive influence around us that draws a more positive environment into our sphere of influence. If we begin to focus on dreams and their meanings in our lives they will begin to increase and we will prosper from understanding the destiny our dreams reveal to us.

Dreams can help us solve our problems and the problems of others if we are able to understand them. Dream recall is a skill that is learned as we diligently apply ourselves. To interpret a dream we must first be able to recall or remember its details. When we apply the wisdom we have received from the dream, God is able to direct the paths of our lives. Here are some basic guidelines in "understanding the dream." Eighty-five percent of the time dreams deal with the individual who is dreaming, rather than with others external to the dreamer. God speaks to us in a language of signs and symbols that we have to learn to understand. Dreams often show us blind spots and areas of weakness in our lives that may need change or work. Because eighty-five percent of all dreams are about the dreamer, our presence in a dream has meaning. Seeing or observing ourselves as a dream character often signifies that we are at peace with ourselves and readily accept the qualities and identify with them. Seeing other characters represented in our dreams indicates that there are qualities with which we do not consciously identify. By uncovering the language and symbolism of dreams we can discover many things. Some of these are:

- The relationship between the world and ourselves around the time of the dream.

- The "global" issues (physical and emotional challenges) that we face.

- Our subconscious beliefs and reactions.

- The condition of our body at the time of the dream: Are we tired, stressed, fatigued, or are we rested and refreshed?

Solving our problems through a dream occurs when God gives us a word of knowledge or revelation from a dream or even about the dream itself.

Mr. Johnson is a highly paid mechanical engineer. He is often hired by large production companies to troubleshoot their assembly lines when things break down. When the machinery is not functioning at peak performance or has to be shut down for any reason it causes a great loss of income to the company. Mr. Johnson was retained to solve a problem at one such company. He ran the usual diagnostic test and observed the machinery running. He was unable to pinpoint the problem. That night he prayed and asked for the answer to come to him in a dream. He then had a dream. In this dream Mr. Johnson was shown a panel on one of the machines. He watched the panel being removed. There he was shown a nut that had fallen off of its bolt; it was lying between two levers. This nut was prohibiting the proper connection and range of motion thus slowing down production. The next morning he confidently went to the plant manager and asked him to shut the assembly line down. The manager argued with him, yelling that a shut down would cost thousands of dollars as it would be stopping production. "How long will this take?" the manager asked. Mr. Johnson replied, "About five minutes, maximum." The order was given and the production line came to a screeching halt. Mr. Johnson took his wrench and screwdriver, opened the panel and located the missing nut. He put the nut back on the bolt, tightened it and replaced the panel. He then announced that his fee would be $10,000. The manager yelled, "WHAT? You want me to pay you $10,000 for replacing one nut?" And with that Mr. Johnson said, "No, not for replacing the nut, but for knowing where the nut was located and that it needed to be replaced." He was paid, the assembly line was restarted and the production company was able to recoup the time that was lost.

There are many different types of dreams, so they will all have different meanings and applications depending on the person, the setting and the environment. Dreams also have different sources. They can come from God, the busyness of the day or from our soul's desires. Our physical bodies can even communicate to us in dreams. Evil or demonic forces that we allow into our lives by not surrendering certain areas of our heart to God can also be a source from which our dreams originate.

Recurring Dreams

Why do we sometimes dream the same dream over and over? The main reason dreams reoccur is that we have not entered into the understanding of the message yet. So the same dream message continues to play over and over. Sometimes the characters change or the setting changes, but the overall message remains the same. Once we come into the understanding and we apply the wisdom and insight of the dream's meaning to our lives the dream will cease to replay. Oftentimes, through recurring dreams, God is trying to communicate something. When we finally understand what he is saying to us, the dream script will stop repeating itself. Our dreams will change when our behaviors change. We can have several different types of dreams but they all deal with the same underlying theme. A biblical example is Pharaoh's dream of the seven cows and seven ears of grain. *Genesis 41:1–7.*

Nightmares

Why do we have nightmares, and how can we eliminate disturbing dreams? Nightmares are about things in our lives that we fear. We are not to be fearful or run from the enemy or difficulties but face them in God's power and boldness. Once we face and confront our fears they will stop haunting us. The people, places, and events in our dreams hold tremendous significance for understanding ourselves. Nightmares are simply messages from the deepest part of us to our consciousness calling for change. If unheeded, not only may we continue to suffer from the unpleasantness of a "bad" dream, but we run the risk of perpetuating negativity in our waking life.

Sometimes a nightmare can be a wakeup call from God. Oftentimes when we ignore what God is trying to speak to us through dreams, whether consciously or subconsciously we can experience nightmares. These terrors of the night get the point across in a graphic way, in order to make a lasting impression on us, so that we will remember the dream and dig into its meaning.

Universal Symbols

There are universal symbols such as the circle, which represents covenant, wholeness, or completeness. But sometimes only the dreamer knows the meanings of the symbols. So in order to accurately interpret dreams, the interpreter should ask questions to find out what personal significance a particular dream symbol holds for that person. Symbols can have totally different meanings to each dreamer. Although they are not as important as people in our dreams, animals can be of large significance as well and sometimes portray our emotional state. People are usually symbolic of our inner person. As a light divides the colors of a prism so a dream will help divide the various parts of our personality. Dreams help us to rightly discern our true selves and to remove the mask that we wear to protect ourselves from our world. Dreams help us to learn to listen to God's voice through symbolic language. They enable us to cooperate with God's greater purpose and plan for our lives. Dreams help us to reach our untapped potential by bringing us into harmony with ourselves, God, and others. They enable us to get at the heart of the matter.

If we want God to speak to us through dreams and visions,

he will. God is not a respecter of persons. Abraham, Jacob, Mary and Joseph, Peter, the Prophets, Gideon, Solomon, Daniel, Joseph, and heathen Kings were all lead by dreams and visions, so we are in good company. We must pursue God and learn the way he speaks through dream symbols and night parables. We should focus on and give attention to our personal dream language. Develop an intimate relationship with the Holy Spirit and he will give insight, revelation and the interpretation for not only our dreams but for the dreams of others as well.

Interpreting the Essence of a Dream's Theme

Identifying the essence or tone of a dream means we are determining the theme, main concept, or message that the dream brings to light.

To capture the essence of the dream, the dreamer should first record the main symbols of the dream removing the extraneous details, objects, and names but retaining the action of the dream. This should be done before the dream is evaluated by point of view or perspective. The theme or main concept of the dream will provide the focus of what or who the dream is about.

Each person has a unique dream vocabulary that has been assigned specific meanings depending on the dreamer's life experiences. Personal symbols in dreams are joined with surrounding details that give them life and dimension. While to some a candle symbolizes romance, ambiance, and beauty, to others it may symbolize their only source of warmth, poverty, and shame. Dogs are known as "man's best friend." This interpretation may apply to dog lovers but not to the person who was viciously mauled by an angry dog as a child. Animals are used in dreams to symbolize our good and bad character traits.

Children and babies often represent a new phase or beginning, immaturity, or childishness, innocence, purity, naivety, spiritual fruit, or something that is very dependent upon us for its well-being.

The dreams that God formulates to speak to us in our sleep are oftentimes very precise. They efficiently address multiple areas, layers, issues, and topics as they reveal concealed knowledge and hidden mysteries come to light through one short dream. It is not unusual for one dream to address both a personal concern and a universal meaning that can be applied to other situations. A dream can forewarn by predicting the future and enable the dreamer to prepare by removing health issues or character flaws or to solve a problem that is arising. We associate dream symbols with our personal experiences and the memories those experiences inspire. The symbols that appear in dreams evoke certain reactions or responses from the dreamer based on that person's individual makeup.

The dreamer will often ask more questions when the interpreter is only giving the essence of the dreams meaning. This technique will keep dialogue and communication flowing between the dreamer and the interpreter. There is an art to giving just enough to keep the person interested but not outlining each and every symbol by definition or rote memory. There must be a flow of the Spirit and not just head knowledge that is given in the interpretation of dreams.

To arrive at the essence or theme of a dream, remove all of the unnecessary information such as extraneous details, descriptions of things and places, and names. The theme is going to surround the action or focus of the dream that will lead to the understanding of the big picture.

Interpreting Keys

Keys to interpreting dreams are found by focusing on the symbols that cause the most emotion in us as we recall the dream. Interpreting a dream is like solving a riddle or putting a puzzle together. The dreamer attempts to fit the pieces together until the perfect fit is attained. This is done by comparing and contrasting symbols; asking questions— "Why this symbol and not another?" and making associations between symbols. An example is, if someone says the word cow some may think milk or beef, others may think bull. The color of the cow will give us a more specific indicator as to its meaning and function in the dream. If the cow is colored blue it could recall a childhood toy cow we loved. What about the word house? Some people envision an estate; others

Chapter Four
Biblical Foundation for Dreams

Dreamers of the Bible

A warm breeze gently lifted the gossamer veil and it lilted toward the bed chamber of the king. He lay restlessly on his royal silk covers hoping to catch a few hours of rest before his vizier could impose another matter of court on his beleaguered mind. He thought of his new prize: a lovely, graceful woman, the sister of a wealthy traveler. She came to the king's court last week with her brother. "Abraham" was the brother's name, and the king could not get her out of his mind. Abimelech was going to increase Abraham's wealth by making Sarah a part of the king's harem.

Abimelech hung between blessed sleep and his pleasant thoughts of Sarah until he finally succumbed to the visions of the night. His dreams, though, were not pleasant. A smoky, eerie presence hovered over his bed and hung in his thoughts. This was a new sensation, a mysterious presence. This Spirit had never visited him before. The warm air quickly grew thick and a cold sweat bubbled up on the rulers' furrowed brow. His head lay heavy upon his velvet pillows as they darkened from his salty, oily sweat dripping off the curled side burns above his ears.

A voice spoke to the frozen figure as Abimelech clutched at his covers, his feet twitching ever so slightly as he tried to find footing in the troubling visions he now perceived.

He could see Sarah standing before a man with strange garments. He wore white linen and a large turban with a gold band holding it to his head. Abimelech had never seen this dress but he instinctively knew he was a religious figure, some kind of a priest. Sarah was being wed to another man. She was not his. Sarah was another man's wife. She was already married. It would be wrong to take her. And the man, Sarah's husband, who was he? A sudden jerk shot Abimelech straight up in bed, an involuntary gush of air groaned from deep within his throat. Beads of sweat congealed on his face. His hands still shaking in fear from his encounter, Abimelech ordered his servants to call for Abraham at the first sign of dawn. In a few hours, Abraham would tell all.

Throughout Scripture, God spoke to both godly and ungodly people through dreams and visions. In fact, a third of the Bible deals with dreams, visions, and the impact the interpretations have on the dreamers' life stories. God warned Abimelech, an ungodly ruler, in a dream, when he appeared in the dream and said, *"Behold, you are a dead man because of the woman whom you have taken, for she is married"* (Genesis 20:3). God also told the king that he knew Abimelech had intended to take the woman to be his wife in integrity of heart. The ruler did not know that she was another man's wife. God revealed the truth to Abimelech during a dream. Abimelech, a pagan king, came close to committing a transgression against his own laws. God spared him this disgrace and humiliation by causing a vision of the night to warn him. Abimelech responded with integrity and wisdom, quickly returning the beautiful Sarah to her rightful husband. In the same way, God directs our paths through dreams, letting us know when we may be outside of his plan, even when we have erred unintentionally. God warns us because he loves us, and he wants to build a relationship with us based on trust and guidance through a supernatural display of his direction in our lives. God wants to reveal his plans of destiny; plans about events only he could know.

Nebuchadnezzar is another ancient and pagan king who encountered God in the night season.

Nebuchadnezzar, a king who did not even believe there was a Creator, saw an extrinsic dream that revealed God's future plans for a later time in the world's history.

Onar Dreams

What is an Onar dream? *Onar* is a Greek word that means dream. There are five onar dreams mentioned in the gospel of Matthew. An onar tends to indicate more literal images, like a vision rather than a complex metaphorical dream. Angels often appear and interact with the dreamer giving messages of instruction and direction. At times, the angelic encounter provides a heavenly picture message delivered to the dreamer in a vivid, lifelike, visionary type format.

An even better known onar dream was illustrated through the Bible character Joseph. The earthly father of Jesus was warned in an onar dream that saved the lives of his family. In this dream an angel appeared to Joseph and told him to take baby Jesus and Mary to Israel because those who wanted to kill Jesus were no longer a threat (*Matthew 2:19–23*). In the same way, God can direct our paths to different geographic regions through dreams.

King Herod called the Magi secretly to find out the exact time the brilliant star appeared in the heavens announcing the birth of a King. Herod sent the wise men to Bethlehem requesting they make a careful search to find the baby Jesus. Herod commanded them to report the new king's location so that he too may go and worship him. The star led them to a house where they presented their precious treasures and gifts of gold, frankincense, and myrrh. They found and worshipped Jesus and being warned in an onar dream not to report to King Herod, they returned home another way.

Years later, King Herod's death released another angelic dream visitation for Joseph. While in Egypt the angel of the Lord entered Joseph's dream (an onar) once again saying, *"Get up, take the child and his mother and go to the land of Israel, for those who were trying to take the child's life are dead."* Joseph heard that Herod's son Archelaus was ruling in Judea so Joseph was afraid to go there. He was warned in another onar dream, so he withdrew to the district of Galilee, to live in a town called Nazareth. This fulfilled two prophecies that first Jesus would come out of Egypt, and secondly, that Jesus would be called a Nazarene (*Matthew 2:7–23*).

The birth and life of Jesus Christ was a historic event that was divinely orchestrated and directed by visions, dream events, and encounters with angels.

Mary, the mother of Jesus was a young virgin girl who lived in Nazareth, a small town in Galilee. She was pledged to be married to a simple carpenter called Joseph. He was a descendant of King David. Joseph was a man of strong moral character who was ruled by a compassionate heart. During their engagement, Mary was visited by the angel Gabriel who proclaimed, *"Greetings, you who are highly favored! The Lord is with you." "Do not be afraid, Mary, you have found favor with God. You will be with child and give birth to a son, and you are to give him the name Jesus. He will be great and will be called the Son of the Most High. The Lord God will give Him the throne of His father David, and He will reign over the house of Jacob forever; His kingdom will never end." She was perplexed and responded, "How will this be," "since I am a virgin?" Gabriel answered, "The Holy Spirit will come upon you, and the power of the Most High will overshadow you. So the holy one to be born will be called the Son of God" (Luke 1:26–38 NIV).*

The angel's words were true. Mary conceived of the Holy Spirit before she and Joseph were married. Because Joseph her husband was a righteous man, and did not want to expose her to public disgrace, he had thought that he would divorce her quietly.

But after he had considered this, an angel of the Lord appeared to him in an onar dream and said, *"Joseph son of David, do not be afraid to take Mary home as your wife, because what is conceived in her is from the Holy Spirit. She will give birth to a son, and you are to give him the name Jesus, because he will save his people from their sins."*

All this took place to fulfill what the Lord had said through the prophet: "The virgin will be with child and will give birth to a son, and they will call him Immanuel"—which means, "God with us."

When Joseph awoke, he did what the angel of the Lord had commanded and took Mary home as his wife. But Joseph had no union with her until she gave birth to a son. And he gave him the name Jesus.

Spousal Dreams

Husbands and wives may also have dreams that are meant to be shared with each other. Oftentimes God uses the dreams of a spouse to bring confirmation of something he is doing in the other mate's heart, mind, or life. One such biblical example is the dream of Pilate's wife, Claudia. Her dream concerned Jesus and the images must have been horrific. She dreamed such a disturbing onar dream she was denied sleep and exhausted after wrestling all night with the vision. She saw that Jesus was an innocent man. After rising from the dream, Pilot's wife told her husband to have nothing to do with Jesus because he was a just man

(Matthew 27:19). Scripture tells us that after Claudia's warning, during Pilot's confrontation with Jesus, Pilot tried to remove himself from his unjust sentence by "washing his hands" of the conviction of Jesus.

Could Claudia's dream encounter have appeared something like this?

Claudia leaned on the cold stone balcony. It was her favorite spot to watch the city below, but not tonight. This was the second time she found herself here gazing into the darkness before dawn. Her thoughts raced like wild horses tied to chariots loosed from a fight.

Before leaving Rome, her blessed city, she had heard so much about the Jews and their beliefs. But during her husband's long ruler-ship over this tiny province of Judah she had grown to know many Jews. Yes, they were strong willed and independent thinkers who held tightly to their religion, held to it as if their very life depended on it. Their fastidious adherence caused her much wonder.

Some of her servants, being Jews, knew the stories told by the rabbis or religious teachers. Claudia would ask them to tell her of their beliefs. She had heard of Moses and his claim that another leader, like himself, would come to rule. Claudia also heard the rumors whispered behind her back that the Messiah was expected soon and many believed he already lived in Israel. This fact was both frightening and exciting to Claudia. It would prove their religion had true prophets and it would also prove dangerous to her husband, and herself.

Knowing the story about Moses did not comfort her tonight. Twice Moses had come to her this very night. Twice the chills ran all over her skin. Twice she found herself grasping the pillars on her veranda trying to calm her racing heart.

The first time Moses appeared in her dream he was carrying heavy tablets. There was strange writing on them. She could only make out a few letters of the Hebrew alphabet. She reasoned that these must have been the Testament, the Law that Moses brought to these people. Moses cradled the large, foreboding stone slabs in his arms. He almost cradled them like a child. His eyes were sad but full of expectation. Claudia noticed his gray beard and how strong and healthy Moses looked. Reasoning to herself she began to question why he was here. Did he expect something of her? Did he want her to become a Jew and follow the Law? She knew it was right. The Jews she knew lived a very austere and holy life. Not like the decadent life she knew back in Rome. Or was Moses simply on her mind because of the stories she heard during the day?

As she lay dreaming, her thoughts wandered to her former life in Rome, and she thought of the contrast between her former religion and the Priest of Isis and Anubis. Lurid visions of temple prostitutes, both male and female, offering themselves to worshippers crept into her view. Suddenly, Moses stepped forward and threw the stones to the floor. The tablets hit the tile floor with a crash and smashed into a hundred pieces of rock and dust. In an instant her hands flew up to grab the stones and to protect herself from the Law. Her arms springing into the air shocked her out of her sleep but she could still feel a tingling in her hands as her nerves crackled from her sudden stir. This was only the first dream.

Moses' second appearance was even more disturbing. Moses appeared again, bearing the large sapphire-hued stones in his arms. Claudia moved forward to touch them. As her hand extended toward the hard unforgiving edges they suddenly blurred and instead of stone she now reached for cloth. Claudia retracted her hand and stood back as she noticed Moses was not cradling stone any longer, but a man. Her hand flew to her mouth as she recognized this man. It was the same man her servants kept talking about. It was rumored that he was a prophet. He was a healer with great power and words. He stepped down out of Moses' arms. It appeared as if the stone tablets transformed into his glowing garment. He stood in front of Claudia with those same sad, expectant eyes of Moses. But this man they called Yeshua, held his arms out to her, almost beckoning her.

Claudia felt such love and acceptance from this miracle healer. He looked right at her. He peered directly into her heart. Claudia wanted to shrink from his all-knowing gaze, but her eyes were held captive. She could not avert her eyes. He knew who she was in her innermost being. She felt compelled to move forward, to melt into his forgiving embrace and rest in his arms, but before she could move Moses quickly stepped back and once again violently threw down the stone tablets of the Law. This time the full impact of the stone slabs were hurled against Yeshua's back, tearing his flesh as they shattered. In revulsion and remorse her sleep was torn from her as she awoke to the sound of a thunderous crack of a metal tined leather whip.

Claudia jumped out of bed and ran to her balcony. She was just in time to see a large contingency of high Jewish officials dragging a group into the courtyard where her husband heard complaints and judged the people. Her eyes caught sight of one man and she froze like the cold static pillar standing next to her. Yeshua! His name slipped from her mouth. Even though he looked beaten and haggard, she knew it was the man in her dreams. Those who taught the law were bringing Yeshua to her husband's court of law. She had to warn her husband Pilate of her dreams and of the healer Yeshua's innocence.

Overcoming Fear and Inferiority Dreams

Gideon overcame his fear and inferiority complex. He became the leader of 300 valiant warriors by understanding his enemy's dream. The adversary of Gideon dreamed that a loaf of barley bread tumbled into the Midian camp, and the loaf struck a tent with such force that the tent collapsed. Gideon's enemy revealed the meaning of the dream. The collapse of the tent was *"nothing else but the sword of Gideon … Into his hand God has delivered Midian and the whole camp."* After hearing this dream and its interpretation, Gideon had the confidence to follow the LORD's instruction. By culling his army of over twenty-two thousand men down to a streamlined, faith-filled remnant of three hundred soldiers, God, not man, received the glory for defeating the enemy. Gideon and his men fought, but God gave the line of attack, and won the battle. Victory is not achieved on the broad expansive thoroughfares of life, but on the narrow, succinct paths. Dreams only seem impossible when we view them through eyes of fear. When we behold their wisdom with eyes of faith they become a living reality. Facing the ugly monsters in our dreams takes courage, but conquering those same monsters in our waking life requires trust and humble submission to God. *(Judges 7:13–18)*

Destiny Dreams—Jacob's Ladder

Creative Illustration

The voice of his beloved mother still rang in his ears. Her desperate pleas for him to take care and leave quickly prodded him along the rock-strewn road. He would obey his parents' desire for him to visit his cousin. There he would find safety for his life. There he would find a wife—one of his own clan. He moved quickly and ate sparingly from the goatskin filled with thick creamy camel's milk. The need for a wife was a good cover. The real reason he fled for his life was the just anger of his brother, Esau. He needed to find a place to sleep. The sun was setting.

His brother was furious and wanted him dead. It was a tricky plan, but all had gone as his mother had hoped. He was now blessed by his father and was on his own, if only he could get safely away from his brother. Esau was a bloody man; always hunting and killing. He thought of the skins hanging around the walls of his father's tent and strewn on the ground to conceal the desert below. The stagnant smell of dead animals clung to the hair of his brother's arms. The remembrance of his brother's heavy odor added to the weight of the air that hung so deep around his neck this night.

Jacob neared Haran and lay down with a stone under his head. The flight into the night must have tired him more than he knew as he felt his eyelids drowsily slide over his eyes. Exhausted, he quickly fell into sleep and started to dream. This was not an ordinary dream. He had never encountered this scene before. Usually he dreamed of bleating sheep and goats and caravans of camels, but in this dream the sky was clear and the stars danced. Their brilliance was mystical and they appeared larger than usual. They hung so close he thought he could reach up and touch them. As he gazed at the dream in wonder he saw a mystery in the night sky. The night appeared to split open as if a gate was swung wide. This was not a bright star. It was much too brilliant and blinding to be a star. And the strangest vision was the form of a man beckoning to Jacob from the opening in the night sky. The illuminated figure stood at the pinnacle of what appeared to be a gleaming golden trellis or something more like a ladder.

Angels were moving up and down this translucent ladder almost effortlessly. Their incandescent wings were moving but it didn't seem like they were needed to travel toward heaven or earth. They were both ascending and descending on this golden bright ladder, when the man at the top of the ladder spoke. His words sounded like that of his father's blessing but this voice was more inspiring, more gripping. The sound was kind, yet it had such commanding depth and gravity that it sounded to Jacob like the voice of a King who was used to being heard and obeyed. What the voice said pierced his heart and he hung on every word. He knew this was something special. He knew it was more than just a dream. He knew he had to remember what was said and that it would make a difference in his life, but there was little doubt he could ever forget the blessing uttered over him that night.

"I am the LORD, *the God of your father Abraham and the God of Isaac; the land on which you lie, I will give it to you and to your descendants. Your descendants will also be like the dust of the earth, and you will spread out to the west and to the east and to the north and to the south; and in you and in your descendants shall all the families of the earth be blessed. Behold, I am with you and will keep you wherever you go, and will bring you back to this land; for I will not leave you until I have done what I have promised you."*

When Jacob awoke he was trembling all over and could not keep his hands from shaking. *"I will call this place the House of God, for surely, God is in this place."* But no one had ever told Jacob that God dwelled here. Jacob set up the stone that was under his head and poured oil on the top of the stone and called the place Bethel.

Jacob knew the dream packed a power and a destiny he could not explain but it moved inside him and the blessing kept running over and over in his mind. In answer to the man at the top of the ladder who stood in the open gate, Jacob promised that if God would make these things come to pass, then the LORD would be his God. In his heart Jacob knew it would happen and to show his passion Jacob made a promise to give God a tenth of all that was given to him. The one thing that Jacob could not explain because it escaped his understanding was how his life would touch every family on earth. This seemed too much to believe but it was a wonder that filled him with hope to think how it would come to pass.

Jacob is often portrayed as a deceiver, a trickster or one who took

73

any means or measures necessary to obtain the upper hand. Jacob went after Esau's birthright and blessings, even if it meant he had to cheat, lie, and steal. But, on closer observation it becomes evident that Esau willingly surrendered his birthright for a simple bowl of soup; a most costly and immoral mistake. Jacob merely obeyed the commands of his mother Rebekah to gain the first born blessing. Jacob protested that his actions, if discovered, could appear as deception and could bring a curse. His mother said she would gladly bear the curse so Jacob could gain the blessing of the first born. Yet God loved, sought out, and revealed himself to Jacob and he hated the immoral, godless Esau. God knew Jacob, a man of peace, would pursue him with passion. *Hebrews 12:14–17* tells us if we desire to see God we must *"Pursue peace with all men, and the sanctification without which no one will see the Lord. See to it that no one comes short of the grace of God; that no root of bitterness springing up causes trouble, and by it many be defiled; that there be no immoral or godless person like Esau, who sold his own birthright for a single meal. For you know that even afterwards, when he desired to inherit the blessing, he was rejected, for he found no place for repentance, though he sought for it with tears. NASU*

Jacob's sin, character flaws, and weaknesses did not cause God to rebuke, reject or desert him. It did, however, cause God to reveal himself to Jacob in an amazing spiritual encounter. The LORD stood at the top of a heavenly ladder connecting heaven to earth. This heavenly door or gateway acted as an entrance for the angels to reach into Jacob's destiny and dreams. The answers to the things we are missing or lacking in our character and lives are all held in heavenly chambers for us. Angelic messengers are able to ascend and descend eternity's ladder to deliver gifts, messages of knowledge, wisdom, and spiritual vision to man.

Strategies for Gaining Wealth Dreams

Divine strategies for success are created from the dream fibers of moral excellence, character, integrity, and love.

God gave Jacob the ability to gain wealth through a dream. Jacob worked for Laban for many years, and Laban was a controlling and manipulative master. The time came for Jacob to move on and begin to provide for a family of his own. In a dream, God showed Jacob that he was to ask Laban for all of the newborn speckled, streaked, and gray-spotted lambs and rams. Jacob was owed payment that he'd so tirelessly worked for over the years. Laban agreed to give him the livestock he asked for because the streaked, speckled and gray-spotted rams were considered outcast and undesirable in the agricultural industry of that time. No one wanted them and they were not valued. Just as Jacob saw in the dream, the majority of the lambs and rams were born speckled, streaked and gray-spotted (*Genesis 31:10–43*).

Spiritually, what happened in Jacobs's dream was this: the angel of God visited him to answer his prayers for deliverance. The angel enabled him to see the divine strategies to prosper even while working under the controlling, manipulative hand of Laban. One lesson that can be taken from this story is that God is able to use what seems to be a throw-away remnant and make it into a lucrative source of income. This lesson applies to humanity today. God is still fashioning lives that are prospering and bringing him glory from broken, rejected, outcast people. Jacob was told to "*Lift your eyes now and see all.*" He was given a visual plan he could see in his dream. We are changed when we behold God's idea of what we could become, even when it does not fit into society's mold of thinking. God's ways and thoughts are higher and it is God who sends wealth. Proverbs further drives this point home by showing us that with God are riches, honor, wealth, and prosperity; and with God our treasuries are full without the trouble of striving to attain it (*Proverbs 8:18, 21* and *10:22*). Believe in your heart's desire, and your dreams will guide you to ascend mountain heights of faith and prosperity.

Wisdom Dreams

The LORD *sends poverty and wealth; He humbles and He exalts. He raises the poor from the dust and lifts the needy from the ash heap; He seats them with princes and has them inherit a throne of honor. (1 Samuel 2:7–8 NIV).*

The revelation in this verse was God's message to Solomon, the wisest man in history. Solomon entered into revelatory dialogue with the

Lord in his dream. He was given a spiritual ear to hear, and a heart of wisdom to understand and discern the voice of the Lord.

Solomon: *"So give Your servant an understanding heart to judge Your people to discern between good and evil. For who is able to judge this great people of Yours?"*

It was pleasing in the sight of the Lord that Solomon had asked this thing.

God: *"Because you have asked for a wise and discerning heart, I will also give you what you have not asked: riches and honor. There will not be any among kings like you for all of your days."*

Then Solomon awoke and it was a dream. He went to Jerusalem and stood before the ark of the Lord's covenant and sacrificed offerings to the Lord (*1 Kings 3:9–15*). Through this encounter with God, Solomon understood a heavenly principle of sacrifice and return. The more you offer to God, the greater the return. Multiply sacrificial giving and God will multiply the return.

Dream Interpreters of the Bible

Daniel

Daniel of the Bible was not only a dreamer himself, but he also interpreted the dreams of others. King Nebuchadnezzar was one such recipient of Daniel's dream interpreting gift. The king had a troubling dream which none of the mystics, sorcerers, and occult leaders in his kingdom could interpret. But Daniel, led and inspired by God, sought the Lord for the interpretation through which he astonished the king and his court.

Daniel replied, "No wise man, enchanter, magician or diviner can explain to the king the mystery he has asked about, but there is a God in heaven who reveals mysteries. He has shown King Nebuchadnezzar what will happen in days to come" (Daniel 2:27–28 NIV).

King Nebuchadnezzar dreamed that a statue stood before him. It was awesome in appearance, and its head was made of gold. Its breast and its arms were silver, and its belly and thighs were made of bronze. Its legs were iron, and its feet were partly iron and partly clay. The king continued looking at the statue until a stone was cut, without hands, out of a nearby mountain. The stone struck the statue's feet and the entire statue crumbled. The wind blew the dust of the statue away so that not a trace of it could be found. Then the stone that struck the statue became a great mountain and filled the whole earth. Daniel heard the king's dream and gathered three of his friends to pray and ask God for the interpretation, so that he could interpret what the sorcerers could not. After prayer, Daniel's interpretation of the king's dream was this:

The statue's head of gold was the king himself to whom God had given authority over all of the land. Daniel went on to say that after Nebuchadnezzar, another kingdom would arise that was inferior to his— represented by the silver breast and arms of the statue. Then a third kingdom of bronze would rise up, indicated by the belly and the thighs. The forth kingdom was to be one of iron and it would crush and break all things, as iron does. The clay was representative of the mixing of the offspring of man with the iron, or the kingly heirs. This indicated the lack of cohesiveness and, therefore, weakness of the last kingdom. The kingdoms of this world will become the kingdoms of our God and King.

Inasmuch as you saw that the stone was cut out of the mountain without hands, and that it broke in pieces the iron, the bronze, the clay, the silver, and the gold—the great God has made known to the king what will come to pass after this. The dream is certain, and its interpretation is sure (Daniel 2:45 NASU).

Then the king had a second dream and remembered Daniel's interpretation of his first dream:

I saw a dream which made me afraid, and the thoughts on my bed and the visions of my head troubled me. Therefore I issued a decree to bring in all the wise men of Babylon before me, that they might make known to me the interpretation of the dream (Daniel 4:5–6).

Then the magicians, the astrologers, the Chaldeans, and the soothsayers came in, and I told them the dream; but they did not make known to me its interpretation. But at last Daniel came before me (his name is Belteshazzar, according to the name of my god; in him is the Spirit of the Holy God), and I told the dream before him, saying, "Belteshazzar, chief of the magicians, because I know that the Spirit of the Holy God is in you, and no secret troubles you, explain to me the visions of my dream that I have seen, and its interpretation" (Daniel 4:7–9 NKJV).

The occult prognosticators are not able to reveal God's hidden mysteries because they cannot enter into the realm of God's light. They operate in the darkened soul realm, out of the Tree of the Knowledge of Good and Evil. They have not been enlightened to know truth. Only believers who are full of the Spirit of God can interpret a Spirit-given dream through the Tree of Life, Jesus. Daniel gathered his friends and they sought and worshipped God for the interpretation of the king's dreams. Daniel was able to receive revelation, insight and knowledge from God because he was a man of prayer.

An interesting detail that we find in Scripture is that in his own dreams, Daniel wrote down the main facts. It is not necessary to write down every small exacting detail of a dream, just the main things that stand out—colors, images, people, names, etc.

In the first year of Belshazzar king of Babylon, Daniel had a dream and visions of his head while on his bed. Then he wrote down the dream, telling the main facts (Daniel 7:1).

Joseph

Joseph is another amazing dreamer and dream interpreter of the Bible. His life was literally mapped out by his own God-given dreams and the dreams he interpreted for others. Joseph's dreams foretold his destiny though a map of parabolic metaphor. In time, the powerful imagery revealed meaning that moved his heart and changed the destiny of the dreamer as well as those around him. In short, God used Joseph's dreams to guide him. He gave him the gift of interpretation to lead and guide others, and favor to eventually guide a kingdom. This unique journey of a relationship with God led Joseph down, down, down to the pit, to slavery, to the dungeon, and finally up to stand before the palace's throne to rule by Pharaoh's side.

God gave Joseph an understanding of dream symbols. Joseph practiced his gift at the bottom rungs of society before God promoted him to the top where he stood before royal kings. Joseph was seventeen years old when he had a prophetic dream about his life as it related to his family and the tribe of Israel. The number seventeen means victory, spiritual order, and election. God elected to wait until Joseph was seventeen to give him two significant dreams that brought his life into spiritual order *(Genesis 37:2–4)*. If we will believe and fight for the dreams that are given to us in our youth they will come true and carry us through life!

The patriarch Jacob gives the account of Joseph's dreams. Joseph was Jacob's favorite son, who was born to him in his old age. To display his special love for Joseph he had a richly ornamented and embroidered color saturated coat designed for him. The multi-colors of his coat may have been inspired by the rich colors of the rainbow, which could indicate the hand of covenant resting upon Joseph. God's covenant word points to the time when God promised his Spirit would be poured out upon all flesh *(Acts 2)*. In *Isaiah 11:2* it speaks of the seven spirits of God which sequentially correspond to the seven colors of the rainbow. These same seven colors are also displayed in the fiery flames of the lampstands in the book of Revelation. We will discuss colors more in depth in the chapter on color to follow.

Joseph's stepbrothers saw that their father loved Joseph more than any of them. The jealousy in their hearts caused them to hate him. One of Joseph's responsibilities was to tend the flocks along with his stepbrothers. His brothers had nothing good to say about him. Returning evil for evil, Joseph often brought their father bad reports about them.

Like many in the Middle East, Joseph was given to dreams. Lacking maturity, humility, and wisdom he spouted them off to his brothers who took issue with his hasty, arrogant dreams. He said to them,

"Listen to this wonderful dream I had: We were all binding golden sheaves of grain out in the field (circle of influence, life) *when suddenly my*

bundle rose and stood upright elevated above yours, (promotion to a high place of leadership) *while your sheaves humbly gathered around mine and bowed* (submitting to his authority, servanthood) *down to it."*
His brothers snarled at him, "Do you intend to reign over us? Will the likes of you actually rule us?" They hated him all the more because of his dream and what he had said.
Shortly thereafter, Joseph had another dream, and he told it to his brothers. "Listen," he said, "I had another dream, and this time the sun and moon and eleven stars were bowing down submitting to me."
When he told his father and his eleven brothers, his father reprimanded him and said, "What is this dreaming you do? Will your mother (moon) *and I* (sun) *and your brothers* (stars) *actually come and bow down to the ground before you?"*

His brother's envy and jealous hatred toward him grew, but his father kept brooding and pondering over the matter of Joseph's dreams of destiny. Jacob may have recognized that God's hand was on Joseph in a special way even from his birth.

This second encouraging dream depicts Joseph's family members in a positive light. The chosen heavenly symbols of the sun, moon, and stars depict their great abilities to shine above others. God planned for them to become the patriarchs of the nation of Israel. This second dream reveals the vast magnitude of Joseph's rule and influence over the nations of the world, not just his own family.

When Jacob was presented with Joseph's blood-soaked garment, had he properly discerned the two dreams, he would have realized that Joseph had met with his stepbrothers' wrath and foul play. Jacob would have realized Joseph's death was only staged. Jacob should have known this because of the two repeating dreams and the *law of double meaning* that affirms destiny. When a dream from God is repeated it indicates that God is establishing that thing and it will shortly come to pass. Jacob believed the lie, assumed the worst, succumbed to his grief and despair and fell into depression. He refused to be comforted by his remaining children. God intends for us to get hold of our emotions, and stop letting them run wild blowing things out of proportion. God wants us to be led by the Spirit and respond accordingly.

These two dreams set Joseph, his brothers and the lineage of Jacob (the nation of Israel), on a course that would lead them into captivity in Egypt and deliverance from the famine. God had programmed Joseph's future path in his dreams that led him to fulfill his destiny as an Egyptian ruler.

The Bible story in *Genesis 40:1–23* tells of two individuals who had similar dreams about their jobs in the King's palace on the same night but with two very different interpretations and drastically different outcomes.

The Pharaohs of Egypt commanded great power and presence. Their servants' lives often hung in the balance. To simply frown in Pharaoh's presence could result in a death sentence. The King's official cupbearer and baker had offended their master. He was enraged so he summoned the captain of the guard to arrest and confine them to the same prison as Joseph. The captain knew that there was something uniquely special about Joseph. It was evident that the hand of the Lord rested on him. God prospered Joseph with great favor. The Captain assigned Joseph custody of the butler and baker. The same night, while in the cold, dark prison God gave the imprisoned cupbearer and baker a dream—and each dream had a distinct meaning of its own.

As the sun was beginning to peek over the horizon Joseph made his usual prison rounds. He came upon the damp sweltering cells of Pharaoh's officials. He found them both dejected and bewildered.

"Why are your faces so sad today?" he asked. "We both had dreams," they answered, "but there are no fortune tellers or magicians to interpret them, there is no one who is able to interpret dreams in this god forsaken prison." Then Joseph said to them, "Interpretations belong to God and the one true God alone! Tell me your dreams."

The chief cupbearer stepped up to tell Joseph his dream first. He began, "In my dream I saw a vine in front of me, with three branches that quickly budded, blossomed and its clusters ripened into beautiful grapes. In my hand was Pharaoh's golden jewel laden cup. I quickly squeezed the ripe grapes into Pharaoh's cup and placed it in his hand."
Joseph said, "The interpretation of your dream is this:

The three branches of the vine represent three days. You will be honored and restored to your former, trusted position in Pharaoh's palace as his official cupbearer. In three days, you will once again place the King's wine cup in his hand. What great news! Your prison sentence is ending and your life is getting ready to turn around. Please show me kindness by doing me a favor and remember me to Pharaoh and get me out of this dungeon, as I am innocent.

Let's examine some of the symbols in this dream and what they mean. How did Joseph come up with his favorable interpretation for the cupbearer? We know from Scripture that Jesus is known as the true vine and we are the branches. The cupbearer saw the vine positioned in front of him, which would indicate something in the future. Vines are living, leaves are for the healing of the nations, and clusters of grapes are fruitfulness, a gathering of people, as well as representative of wine. Wine often represents something that brings joy. The branches are three days of time indicated by the quick progression of the buds, to blossoms, to ripened clusters of grapes. Three is also the number of the Holy Trinity, completion, fullness, kindness, entirety, and the Godhead. In the cupbearer's dream his hand reaching out to Pharaoh represents service, relationship, agreement, and a powerful connection. He quickly blends the grapes by squeezing them into the King's cup representing him being restored to blend in with the officials of the King's court.

> John 15:5 "I am the vine; you are the branches. If a man remains in me and I in him, he will bear much fruit; apart from me you can do nothing" (NIV).

Creating a clear theme or moral for this dream can be summed up in one or two sentences that will bring out its essence or message.

The Dream

From *Genesis 40:9–11*
> In my dream, behold, a vine was before me; And in the vine were three branches: and it was as though it budded, and her blossoms shot forth; and

the clusters thereof brought forth ripe grapes: and Pharaoh's cup was in my hand: and I took the grapes, and pressed them into Pharaoh's cup, and I gave the cup into Pharaoh's hand.

The interpretation of this dream in a nugget or theme in one sentence would be: You are going to receive the fruits of restoration in your life.

Now we can imagine the excitement of the chief baker when he heard Joseph give the cupbearer such an encouraging interpretation. Leaping to his feet, he firmly grasped Joseph by the arm and announced, "I also had a dream last night about my former job! In my dream I had three baskets of bread. The baskets were full of the Pharaoh's favorite baked goods and delicacies, but the birds were eating them out of the top basket on my head."

Joseph pondered the dream's interpretation in a moment of silence. How would he formulate the message in a gentle way to break the bad, or should we say "deadly" news to the baker? "I am sorry, my friend, but this is what your dream means: The three baskets also represent a three day time period in which you will be brought before Pharaoh. But, within those three days Pharaoh will put a noose around your neck and hang you from a tree where the birds of prey will eat away your flesh." The baker's stomach sank as he fell to the floor in horror from the devastating blow delivered by the stinging message of impending doom.

Once again let's examine the symbols and their meanings to determine how Joseph knew the manner and timing in which the baker was going to die. In each of these dreams we must take into account the cultural norms of that day. Because there were no refrigeration systems, people went to market carrying baskets that would hold a day's supply of food. Thus Joseph saw God's association with the three baskets representing three days' time. Also notice that the baskets were located on the cupbearer's head and the birds were removing or eating the bread (flesh) out of them. Bread is symbolic of life, the body, flesh, provision, and the Word of God. Jesus said in *Luke 22:19, "This bread is my body broken for you take and eat."* As we seek for understanding in Scripture we will find different levels of symbolic, literal, and hidden mysteries revealed in the parables and ancient stories.

Pharaoh's birthday was celebrated with a feast for all his royal officials. In that year, the King's extravagant celebration took place three days after the interpretation of the cupbearer's and chief baker's prophetic dreams. As their prophetic dreams foretold, Pharaoh called the cupbearer and the chief baker from prison into the presence of his royal officials. He restored the cupbearer to his former position and he once again was trusted to place the golden cup in the King's hand. But he passed judgment on the chief baker for execution just as Joseph had prophesied.

Dreams often match the theme of what is going on in our waking lives. Most of the dreams we experience do not have a prophetic or futuristic focus. Most of the dreams we have are of an intrinsic nature which means about 80 to 90 percent of the time they revolve around the needs, wants, and desires of the dreamer. To identify the themes of the dreams you experience, simply ask yourself: "What area of my life is this dream reflecting?" rather than asking "What is this dream foretelling?" Start the interpretation process by realizing that the majority of your dreams are going to be about you and the message is going to be for you. When you have reached a proper theme, essence, or interpretation and assigned it to the proper area of your life, you will have 'a knowing' that truth has come. The spirit will always bear witness to a true interpretation; emotions will feel it and the heart will know it, when we are at rest and our mind is not striving. With our minds at rest we are able to arrive at the proper conclusions and answers to our dreams far easier than if we used emotional thinking patterns while we are awake.

Although the butler and the baker were processed and released from prison, Joseph remained behind for two more agonizing, long years. Every time a messenger was sent to the prison Joseph hoped it was his day of deliverance. Finally, the fullness of time came for his release when the chief cupbearer suddenly remembered his fault and unkept promise to Joseph. Pharaoh had awakened from two disturbing dreams the previous night. He had no understanding of their meanings and his counselors were not able to come up with a satisfactory answer.

At the end of two years the Pharaoh of Egypt had a disturbing dream where He saw himself standing by the Nile River. Suddenly out of the river seven cows, sleek and fat, emerged and they grazed among the reeds. After them, seven other cows, ugly and gaunt, came up out of the Nile and stood beside those on the riverbank. The ugly, gaunt cows ate up the seven sleek, fat cows. Then Pharaoh woke up (Genesis 41:1–27).

When he fell asleep again he had a second dream that established the first. This time instead of cows, seven healthy heads of grain, full and good, were growing on a single stalk. After the prosperous ones, seven other heads of grain sprouted—but these were thin and dry and scorched by the east wind. The thin heads of grain swallowed up or replaced the seven healthy full heads. Then Pharaoh awakened and realized that he had dreamed two dreams in one night.

In the wee hours of the morning as Pharaoh lay upon his bed recalling the dream events of the night his mind was perplexed and troubled. So he sent word to gather all the magicians and wise men of Egypt to court. Pharaoh reiterated his dreams to his counselors, but no one could interpret them or bring any insights or understanding to him.

Then the chief cupbearer said to Pharaoh, "Today I remember a promise I made years ago but have been negligent in fulfilling. Please forgive me of my shortcomings. More than two years ago my Lord, Pharaoh was angry with his servants, and he imprisoned both me and the chief baker in the house of the captain of the guard. The two of us had a dream the same night, and each dream had a separate meaning of its own. Now Joseph a young, handsome Hebrew slave was there with us in the dungeon. He had great favor as a servant to the captain of the guard because the Lord was with him. We both told him our dreams, and he interpreted them for us, giving each man an accurate interpretation of his dream. The things he declared turned out exactly as he interpreted them to us: I was restored to my royal position in the palace, and the baker was hanged."

So Pharaoh dispatched an escort to quickly deliver Joseph, from the dungeon. When he had bathed, shaved and changed his clothes, he stood before Pharaoh. The fulfillment of the dream he had so many years ago was now being birthed into existence. God was bringing the impossible into play by positioning his chosen into the leading role of a nation before kings and noblemen.

Pharaoh said to Joseph, "I had a dream, and it angers me that none of my counselors and magicians can interpret it. But my cupbearer said, 'You hear dreams with spiritual ears of understanding and wisdom and can immediately interpret them.'"

"I cannot do it in my own strength or abilities," Joseph replied to Pharaoh, "but God will give Pharaoh the answer and wisdom he desires through his servant."

Then Pharaoh told his two dreams to Joseph,

"In my dream I saw myself standing on the bank of the Nile, when out of the river there came up seven cows, fat and sleek, and they grazed among the reeds. After them, seven other cows came up—scrawny and very ugly and lean. I had never seen such ugly cows in all the land of Egypt. The lean, ugly cows totally devoured and ate up the seven fat cows that came up first. But even after they ate them, no one could tell that they had done so; they looked just as thin, gaunt and ugly as before. Then I woke up with a terrible feeling of dread."

"In my second dream that immediately followed the first I also saw seven heads of grain, full, strong and good, growing on a single stalk. After them, seven other heads sprouted—withered, thin and scorched by the east wind. The thin heads of grain swallowed up the seven good heads. I had the same dreadful feeling of some impending doom. I told this to the magicians, but none could explain it to me."

Joseph took a deep breath and focused on Pharaoh's face and said,

"The two dreams of Pharaoh are one and the same. God has revealed to Pharaoh through these [extrinsic] dreams what he is about to do in the land of Egypt and surrounding areas. The seven good beautiful cows are seven years of plenty and abundance, and the seven good heads of golden grain are seven years of bounty; it is one and the same dream. The seven lean, ugly cows that came up afterward are seven years of drought and destruction, and so are the seven worthless heads of grain scorched by the dry east wind: They indicate a seven year cycle of severe famine, plague, drought and devastation."

My words to Pharaoh are true. God has shown the King what he is about to do so you may prepare. Seven years of great abundance are coming throughout the land of Egypt, followed by seven years of hardship and famine. This drought and famine will be so extensive all the abundance in Egypt will be forgotten, and the land will be ravaged and desolate. The reason the dream was given to Pharaoh in two different symbolic forms is that the matter has been firmly decided and established by God, and will shortly take place. Genesis 41:28–47

"Now, God has clearly revealed the meaning of these dreams, let Pharaoh appoint a discerning, wise man to be in charge of the lands of Egypt." He continued, "Let Pharaoh appoint commissioners over the land and provinces to take a fifth of the harvest of Egypt during the seven years of abundance. Commissioners should collect all the food under the authority of Pharaoh, during these abundant, good years that are coming and store up the grain, to be kept in the cities for food. This food should be held in reserve for the country, to be used during the seven years of famine that will come upon Egypt, to prevent its ruin by the famine."

The plan seemed good to Pharaoh and to all his official counselors. So Pharaoh asked them, "Are there any among us like this man, one in who the Spirit of the living, all knowing God exist?"

Then Pharaoh said to Joseph, "Since God has made all this known to you, there is no one so discerning and wise as you. Joseph you shall be in charge of my palace, and all my people are to submit to your orders. Only with respect to the throne will I be greater than you."

So Pharaoh announced to Joseph and his court, "I hereby put

you in charge of the whole land of Egypt." He slid his royal signet ring from his finger and placed it on Joseph's finger. His servants dressed him in robes of fine linen and put a heavy, decorative gold chain around his neck. Pharaoh had him ride in a horse drawn chariot as his second-in-command, and men of honor shouted before him, "Make way!" Thus he put Joseph in charge of the whole land of Egypt.

So how did Joseph get to this point? Can we expect God to perform this same kind of action in our lives? God continued to build upon Joseph's road map in the higher rungs of society by giving Pharaoh troubling dreams which Joseph was asked to interpret. Joseph's encounter with the butler and the baker was groundwork for the later promotion. This was necessary to fulfill his destiny and complete the dream map that led to provision for all of Egypt when they needed it most. Through this network Joseph's gift made room for him. Because Joseph went through God's process of humiliation he met the baker and the butler, who knew the King and remembered at just the right time that Joseph had a gift. As God planned in the fullness of time and when Joseph's gift was mature, he was remembered and elevated to a position of rulership.

Dreams impacted the government rulers and all of society in ancient days just like dreams and their interpretations are making an impact on the modern leaders and marketplaces of our day. Joseph was thirty years old (the number 30 signifies the beginning of ministry) when he entered the service of Pharaoh, King of Egypt. Joseph went out from Pharaoh's presence and traveled throughout Egypt carrying out the strategic plan God revealed in Pharaoh's extrinsic dreams. Joseph was 37 (37 means first born) when his brothers bowed before him in Egypt seeking grain for their families. Joseph's character development took a twenty year process. The difficult journey from the pit to slavery to prison and finally to the palace spiritually prepared him to be first and foremost a man of strong character and integrity, and a true servant who was humble yet mature in his gifting and abilities to interpret dreams.

King David Tells Joseph's Story

He sent a man before them—Joseph—who was sold as a slave. They hurt his feet with fetters, He was laid in irons. Until the time that his word came to pass, the word of the Lord tested him. The king sent and released him, the ruler of the people let him go free. He made him lord of his house, and ruler of all his possessions, to bind his princes at his pleasure, and teach his elders wisdom (Psalm 105:17–22).

We have told you the end of the story, but have touched only briefly on the beginning. Before Joseph reached his happy ending he endured a time of testing. Thirteen years (13 means rebellion, depravity, backsliding, revolution, corruption but, it also means love in 1 Corinthians 13) of testing in prison to be exact. Through God's testing of Joseph a theme emerges which defines one of God's top priorities for us—to refine our character so that we will be perfected, rooted, and grounded in love. It was necessary for Joseph to endure the hardships initiated by his brothers in order for him to be in the right place at the right time to fulfill his destiny. Before promotion comes, testing is necessary. As seen through Joseph's life, the jealousy and wickedness of man developed his strength of character and skill. In the fires of affliction Joseph was prepared for his divine destiny. Similar to the life of Joseph, during times of testing God uses our negative circumstances to refine our hearts and motives, while protecting us in the process—it is a controlled fire like a glass blower refining his art. This process gives us the beauty, character, and maturity needed to walk in abundant blessing and prosperity.

When Joseph was taken to Egypt his master Potiphar purchased him as a slave. He soon recognized the Lord was with Joseph and Joseph was a successful man because the favor of the Lord made all he did to prosper. Joseph also found favor in his master's sight and served faithfully overseeing his whole estate. One area where God tested Joseph involved Potiphar's wife. Had Joseph failed this test, it may have frustrated or even changed the course of his destiny.

That she caught him by his garment, saying, "Lie with me." But he left his garment in her hand, and fled and ran outside (Genesis 39:12).

In the fullness of time as he was faithful wherever the Lord sent him to serve, Joseph was promoted from the prison to the palace.

Now therefore, let Pharaoh select a discerning and wise man, and set him over the land of Egypt (Genesis 41:33).

The seven years of plenty which were in the land of Egypt ended, and the seven years of famine began to come, as Joseph had said. The famine was in all lands, but in all the land of Egypt there was bread. So when all the land of Egypt was famished, the people cried to Pharaoh for bread. Then Pharaoh said to all the Egyptians, "Go to Joseph; whatever he says to you, do." The famine was over all the face of the earth, and Joseph opened all the storehouses and sold to the Egyptians. And the famine became severe in the land of Egypt. So all countries came to Joseph in Egypt to buy grain, because the famine was severe in all lands" (Genesis 41:53–57).

Joseph was 30 years old when he saw the fulfillment of his initial dream from age seventeen (which revealed his family bowing at his feet); he was 37 when he saw his brothers again. For the first time in thirteen years he was able to say with forgiveness in his heart, "You meant it for evil but God meant it for good."

Today, God is giving warning dreams to us of disasters to come on the earth like bird flu, floods, earthquakes, plagues, and destruction. He is also showing us the good things that are to come, and most importantly what is in our own hearts, be it good or evil. He is releasing Joseph's gift for dream interpretation, favor, understanding and wisdom to funnel the wealth of the world into his Kingdom. In Joseph's life, this wealth was to feed Egypt in a time of hardship. In our lives, we must seek the Lord for the purpose of our obedience. A pattern of how God works is revealed in Joseph's map of dreams. First the vision or dream comes. Then God gives us revelation about the dream's meaning and often a promise of what is ahead. Then the problems and testing begin before the provision and fulfillment come.

Evil Counterfeits vs. Godly Dream Interpretation

Psychics, mediums, witches, Wicca, and the New Age movement are the counterfeits found trapped in the dark deception of the occult. A biblical example of a person turning to an evil source rather than looking to God for the interpretation of spiritual mystery is King Saul. He sought the supernatural through the banished Witch of Endor because God would not answer him by dream, Urim, or prophet.

> *And when Saul inquired of the Lord, the Lord did not answer him, either by dreams or by Urim or by the prophets. Then Saul said to his servants, "Find me a woman who is a medium, that I may go to her and inquire of her." And his servants said to him, "In fact, there is a woman who is a medium at En Dor." So Saul disguised himself and put on other clothes, and he went, and two men with him; and they came to the woman by night. And he said, "Please conduct a séance for me, and bring up for me the one I shall name to you" (1 Samuel 28:6–8).*

> *Then the woman said, "Whom shall I bring up for you?" And he said, "Bring up Samuel for me" (1 Samuel 28:11).*

The practice of going to mediums or to the occult is strictly forbidden. God is a loving but jealous God who affectionately protects us from anything that would cause us harm. His desire has always been for us to eat of the spiritual "Tree of Life," which is Jesus. He does not desire for us to eat from the "Tree of the Knowledge of Good and Evil." The blessings God releases to us when we seek him for the supernatural are far stronger than the curses that are released when we pursue the occult realm. The end of Saul's story depicts a tragic outcome of a nation's leader who sought guidance from the realms of darkness. Ignoring the laws of his own country and the outlines of the Bible, Saul delved into the forbidden dark realm and reaped more than death. The consequences of his disobedience forced the loss of the rule of his kingdom not only for himself but also his son. It wrenched his destiny from his hands and left his family without a kingdom, rule, or honor.

Dreams of the Bible and the 21st Century

And it shall come to pass afterward that I will pour out My Spirit on all flesh; your sons and your daughters shall prophesy, your old men shall dream dreams, your young men shall see visions (Joel 2:28).

How is it possible for God to still speak this way in today's time? Even if there was a doubt about dream revelation in the 21st century, Scripture prophetically covers future bases to address our misunderstanding. God is the same yesterday, today, and forever. In the second chapter of the book of Joel there is a prophecy that depicts the outpouring of God's Spirit on all flesh. *Acts 2:17* tells the same story, establishing the beginning of this Old Testament prophecy in Joel, and bringing it into our time. These passages also speak of a time when wonders in heaven and signs on earth will be shown along with supernatural miracles. If this does not sound a lot like today's experience on the streets it is definitely reminiscent of Hollywood's futuristic interpretation of our world. With movies like *X-Men, Next,* and *Supernatural* we see icons of a time to come. Yet credit is not given to God, it is given to man and evil supernatural entities. The enemy is working hard to counterfeit, mystify, and misrepresent the true supernatural power of God. Yet God's Kingdom continues to manifest, expanding his rule in the earth.

Today's television producers are eager for the supernatural. They are looking for the paranormal and are making movies that the masses are thrilled to consume. However, God's divine plan literally flies in the face of the humanistic agenda and evil attempt to distort our perception of the all-powerful, supernatural God. Christians need to begin to step out in our God-given power to creatively restore those around us who need spiritual, emotional, and physical healing. Prophecy, dreams, and visions reveal the secrets and destiny concealed in a man's heart. As we are obedient to put our faith to the test, God will be glorified for the amazing regenerative and life giving power that he created and gifted to us.

Now is a time in history when God is increasing the presence of the Holy Spirit in the earth. According to the prophecies of Scripture, an increase in dreams and visions is a sign of the day and age in which we live. In today's world heightened sensitivity to God's voice, guidance and direction is vital to hearing and understanding all he has to say to us. The heart of God contains Kingdom mysteries, thoughts and plans that will first have a great impact on the church and then on the world at large. At this pivotal time in history, we must seek his Kingdom first, asking for godly wisdom and understanding. Through seeking Jesus and the Holy Spirit with all our heart we will receive the knowledge that reveals the deeper spiritual meaning of our dreams.

Understanding the Times

We need to be like the Sons of Issachar in the Bible; knowing the times and seasons, they were full of wisdom, discernment, and understanding of God's mysteries. A mystery is "a spiritual truth that one can know only by divine revelation and which cannot be fully understood." When we think of understanding God's mysteries, we may visualize healing the multitudes and moving in signs and wonders and the power of the anointing, but God's thought is that we would embrace the cross, crucify our flesh and die to ourselves. He wants to raise us up in his image so that he can move through us to impact a nation.

> *Let a man so consider us, as servants of Christ and stewards of the mysteries of God (1 Corinthians 4:1).*

Much like Webster's definition suggests, God's mysteries are the hidden, secret morsels of wisdom available to those who believe but are concealed from the disobedient and unbelieving. God reveals his mysteries to those who will seek him for understanding.

> *But we speak the wisdom of God in a mystery, the hidden wisdom which God ordained before the ages for our glory, which none of the rulers of this age knew; for had they known, they would not have crucified the Lord of glory. But as it is written: "Eye has not seen, nor ear heard, nor have entered into the heart of man the things which God has prepared for those who love Him" (1 Corinthians 2:7–9).*

The secret of the Lord is with those who fear Him, and He will show them His covenant (Psalm 25:14).

As we have seen in many ways throughout this chapter, the Bible is full of God-given revelation through dreams, visions, and prophecy. We must study to show ourselves approved so that we can operate in the Spirit of understanding and be spiritually fruitful in today's age of increasing spiritual awareness—which is both good and evil. We must learn from the Holy Spirit to discern between the two and have the character to reject the evil and embrace the true.

> *That the God of our Lord Jesus Christ, the Father of glory, may give to you the spirit of wisdom and revelation in the knowledge of Him, the eyes of your understanding being enlightened ... (Ephesians 1:17–18 NKJV).*

The tangible presence of God residing in our lives enabling us to do the impossible is more important now than ever before in history. We do well to adopt the prayer of Moses in *Exodus 33:13–16*

> *"Now therefore I pray, if I have found grace [favor] in Your sight, show me Your way, that I may know You and that I may find grace in Your sight. And consider that this nation is Your people." And He said, "My Presence will go with you, and I will give you rest." Then he said to Him, "If Your Presence does not go with us, do not bring us up from here." "For how then will it be known that Your people and I have found grace in Your sight, except You go with us? So we will be separate, Your people and I, from all the people who are upon the face of the earth."*

Love for God and mankind will demonstrate his reality and the truth of the gospel.

Chapter Five
Types of Dreams

Dream Interpretation

Is dream interpretation exclusively a New Age practice? Is it possible for Christians to tap into these stories of the night and receive deeper insight into their waking lives? Many people believe that dream interpretation only belongs to the realm of psychics and psychoanalysts. The Bible, however, reveals to us that dreams are one of the ways that God speaks to us *(Job 33:15 & Numbers 12:6)*. The key to understanding God's dream language is that we must use a biblical basis to interpret the symbolism. We must rely on the Holy Spirit as our source of revelation, understanding, wisdom, and proper application.

Most dream interpretation methods and the explanatory books offered today use a Freudian, Gestalt, or Jungian interpretation approach. These methods are not biblical, and according to them, a dream does not come from the Spirit of God, but rather, exclusively from our own soul or psyche. Therefore, if we try to apply their methods to a dream already interpreted in the Bible, we will not interpret it in the way God intended. It is not recommended to use dream-symbol resources that derive their meanings from Freudian, Gestalt, or Jungian methods as they are based in a humanistic philosophy and approach.

Genesis 40:8 clearly states that the interpretation of a dream comes from God. God spoke to the prophets through dreams and visions. Two principal people in the Bible who actually interpreted dreams were Joseph and Daniel. King Nebuchadnezzar and Pharaoh both had dreams, and no one could interpret them except Joseph and Daniel— who realized that the true interpretation came only from the Spirit of God or the Tree of Life, who is Jesus. In both instances, the popular dream interpretive methods of that day could not correctly interpret a dream from God *(Genesis 41:8 & Daniel 2)*. We have found that this is still the case today.

Dreams are Symbolic Night Parables

Jesus often taught people by using parables, which are stories with a deeper spiritual and moral meaning. His disciples asked, *"Why do You speak to them in parables?"* He admonished his disciples that they must be able to interpret parables and understand this type of symbolic thinking in order to uncover the mysteries of the Kingdom.

> *Because it has been given unto you to know the mysteries of the kingdom of heaven, but to them* [the world] *it has not been given ... But blessed are your eyes for they see, and your ears for they hear; for surely, I say to you that many prophets and righteous men desired to see what you see, and did not see it, and to hear what you hear, and did not hear it (Matthew 13:10–17).*

These mysteries are hidden in the realms of the Spirit. Therefore, worshippers of God must worship him in Spirit and in truth to enter into this realm of mystical understanding and enlightenment. It is the Spirit of truth that will lead and guide us into all truth.

> *John 14:17–18 says, "The Spirit of truth, whom the world cannot receive, because it neither sees Him nor knows Him; but you know him, for He dwells with you and will be in you. I will not leave you orphans; I will come to you."*

God comes revealing mysteries to us through our dreams in our bedchambers at night. There is an urgent call to intimacy with God as never before. The Bible says the marriage bed is undefiled. You don't let just anyone into the sacred bedchambers—only your covenant lover. Yet, at night the lover of our soul comes to visit us with keys to unlock divine mysteries that are hidden in his heart. He longs to share his secrets with his beloved bride. This makes it imperative for us to learn his love language of dreams. Understanding the mysteries of the night will make it possible for us to understand his plans and purposes for our life. *(Jeremiah 29:11).*

Jesus said, *"He who has my commandments and keeps them, it is he who loves Me. And he who loves Me will be loved by My Father, and I will love him and manifest Myself to him (John 14:21).*

Jesus continued, *"If anyone loves Me, he will keep My word; and My Father will love him, and We will come to him and make Our home with him" (John 14:23).*

The Holy Spirit comes to reveal the Father and Jesus the son to us in our dreams. If we love God with our whole heart he will take up his residence within us and reveal to us the mysteries of his everlasting Kingdom.

For centuries the church has been walking on the same level of spiritual understanding. Revelation knowledge of the mysteries of the Kingdom remain sealed in the heart of God. He desires to bring these hidden secrets to the forefront through dreams to unleash their power in a dark world. God's eyes are searching for those with a wholehearted devotion to seek him out—those who have allowed the refiner's fire to passionately purify their hearts and to cleanse their hands to perform miracles. These are the ones through whom he can show himself strong.

2 Chronicles 16:9a For the eyes of the Lord move to and fro throughout the earth that he may strongly support those whose heart is completely his (NASB).

Daniel was known as a man in whom the Spirit of the Holy God dwelt with an excellent spirit, full of knowledge, understanding, interpreting dreams, solving riddles, and explaining enigmas. His spiritual intimacy enabled the deep of God to reveal deep and hidden mysteries to the deep in Daniel alone. No secret troubled him and he was able to explain the handwriting on the wall, visions, enigmas, and dreams. World rulers said of him, "the Spirit of God is in you; light and understanding and excellent wisdom are found in you."

The word of God severely tested and tried Joseph until it finally made him fit to be released from the shackles that bound him and propelled him into his destiny in front of kings and rulers. Daniel and

Joseph were able to discern and reveal mysteries to all who came before them, great and small. Where are the gifted dream interpreters who are called to stand before the Pharaohs of our day?

Dreams are symbolic and are basically night parables. The first place to look to understand the symbols found in our dreams is the Bible. For instance, depending on the context in the dream, a tree can represent a righteous or an evil leader *(Daniel 4:22)*, and a snake can mean lies and deception *(Genesis 3)* or healing *(Numbers 21:8)*. This is where the medical community got the symbol of a snake on a pole. But what do we do when we come across a symbol in a dream that is not defined in the Bible? For example, we don't find automobiles or airplanes mentioned in the Bible. However, chariots and horses are mentioned which are also modes of transportation. We must then learn to think metaphorically, asking the Holy Spirit to reveal why a particular symbol was chosen and its corresponding meaning.

Jesus gives us some insight into how to understand things symbolically.

> *Matthew 16:5–7 says, "When they went across the lake, the disciples forgot to take bread. 'Be careful,' Jesus said to them. "Be on your guard against the yeast of the Pharisees and Sadducees." They discussed this among themselves and said, 'It is because we didn't bring any bread.'"*

Jesus was attempting to help the disciples to think and understand Kingdom principles on a deeper level, but they were thinking literally and not symbolically. Jesus went on to say:

> *"How is it you don't understand that I was not talking to you about bread? But be on your guard against the yeast of the Pharisees and Sadducees." Then they understood that He was not telling them to guard against the yeast used in bread, but against the teaching of the Pharisees and Sadducee (vv.11–12)*

Most people miss the fact that Jesus was giving us a major clue to help us understand parables and the symbolism found in dreams. Yeast causes things to rise; so the hidden meaning here is that the teaching of

the Pharisees causes pride to rise in their political standing and hypocrisy to spread in their religious life. *(Luke 12:1).*
Sin and a little of man's traditions and false teachings have the power to ruin or corrupt the whole.

Applying this type of metaphoric thinking to symbols that are not clearly defined in the Bible can help us unlock God's hidden messages in our dreams. A car can represent our life or career. A jet plane can represent a business, corporation, church, or a ministry. Being late can symbolize a warning not to miss something important. Taking an exam can give us a clue that we are being tested.

After interpreting multiplied thousands of dreams for people, Breath of the Spirit Ministries and its dream interpreters have noticed that there are a few common dream themes. Some of the common dreams are flying, teeth falling out, falling, and going to the bathroom, to name a few. I began to recognize that the meanings of these dreams highlight where many people are spiritually. For instance, flying indicates a high destiny in God and revelatory giftings; teeth coming loose or falling out may mean there is a need for wisdom or advice because of indecision. Falling may indicate feeling out of control of a situation; going to the bathroom is the need for spiritual cleansing or flushing (forgiveness).

A Relational Goldmine

As we understand the meaning of dreams, we can help other people find their destinies in God. Although not all dreams are from God, people everywhere are having dreams. Many of the dreams which people share with us have been divinely given.

Acts 2:17–18 reveals that prophecy, dreams, and visions will become more of a strategic part of God's methods of reaching people in these last days.

Breath of the Spirit Ministries continually leads prophetic and dream interpretation outreach events into the community at large and advises professionals in the business field. Accurate dream consultations have saved businesses from disaster and financial losses. We are finding that people everywhere are very interested in knowing what their dreams mean. As they share their dreams, they reveal the secrets of their hearts.

Their walls of resistance come down and they become very open to talking more about God and their spiritual condition. Because people today consider themselves spiritual, being able to hear their dreams accurately interpreted through the Spirit of God is proving to be a relational goldmine. Dream interpretation is one of the tools God is releasing to enable us to become more culturally relevant.

Types of Dreams

There are many different types of dreams. Note that dreams typically blend into one another, so it is not always easy or even necessary for the dreamer to define the dream completely upon waking. This chapter addresses some common categories dreams fall into. It also provides dream symbol meanings on a universal or common level. Remember, dream language is specific to the dreamer. That means if the full revelation of the dream is not immediately clear, the true interpretation must be filtered through the mind and experiences of the dreamer with the guidance of the Holy Spirit. Frequently, a dream leaves us with a basic impression so that we know it is an important dream event and the encrypted symbolism is revealed later.

Angel Dreams

Angels are still very present in dreams today. These winged cherubim and seraphim are symbols of God's intervention in our lives. These holy messengers bring spiritual insight and direct the dreamer onto the correct path in life. It is interesting to note that often angels appear as regular human beings in our dreams and rarely manifest in all of their glory but hide their heavenly features behind an everyday appearance. Often they come along side to lead, guide, and direct us in our dreams. People refer to them as "faceless" because they do not retain recollection of their facial features.

Animal Dreams

The animals that appear in our dreams have significance. Some animals we love and are easily drawn to while others we fear and run from. When an animal appears in a dream the dreamer should ask the following questions: Are they domestic, family pets, tamed or wild? What characteristics, attributes or functions do they perform? Do I like and feel positively toward them, or do I dislike and feel negatively toward them? Does this animal appear in the Bible, and if so, in what context? The animals that visit our dreams can have direct correlation to the way we are acting or behaving in our lives.

Buildings

The buildings in our dreams are significant and should be noted because they reflect specific areas in our lives. Childhood homes often indicate unresolved issues from the past that need to be addressed as they are now affecting areas in the dreamer's life today. Houses or buildings in disarray or in need of repair indicate areas in the dreamer's life that need supervision, cleaning up and redirecting. Chaos and confusion in past dwellings indicates that these types of disturbances may shortly recur in the dreamer's present life or situation. Dreams of the workplace, the buildings, such as factories or office complexes often deal with co-workers and social relationships where open communication is needed. The general or instinctive associations the dreamer assigns to the different locations in a dream helps reveal the specific meaning or symbolism of the dream.

Calling Dreams

A *calling dream* will allow the dreamer to see himself or herself accomplishing great feats. Usually in this type of dream, the person dreaming is not presently aware that he or she is capable of possessing the type of skill, gift, or ability they see themselves demonstrating in the dream. This type of dream is a revelation of calling and an invitation to enter into the preparation process for a new field, job, ministry, relationship, or gifting if the call is answered.

Chasing Dreams

Dreams where we are being chased erupt from feelings of fear, anxiety, stress and pressure in our waking life situations. These dreams are more common among women who fear violence and sexual attack, because they feel physically vulnerable. Both women and men instinctively picture themselves running as they attempt to retreat from the perceived physical threat in the dream. The pursuer wants to bring harm in some way. At times people may fear that the attacker intends murder. In these dream scenarios it is sometimes difficult to get our legs to work as fast as we would like. They seem to be almost paralyzed with some great weight. We continually try to outsmart, outmaneuver, hide, and run away from the attacker(s). Chasing dreams are part of our coping mechanism that helps enable us to handle various forms of fear in life. The chasing dreams will continue as long as we continue to run away or avoid the fearful life situation. To conquer our fears we must determine what they are and then confidently face and confront them. We must ask ourselves what or who am I afraid of? Why do I fear? At times we are afraid of ourselves, of our own feelings of anger, jealousy, rejection, or intimacy and love. Our emotions can appear as threatening figures. Ask your pursuers why they are chasing you? Am I consumed with my own emotions of love, jealousy, or anger? Am I exhibiting self-destructive behavior or open hostility? Our subconscious actions or memories at times threaten to hinder or harm our relationships and career opportunities. Chasing dreams are one way our conscience brings negative actions to our attention.

Cleansing or Self-Condition Dreams

Cleansing dreams usually take place in a publicly exposed or private bathroom setting: on the toilet, in the shower or tub, shaving, putting makeup on in the mirror, combing hair, or brushing teeth. Cleansing or self-condition dreams allow the dreamer to know which areas of his or her life need to be purified, refined, or purged of sin, unforgiveness, bitterness, guilt, shame, or any other unhealthy or unclean thing.

Clothing

Concerning the meaning of clothing in a dream, ventures or enterprises embarked upon will be successful or fail depending on the apparel's color or appearance. Clean, new, or elegant clothes indicate prosperity. Torn or soiled garments may represent deceit or harm to character or virtues. Starched clothing may indicate the necessity for professionalism or, it may show a need to be flexible. Threadbare rags symbolize poverty, or being poor in spirit, attitude, character, or virtue. The dreamer's moods, attitudes, or state of mind can also be reflected by the clothes that are worn in a dream. The reason certain clothes are chosen vary depending on the dreamer's type of work, social engagements, status in life, belief systems, and even whether the dreamer is in a serious relationship or dating. Clothes are often the shields we hide behind or flaunt in front of people. The clothes and their colors that are being worn by the dreamer and others in the dream will provide a plethora of information. Also, if the dream depicts clothes in the closet, on the floor, on clotheslines and washing rooms, these indicators will also provide valuable clues about whether the clothes represent symbolic renderings or are pointing to something we, or others in the dream, actually wear (part of our nature) or whether it has been cast aside (part of our past).

Color Dreams

Color dreams can be split into two categories: spiritual or soulish. Bright red, green, and blue colors in dreams indicate something of a spiritual nature; whereas yellow, orange, violet, or indigo tend to point to the issues of the soul, i.e., the mind, will, or emotions. Colors are a very important part of the message of a dream. The intensity, hue, and contrast of the colors should be observed as symbols to be interpreted. Also, any color that is obviously being emphasized in the dream should be taken into account with thoughtful consideration. Gray scale or black and white dreams are indicators of things from the distant past, unpleasant, painful memories or difficult conflicts, struggles and trials that may be once again surfacing. One thing we must remember about colors in dreams is that spiritual dreams come from God, who is the Father of lights. He blends all the rainbow colors seen in refracted light together to communicate his divine messages to the dreamer.

Confinement Dreams

Dreams of being held down, restrained, bound, entrapped, raped, buried, or held prisoner against our will in a building are all very traumatic, troubling dreams. In dreams like these, the dreamer feels that his or her ability to choose is being limited or totally removed. These types of dreams indicate someone—often an employer, parent, or spouse—is trying to control, manipulate, or take advantage of the person dreaming. The dreamer feels hopeless, trapped and powerless in a situation that is beyond his or her control. Confinement dreams create anxiety because there does not appear to be any type of resolve or an exit point. This produces several options for the dreamer: separation from those causing the control, direct confrontation, or oppression and depression when the dreamer feels overcome by the stronger person or force in the dream. The dreamer must discern who or what is causing the feeling of entrapment or confinement in their waking life. Once the dreamer has discovered the source that is imposing unwanted limitations, he or she will be free to make the necessary choices to cut off the negative influences being shown to him or her in the dream.

Daydreams

We often have a tendency to be lost in solitary thought. We daydream an average of one to two hours a day. Daydreaming is an unawareness of one's surroundings, classified as a level of consciousness between sleep and wakefulness. It occurs during our waking hours when we enter into a mild trance state, inviting our imagination to carry us away into illusions or visions. As our minds begin to wander and our level of awareness decreases, we lose ourselves in our imagined scenario and fantasy. Daydreaming can be used to gain new options or insights, help us to enter into peace and relieve stressful situations. Daydreams bring us into the creative dimension of the Spirit where we are able to access new ideas and strategies to overcome our present situations. We should learn to embrace and practice these peaceful times of reflection. Daydreams open the doors to inventions, solutions, and increased productivity.

Deliverance Dreams

Deliverance dreams enable the dreamer to shed negative dark influences or rescue the dreamer from negative strongholds in the mind by revealing wrong responses to situations or bad habits. This type of revelation allows the dreamer to work through issues. By introducing light and truth, deliverance dreams reveal a new path, setting the dreamer free from issues that have been holding him or her captive in some way.

Divine Dreams

Direction or *divine dreams* occur when communications or visitations take place with divine beings such as angels who intend to assist the dreamer on some level. They could be bringing messages of wisdom, knowledge, healing, teaching, and answers to prayer.

Dreams of Dying

Can experiencing death in a dream cause death in reality? How would we know? The content of the dream would be sealed with the death of the dreamer. Dreaming of one's own death and funeral or dreaming about the death of a loved one causes worry and tears because death represents a great, sad, and painful loss that is difficult to accept. In dreams, death is rarely seen as a literal prophetic forewarning of someone's natural death, although it can be. Seeing one's grave can indicate the dreamer's time on earth is drawing to a close. This dream may forewarn the dreamer to ensure that his house is in order and the eternal dwelling place of his soul is secure. Dying in dreams usually indicates the end of a chapter in life, or the breaking of a bad habit or a destructive relationship. Dreams of death can actually bring us new insights into life's experiences. Death dreams can also serve as an escape mechanism for dealing with extreme stress. Clues to the inner workings of our minds, assumptions, biases, motivations, and expectations can be gleaned from these types of dreams. Dreaming of someone else's death could indicate that the dreamer is dead to certain positive traits they possess and there is a need to cultivate them again. Nearly any dream of death, dying, or attending a funeral indicates dramatic, major change in life, relationships, jobs, or attitude. Death dreams also enable the dreamer to confront threats, the fear of death, the unknown, or the fear of change.

Epic Dreams

Epic dreams, (also known as *great dreams*) are extremely vivid, lengthy, life-like, and so compelling that the details seem to imprint themselves on the dreamer enabling recall for many years after the dream. These dreams possess many chapters and much symbolism. Upon waking from an epic dream, the dreamer's soul rejoices in discovering something profound or amazing about the world. Epic dreams are often life-changing experiences.

Dreams about Exes

We live in a world where the divorce rate is continually rising. Many people have suffered a painful breakup of what was once a happy home or romance. Our dream interpretation Web site www.MyOnar. com receives many dreams that deal with ex-husbands, ex-boyfriends, ex-wives or ex-girlfriends who continually appear in our clients' dreams. Like any other characters in our dreams, exes may represent aspects that we despised or love about them. If the dreamer is no longer in the relationship or attached to the person, why does this person continue to appear in the dreamer's dreams? Does this indicate that the dreamer still loves or secretly desires to be with the ex? In some cases yes, but in most cases, the pain of the divorce or separation destroyed most of the positive feelings of love. When two people are married or enter into a sexually intimate relationship, the two souls touch during intercourse and the two individuals become bonded as one in their spirits. Their souls share both the positive and the negative aspects of each other, as well as those who were involved in prior relationships with each partner. This connection is called a soul tie and must be broken to stop the reoccurrence of the ex-lover's appearance in the dreams. Although divorce is final with regard to the law, there is still a connection between the two people in the soul realm. Achieving closure and emotional healing from a broken relationship takes time, counsel, and reflection. Dreams are useful instruments to bring negative feelings of unforgiveness and betrayal to the surface so that the dreamer can examine them and choose to forgive the ex. When the forgiveness process is complete, the ex will stop appearing to the dreamer in his or her dreams and the dreamer is then able to release the pain once and for all.

Falling Dreams

Many of us have abruptly awakened right before we hit the bottom of a rocky canyon floor, street, or any place from which we have fallen. We feel the earth's gravitational pull and speed downward to a jolting awakening just before or after we make impact. Most people have experienced these anxiety-filled dreams during the first stage of sleep. Falling dreams are often characterized by jerking actions from the arousal mechanism that awakens us. The dream myth states that the falling sensation is so real that the dreamer will die if he or she does not wake up before impact. Falling dreams may induce a feeling of being overwhelmed, out of control, fearful, confused, anxious, stressed, insecure, and unstable. The dreamer often feels pressured into a situation in which he or she has no knowledge or footing. After losing footing and being knocked off balance, the dreamer begins a downward spiral and continues to plummet through space. Fear of failure, guilt, and shame issues are often represented in falling dreams. Falling dreams let the dreamer know there is a need to call out to God for deliverance from overwhelming situations and to bring resolution to out-of-control areas in his or her life.

Fear Dreams

We fear what we do not understand or the things that we cannot control. Often we fear the future because of its unpredictability and uncertainty. We try to imagine what the future holds, but it is not a reality that can be grasped. In essence, the future is something we should be looking forward to and not dreading. It is not possible for us to control or to know the future. Only God knows the future, though he reveals glimpses of who we are in the future through the dreams he gives us.

Our vain imaginations run wild when we try to consider scenarios of the things we fear may happen, but we really have no way of knowing. We waste a lot of time and energy speculating on, "What will I do if this, or that happens?" Why do we have so much fear in our lives? Fear comes out of a heart that does not believe that God loves us and that he will take care of all of our needs. The person who is controlled by fear instead of faith will have to serve this hard taskmaster. Fear paralyzes us and keeps us from moving forward. So we remain stuck in the past because it is familiar and we already know the outcome. The things, creatures, people, or situations we fear in our dreams will continue to manifest until we are able to conquer and overcome them. Once we face our enemies and place our trust and belief in God's ability to make us stronger, the fear will die.

Flying Dreams

In a flying dream we can feel the rush of the wind and see the landscape below in the distance. We may be able to distinguish vibrant colors, exhilarating feelings of excitement and the buoyancy of movement. Often, when we dream of being chased by some creature or evil person we discover that we have unusual leaping, bouncing, or flying abilities and a sudden inner affirmation that nothing can harm us. People to whom God has given a revelatory gift will find themselves flying over land and sea in their dreams throughout their lives. Flying dreams indicate that the dreamer has been able to overcome or rise above obstacles in life that are trying to hinder progress. Through flying in our dreams, we are given a sense of supernatural power to gain a new or higher perspective from a heavenly vantage point that will ensure future success. Flying higher means that the dreamer is not afraid to make the necessary changes to meet the challenges of life. Flying dreams are very common and can tell us a lot about ourselves and our spiritual condition. A dream in which a person flies may indicate that that person is very creative and has the ability to advance in spiritual understanding and experience. Flying dreams, though symbolic, encourage us to rise above real life situations. Through them we can gain new confidence and even reduce stress as God allows us to conquer our weaknesses.

Though not all dreams are given to us by God, a good number of flying dreams are. We can derive our understanding of the essentials found in dreams by studying the symbols that are already interpreted in the Bible. There are over 200 references to dreams and visions in the Bible. Jesus communicated through the use of a concealed symbolic language called parables. By using parabolic thinking we can safely interpret flying as spiritual advancement. To understand flying dreams in more detail we must look at the context and the role that flying plays in the dream. For instance, the context of flying out of control is negative and indicates the need for greater spiritual discipline in life. But flying with great ease and precision with the ability to control flight indicates that the dreamer is advancing in spiritual growth.

Trying to take off but failing can indicate that there is something that the dreamer is destined to do, but he or she is experiencing setbacks. It is possible the dreamer could be hindering his or her own advancement spiritually or in life. The Lord might be using the dream to let the dreamer know that spiritual or life changes should be made.

Low or high altitude flight can indicate the dreamer's level of spiritual maturity. If dreams consistently depict low altitude flying this means that the dreamer should examine his or her life to find ways to grow spiritually. Flying in high altitudes shows that the dreamer, or the person flying is advancing in spiritual power and that creativity is increasing. Losing altitude is a sign that the dreamer is regressing and immediate attention is needed to empower their prayer or spiritual life.

Flying over a known city or region is usually an indication that the dreamer is to pray and intercede for that area. It can also indicate that the dreamer may have a literal connection to that particular area as well.

Flying above flames indicates that the dreamer is rising above a difficult situation and will not be harmed.

Flight into outer space is a great dream! This tells the dreamer that he or she is moving into high-level spiritual experiences with God.

Crashing or flying out of control is an obvious indicator that the dreamer's spiritual or physical life needs attention. It may be a warning to bring balance back into life to avoid a natural or spiritual disaster.

Floating or being elevated is similar to flying in that the dreamer is rising above or able to observe situations in life from a higher perspective, just like the biblical example of the prophet Ezekiel who was caught up by the hand of the Lord and suspended between heaven and earth.

Flying into or towards bright light shows we are being spiritually enlightened or drawn closer to God's heavenly realms of understanding to receive spiritual insights.

> *Revelation 4:1–2* says, *After this I looked, and there before me was a door standing open in heaven. And the voice I had first heard speaking to me like a trumpet said, "Come up here, and I will show you what must take place after this." At once I was in the Spirit, and there before me was a throne in heaven with someone sitting on it.*

If the light is blinding then it may indicate that God wants to blind you to your own ways to reveal his love and destiny for you.

Flapping arms to fly may mean that the dreamer is using his or her own natural charisma or physical efforts instead of relying on God's grace and power in his or her life.

Flying in a jet or airplane usually represents a church, ministry, company, or organization with which the dreamer is involved. The context can be determined by who else is in the plane. Also note how the plane is acting. Is it taking off or landing? This speaks of increase or decrease. Is it crashing? This may be a symbolic warning of potential loss. Is it going through a storm or turbulence? In this case, the dreamer may be about to experience rough times.

A good example of a flying dream:

In my dream I was flying very high in the sky and I could see huge areas of land and water. I remember thinking, "I wonder if I can dive in the water?" So I took a dive in the water and went very deep and fast and I came back out and was still flying. I thought, I would like to try flying through the wall, and I did and it was painless. I flew through a house and was able to land and walk and then begin flying again. Whatever I thought, I was able to do.

Interpretation: The dreamer is advancing in her spiritual life and God is taking her into deeper things of the spirit. The dream indicates that the dreamer can do everything through God who gives her strength *(Phil. 4:13 NIV)*. When we fly in a dream we should take a closer look at what God may be saying to us. We should learn to examine our dreams and break them down to their simplest form so that we are able to uncover deeper insight into our destinies.

Food (for Thought) Dreams

Food dreams may symbolize the partaking of spiritual, intellectual, or emotional nourishment through new thoughts, experiences, and feelings. Different types of foods served, enjoyed, or detested have particular meanings. For example, eating an apple can symbolize good health, a tranquil spirit, sin of temptation, pleasure, harmony, words of appreciation, or even fertility. However, chewing on something like bubble gum could mean the dreamer is still entertaining childish things that will bring no nourishment. Drinking coffee in a dream could symbolize a wake up call or that stimulating or sobering conversations need to be held. Breath of the Spirit has developed over five nutritional dream symbol cards explaining possible meanings and their spiritual applications in order to give dreamers insights into the spiritual feast that God is serving them in their dreams.

Guilt and Shame Dreams

Many of the choices we make in life arise out of the powerful emotions of guilt and shame. Guilt comes because we think we should have been able to do or say more than we were able to achieve. Shame dreams come when the legitimate needs of the dreamer are not validated. Guilt or shame dreams come when people are devalued or made fun of by friends, family members, or those he or she is in relationship with and or in close proximity to in the workplace, at home, or in social settings. The soul invites us to take responsibility for our life decisions—good, bad, and ugly so that we can be absolved of all guilt and shame.

Healing Dreams

God designed our bodies to communicate to us through dreams. They signal us when chemicals are out of alignment with our bodies even before any physical symptoms show up. Healing may be needed in the physical body, in the emotions, or in a relationship. Healing dreams allow the part of the body that is ailing to communicate the type of nutrition, medicine, or treatment it needs to recover. When the body is dehydrated we often dream of drinking liquid incessantly, but our thirst is not quenched, which often results in waking up to rehydrate.

Healing dreams deliver messages to the dreamer related to their physical, emotional, spiritual, and social health. Healing dreams help us avoid or escape potential health problems. A woman who attended a Breath of the Spirit Dream Encounter Workshop was in so much pain that she had to lie on the floor during the training sessions. She shared a recurring dream of seeing herself running up and down stairs pain-free. Through dreams, her body was giving her a new image of herself to affect the healing process in her life. After receiving prayer, the pain immediately left her body and she was healed.

Houses and Buildings in Dreams

What kind of private home or public building is in the dream? Is the building new and in good condition or old and in need of much repair? Is the whole interior and exterior of the house visible or just certain isolated rooms? What is going on and who is in the house or building and what feelings are being conveyed?

Often the setting of a dream takes place in a house, office, church, restaurant, or other type of building. Houses and buildings generally reflect the dreamer or part of the dreamer's body. For example, the kitchen being a place to prepare food can depict a place of creativity or nourishment of either the body or soul. The attic can indicate areas of thought or confusion and the basement brings up foundational issues.

Identity Dreams

Dreams have an amazing ability to reveal who we truly are because they blatantly reveal ourselves to us. Throughout our lives we continually adapt to new circumstances and situations. We change as we mature and grow older. *Identity dreams* are helpful in allowing us to note our progress as we pass through the different demarcation points in life from childhood, to adolescence, on to adulthood and then into our retirement years. During life each of us will play different and varied roles from being single, to engaged, to becoming a wife or husband, then to a mother or father, and finally to a grandparent. Our careers or lack thereof also play a role.

Identity dreams usually feature our homes—whether this means dwelling places from the past, present, or even future. We can gather a lot of insight from the conditions of these houses. Are they old, run down and in need of repair, or clean, orderly, and spacious with new furnishings? The other dream symbols that frequently appear in identity dreams are purses for women and wallets for men. These two objects allow us to carry our forms of identification, credit cards, cosmetics, and other important items that speak of our individuality in waking life.

As the soul identifies bad habits or character flaws we may dream of murdering that "person" who is representing the personality trait that resides within us. We may try to hide the negativity or cover it up in an effort to remove it from the dream. This may symbolize a desire to remove the character flaws from our real waking lives. Dreams of this nature do not mean that we are becoming murderers or even thinking about murdering people in our waking life. However, they may symbolize the process of dying to some negative aspect of our personality that really does not need to exist any longer.

When this process is complete, we will be able to aspire to new and greater heights. A new identity will emerge similar to a beautiful, colorful butterfly escaping from a cocoon, allowing us new expressions of liberty and freedom.

Lucid Dreams

Lucid dreams occur when the dreamer realizes that he or she is doing something impossible like flying and recognizes that because the feat is impossible, the experience must be a dream. However, after realizing it is a dream, the dreamer chooses to remain in the dream. Most dreamers wake themselves up if they do not like the storyline of their dream. Through practice dreamers can cultivate the skill to remain in the lucid state of dreaming. In doing this, the dreamer becomes an active participant in his or her own dream and has the ability to make decisions in the dream and influence its outcome without waking up. These vivid dreams are related more closely to the vision realm. When in a lucid state, the dreamer can then take control of the dream symbols to manipulate them and affect their progress.

In the realm of lucid dreaming people are often given creative ideas for new inventions. The famous inventor Thomas Edison kept a cot in his laboratory where he regularly took naps. During these brief respites he received multiple answers to perfect his inventions. Many people experience healing in this type of dream. For example, if a person dreams that he or she is confronting someone in a much needed but uncomfortable situation, once the dreamer is aware that he or she is dreaming active participation can actually become practice for the real event.

Money Dreams

When money appears in our dreams it usually foretells of either an increase or decrease in favor. That favor can come in all types of currency. Obtaining coins or change can often represent changes or exchanges that need to take place in the dreamer's life. It can also represent being shortchanged in business or relational situations. Seeing oneself writing a check depicts the ability to write one's own ticket, to carry out our plans or desires with ease. Making deposits into a bank indicates increase or favor is being added to us emotionally, spiritually and physically. However, making withdrawals predicts there will be demands placed upon the dreamer that will cost him.

Naked Dreams

Naked dreams do not indicate that the dreamer has completely lost decency to the point of publicly exposing their nakedness. On the contrary, *naked dreams* are often not about nudity or sexuality but rather indicate an openness, transparency, and vulnerability. Naked dreams may indicate that the dreamer has fears of being rejected if his or her true self is revealed. Naked dreams also point to freedom, openness to new ideas, thoughts, and concepts that are unrestrained. Appearing naked in one's dream can also indicate that the dreamer will be very productive or holds reproductive abilities. Finally, dreams of being naked can indicate that the dreamer does not feel equipped or qualified to accomplish the tasks at hand.

Nightmares

A nightmare is a disturbing dream that causes the dreamer to wake up feeling horror, anxiety, distress, and fear. Nightmares may also cause a suffocating feeling and may come in response to real life trauma or stress. These types of nightmares fall under a special category called Post-traumatic Stress Nightmares (PSN). Nightmares may also occur because we have ignored, repressed, or refused to accept a devastating life situation. Research shows that most people who are regularly plagued with nightmares may have a history of psychiatric problems or suicide in their family line, drug addictions, or a myriad of turbulent relationships. Nightmares are an indication of a fear that needs to be acknowledged, confronted, and overcome. They scream at our subconscious to wake up, pay attention, and make necessary changes.

Number Dreams

God is eternal. He operates outside of time yet he has designed mankind to operate within times and seasons so numbers are a necessary part of our daily lives. If we don't know how to interpret the numbers and letters we find in our dreams we may consider them the most difficult symbols to understand. However, numbers are very meaningful symbols and worth the trouble to interpret.

The location of the numbers provides meaningful clues. The environment surrounding the number will also signal the dreamer of the application, purpose, or context of the number. For instance, seeing a specific date highlighted on the calendar may be an alert to timing and seasons.

If the numbers in the dream seem elusive, or hold a hidden meaning, calculating the numerical value or equivalence of the word or the characters may prove to be helpful because each Hebrew letter is assigned a numerical value. Number meanings in biblical dream dictionaries are generally useful in understanding the numerology behind the definition and can be useful in getting ideas. *Psalm 90:12* states *"Teach us to number our days that we may gain a heart of wisdom."*

We also learned that God established the weight of the wind from *Job 28:25*—a clear indication God creates and communicates with numbers.

Numerology (the study of numbers) relates to dreams in that it is a metaphysical science reflecting certain meanings in the relationship between numbers and living things. This book is not endorsing the practice of divining one's life through calculating birth dates and the numerical meanings of one's name, which is a practice in which many in the world engage. God created the universe through the creative force of spoken words. Everything in our world is scientifically related to words and mathematics.

Literal numbers such as time, birthdates, appointments, payments, street addresses, and house numbers that appear in dreams give great insights. When the numbers are more random, like three swans swimming on a peaceful pond, or seem to contain a mystery, determining the meaning of the number will be helpful.

Helpful hints:

First, try to determine if the numbers that appear in a dream have some special biblical significance by searching Scriptural patterns regarding the number. For example the number three represents the Holy Trinity, complete fullness, kindness, entirety, and the Godhead. The number five represents grace, favor, redemption, atonement, life, the divine name of God, new song, the cross, and the anointing. The interpreter may take double-digit numbers whose meanings are not clearly delineated in Scripture and break them down to a single digit. For example:

54= (5+4) =9 or
88= (8+8) = 16 then (1+6) = 7

Then look up the biblical meaning of that single digit on Breath of the Spirit's dream symbols Numbers card to determine how the meaning of the number relates to the context of the dream. We have already done many hours of research to dig the meanings of these numbers out of Scripture for you.

Participant or Observer in the Dream

If you are the dreamer but you are only an observer, i.e., given a bird's eye view of others playing a role as in a movie, then the dream is not about you. The dream becomes about the dreamer when he or she steps into the dream and becomes an active participant in its scenes. Observers are detached from the dream and simply watch it play out while gaining insight into why certain people act or respond in differing ways. Dream observance may also indicate that the dreamer is experiencing a series of changes or needs to make decisions about the direction life is heading. By observing, one can see the big picture and the way in which things will turn out for the dream's characters. If the dreamer is totally immersed in a situation, observing from the outside often enables the dreamer to watch and learn from other characters in the dream. Observers in dreams predominately use their hearing and seeing senses to gain understanding because they are not interacting in the dream.

Most of the time dreamers find themselves participating in the events in their dreams, which means that the dream is about them. They see through their own eyes, hear spoken words or musical melodies, and interact with the other dream characters' actions and feelings.

People Dreams

The people that come into our dreams have great importance. Often the meaning of their names or their favorite Scripture contains the message for the dreamer. Other times it is the personality, character traits, job position, or the authority they hold that discloses the symbolism of that person's presence in the dream. Asking questions about the people that appear in dreams will give the dreamer introspective insight. People portrayed in dreams are often reflections of the dreamer's own positive personality traits that he or she may not be aware of, but need to discern in order to enhance or develop these traits. Other people in the dream can also display the dreamer's negative personality traits that need to be tempered or eliminated. The dreamer should ask: Do I like or dislike the traits this person exhibits? Then look for those traits to be mirrored personally. Other valuable questions that help reveal the people focus of the dream are: Am I, or others, the focus?, Am I participating in the dream, or just observing? Do I know the people in the dream personally, not at all, or just recognize them? What does this person represent to me? Are their countenances dark or light? The answer to these and other pertinent questions will give the dreamer the needed understanding to interpret the meaning of people in dreams.

Precognitive or Prophetic Dreams

Dreams that predict future happenings or events are called *precognitive* or *prophetic dreams*. Prophetic dreams are valuable tools that help the dreamer build a framework on which to construct a future. Several famous prophetic dreams are found in the words of the ancient wisdom of Hebrew Scriptures. Joseph's life was directed to become the second in command of the nation of Egypt through a dream of his brothers' sheaves of wheat bowing down to his. Joseph's entire family was depicted as the sun, moon, and stars bowing before him. Joseph interpreted both of the prophetic dreams of the imprisoned butler and baker. The butler later introduced him to Pharaoh. Joseph interpreted Pharaoh's prophetic dream about seven years of plenty, followed by seven years of famine with a word of wisdom and counsel revealing heaven's divine strategy to preserve not only Egypt, but to shelter the tribe of Israel so that it could become the nation of Israel.

There are two common types of precognitive dreams—symbolic and literal. Earthquakes or floods in a literal dream would portend an actual natural disaster involving an earthquake or flood. In a symbolic dream earthquakes and floods may symbolize great shakings in world systems like the economy, or changes in the stock market that may result in increase or decrease. Our subconscious mind or spirit is able to receive messages from the Holy Spirit who knows the future. It is obvious that prophetic dreams do come true, but the question still remains, "How?" A common element in precognitive dreams is that of divine revealed truth that releases a foreknowledge of things and subsequent events to come. If the revealed future event is of a negative or distressing nature, the dreamer is being warned in advance and is being called to pray for divine intervention to preempt harm and destruction from happening. Many people reported dreaming or seeing visions of the destruction of the Twin Towers in New York on September 11th, but they did not know what they were seeing. The prayers of those who did recognize the literal prophetic warning were able to decrease the death and destruction. Prophetic dreams are given to help us prepare ourselves for the future and to help us intervene on behalf of others. President Abraham Lincoln learned of his own death through a prophetic dream ten days before John Wilkes Booth took his life, but proper steps were not taken to prevent the assassination.

Prophetic dreams reveal God's intended life script, which allows the dreamer's soul to walk along the designated pre-described path. The dreamer's soul is able to watch future events and experiment with possible outcomes. The soul has already seen the success or failure of these events and now helps direct the dreamer in his waking life to align with his greatest possible destiny.

Recurring Dreams

Recurring dreams repeat themselves with little variation in story or theme although the characters may change to give new clues and insight.

Recurring dreams are usually fueled by the same triggering events. A specific trigger point may be a traumatic event such as a near death experience, a rape or molestation, or the recognition of a particular dream symbol at the onset of the dream. In such an event, the soul can be traumatized to the point that it affects the personality. Emotional pain is just as real as physical pain and they both require active assistance and time to heal. Occasionally these dreams are positive in nature but most often they are distressing and nightmarish in content. Dreams may recur because a past or predicted conflict in the dream remains ignored or unresolved. Once we have understood the message in a recurring dream and found and acted on a proper resolution to the predicament, our recurring dreams will fade away. This is because the answers to the recurring dream are waiting for us to discover them in our waking life.

Running and Chasing Dreams

Running in dreams indicates that we have initiated the fight or flight mechanism in the mind. The dreamer may be trying to retreat from pressures of life, the unknown, difficult changes, extreme stress, or other ordeals that he or she is currently facing. We run from these unknown pursuers who want to harm us. After a night of running, the dreamer may awaken exhausted or feeling anxious and fearful. The dreamer will often try to disappear by hiding or outwitting their attacker after taking to flight but finds his or her arms and legs are extremely heavy, making movements slow and labored.

School or Classroom Dreams

From time to time we all find ourselves back in a school, college, or university setting. In dreams, the classroom is a place of learning, including spiritual, emotional, and social development. Sometimes *school dreams* depict a general setting and other times it is very specific. For example, they may take the dreamer back to a favorite teacher from childhood. Whatever the setting or characters, the emotions we experience in school dreams are mile markers. They reveal the wisdom necessary to understand our repressed emotions about our current situations in waking life. The challenging environment of school is one in which we learn about ourselves through constant feedback from teachers and fellow students. Our positive or negative attitudes about changes and learning are often reflected in school dreams. For some of us these are happy memories of being successful and achieving high scores. For others these dreams seem like nightmares with the cruel teacher looming overhead, assigning massive amounts of homework, reports, and tests that would ensure failure. School dreams may stir up old anxious feelings of inferiority, lack, shame, conflict with authority figures, or possibly resistance to new ways of thinking, revealing our narrow-minded approach to life. Emotional scenarios are brought up in school dreams for a significant reason. The dreamer needs to correlate them to current thoughts and social or job situations. This will aid in the discovery of necessary changes or the solutions to conflict and shortcomings.

For example, people who are comfortable with the process of learning and who enjoy studying and discovery will have an ability to apply what they have learned to their waking life. Our subconscious uses the information gathered in the classroom setting to bring up important issues that relate to our current thoughts. Pay close attention to any written words that may appear on chalkboards, overhead projectors, autobiographies, assignments being giving by the teacher, and the way other students are behaving or responding in school dreams.

Sealed Dreams—Déjà vu Dreams

Job 33:14–17 Indeed God speaks once and then again but no one notices, hears or understands His message, in dreams, in visions of the night when deep, sound sleep falls on men as they lie slumbering on their beds. Then God opens their ears in times like that and seals their instructions, giving them wisdom and causing them to change their minds, so they will turn away from their misconduct, and keeping them from pride, and warning them of the penalties of sin, and keeping them from falling into some trap(author paraphrase).

Sealed dreams are not remembered because God seals them in our subconscious until the preparation process is complete in us. Then the seal is broken. Upon hearing, seeing, and walking through a situation in life our past dream is recalled and remembered. That is why some call this a *déjà vu* (or already seen) experience. Years ago the dreamer dreamed the experience, interacting with the characters of the dream. It was sealed and forgotten. In the fullness of time, when the dreamer is walking into the situation in real time, the near memory is triggered and the dreamer recalls the previous dream events. He then follows the script that was written in the past, in the dream. This invokes the feelings of "I've been here or done this before."

Signal or Trigger Dreams

Signal dreams provide indicators through which a certain recurring dream symbol appears in a dream. The appearance of this symbol helps to signal or alert the dreamer's understanding of the dream's message from previous experiences. These signals let the dreamer know how to solve problems or make good decisions.

Teeth Falling Out

Losing teeth in dreams is a very common occurrence indicating insecurity, inadequacy, and loss of personal power. Losing teeth in a dream is often associated with feelings of biting off too much or experiencing extreme pressure, forcing the dreamer to continually chew on or mull over his thoughts. It could also symbolize problems in the decision-making process or a lack of wisdom or understanding with no realization of relevant issues, resulting in frustration and stress. Teeth dreams also reflect a poor self-image, a fear of losing face, being embarrassed, or growing old and losing one's attractiveness. It can also indicate that the dreamer is worried about what others think. When teeth begin to fall out in a dream, take proper measures to adjust schedules and responsibilities and release areas of undue pressure. Becoming aware of stressful situations in life is the first step toward decreasing these levels of stress. Dreaming about losing teeth also has a medical explanation, as dentists have observed that patients who dream about losing their teeth actually grind their teeth during sleep. In this case the teeth are, in all actuality moving or being loosened. Although it is sometimes hereditary, grinding teeth while sleeping may also indicate heightened levels of stress.

Vehicle Dreams

The vehicles or mode of transportation that appear in our dreams are very significant indicators of the influence we carry in life, our feelings about ourselves, and our current level of power or authority. The condition of these vehicles illustrates how well we are flourishing in our current happenings. The model or make can point to certain time periods in history. The following questions will help the dreamer gain useful insights about vehicle dreams.

How do you feel in the dream and upon waking? Who is driving the vehicle? Are you at the wheel? If so, this may indicate you feel confident and in charge of your life at that time. If someone else is driving your vehicle, beware of that particular person. You may have surrendered the control of your life or decision-making ability to them.

The majority of the time the person driving is the one in control. If the dreamer is limited to the backseat then someone else is exercising or governing the direction of the dreamer's life. This may be accompanied by feelings of helplessness, anger, resentment, or loss of control, which can lead to depression, unless the person driving is Jesus.

What is happening with the vehicle? Are you gliding along peacefully in a plane or recklessly driving a car in reverse down a crowded highway? If you wreck, spin out of control or crash your vehicle, this is a sure indicator of conflict—be aware of strong, raging, emotions. Perhaps you are fearful or having feelings of being overwhelmed. It could indicate a need for relational mistakes to be corrected.

Pay attention to the type of vehicle. For example, is it a car, truck, van, bike, boat, train, or plane? Remember that its color will have significance as well as its working condition. Is it an old antique or stylish new space-age mode of transportation? The physical characteristics such as the size and special abilities of the vehicle will provide clues about what the dreamer believes about his or her current situation. The vehicles can also indicate things about the health of the body and the direction in life that person is taking. If the vehicle is old, worn out, beat up, punched in with dents, decaying in a pile of rust with the bumpers falling off, it may be a wake-up call. This could indicate that the dreamer needs to strive for an improved condition in his or her physical, mental, emotional, and spiritual well-being.

Visitation Dreams

Have you ever dreamt of a loved one that has passed on? Or has a friend (or even an enemy) from the past seemingly resurrected in your dreams at night? This is a very common dream because we still think of them even though we have lost relational access to them. We no longer experience or see them in our waking lives, so why would we dream about them? It is possible that our subconscious minds are simply using the person who has passed away as a dream character to illustrate an aspect of the dream's message, just like any other dream character or symbol. In this type of dream there tends to be overwhelming emotions and a "knowing" that usually does not come about in a regular dreamOften when images of our deceased loved ones visit in our dreams we recoil. The apprehension is because we believe we are practicing the forbidden practice of necromancy or talking to the spirits of the dead in order to predict the future by using black magic. This is not what is actually happening. We are not engaging in talking to the dead, calling up spirits, or necromancy. This common dream phenomenon is simply a dream symbol taking on a form with which we are familiar. For example, my earthly father died Tuesday, August 17, 1999. Before his death, I would counsel with him to receive from his gift of wisdom. Now, after his death when I am in need of wisdom and counsel I pray to God, my heavenly father. The answers to my problems sometimes come through the dream symbol of my father's countenance entering into my dream. It is much easier for me to receive his comforting presence in my dream offering godly wisdom and solutions to my troubles than to have the omniscient God himself invade my dream in all his glorious splendor and magnificence.

If a dead body is discovered in a dream, the dreamer should try to identify the gender, age, and any distinguishing characteristics. Same gender bodies that are either younger or older usually relate to some aspect of the dreamer's identity that he or she is rejecting or trying to change. An opposite gender body could point to the dreamer having relational difficulties. If the dead body appears to have a lot of qualities that the dreamer possesses, the dream may be revealing areas in the dreamer's life that need attention or that the dreamer feels are out of reach.

Observing someone dying in our dream is alarming because it seems so real. After a dream like this, the first line of defense is always to pray for that person's health and well-being and then begin to ask questions about ourselves and the person in the dream. For example: What is my perception and feelings toward my boss or other authority figures in my life at this time? Do I hold any level of anger, hostility, bitterness, resentment, or ill feelings toward them? Was the person in my dream abusing harmful, addictive substances, acting in an inappropriate fashion, or not being financially responsible? Is this a family member, close friend, or work associate? How will I be affected by their death? Which outstanding characteristics does the dying person possess that are similar to or different from my own characteristics?

When loved ones surprise us by seemingly returning from the dead in our dreams or visions of the night they are often very vivid, frightening, and memorable experiences that are called *visitation dreams.* Some psychologists call these *Return to Life* dreams.

Visitation dreams act as catalysts that enable us to make drastic changes or transformations in our lives because of the emotional needs or concerns of our hearts. These dream experiences engage our imaginations, emotions, feelings, and memories of our past history and encounters. Our imaginations are able to create positive images and receive God's healing from the pain of loss and grief. Visitation dreams enable us to remember our loved ones as they were when they were living. They usually appear in their perfected heavenly bodies, healthy and whole and in the prime of their lives. When a loved one is torn from this world we sometimes regret not being able to say, "Good-bye," or "I love you!" along with all the things we wanted to say to them. In a visitation dream, the dreamer can receive closure and healing from these issues by simply communicating love and sharing feelings. Often, the dreamer experiences a release from feelings of failure, shame, or the guilt of not adequately communicating their love or appreciation to a loved one. The message is usually, "I am happy and at peace; I forgive you, I want you to move on, and live your life to the fullest."

An Example of a Visitation Dream:

I recall a woman coming to me sobbing. She confessed to me that she had sought out a medium in order to get in touch with her beloved mother who was snatched from her in a tragic drowning accident. She never had the opportunity to say good-bye or express her heartfelt love before the passing of her best friend. She had agonized and grieved for years with no relief or consolation over her deep pain. I expressed my concern about her seeking the dark realm to attempt to communicate with her deceased mother. I explained to her that God alone held the keys to life and death. For believers, to be absent from the body was to be present with the Lord. I told her the realm of darkness is not able to communicate to our loved ones who have gone into their heavenly reward. They can only communicate with familiar spirits that peep and mutter. I lead her through a prayer of repentance for seeking that which the Bible forbids. I encouraged her to pray and ask God to allow a vision of, or the memory of her mother to visit her in a dream, to bring the needed healing and release from her pain and grief. Months later on a trip to Israel she came to me with a new composure upon her face. A new joy and gladness was evident. Grief no longer held her bound. She shared that God had answered her prayer. The image of her beloved mother had entered her dream that night with a reassuring message, "I am with the Lord, and my happiness has been made complete in him. I don't want you to sorrow for me any longer but go on with your life and serve him in gladness of heart."

Dreams that occur during REM sleep cycles are an important part of disassembling grief, resolving denial and confusion, and entering into the transformational healing process. REM dreams allow the dreamer to experience the same types of emotions and brain activity as is normal during waking times. The bereaved must forgive and release themselves from any disappointments or shortcomings in order for them to grow and become who they are called to be. Now the bereaved person can begin to let go of internal pain by releasing the loved one and the function or role that the loved one held in the dreamer's life. We will always have our memories of our loved ones and now they can be held in our dreams and remembered without regrets and pain.

Visitation dreams are a resource that gives us valuable information about ourselves and about where we are in the grieving process.

Warning Dreams

Dreams that warn of impending bad decisions affecting things to come in the future, with regard to our health, or our negative attitudes allow us to prepare ourselves to meet the challenges of tomorrow. They give us time to avoid potentially disastrous events. To be forewarned is to be forearmed. A lot of people saw indicators of the recent stock market crash in dreams but did not know what they were seeing so they did not respond correctly.

Water Dreams

Everyone dreams of water in some shape or form, whether it is oceans, rivers, lakes, rain, or snow. Dream symbols involving water should always be considered as part of the core message. Think of water as the underlying emotion, teaching, spirituality, and healing in the dream. Is the water clear or muddied, calm or rough? Is the rain a light spring mist or a torrential downpour? A stream or river could be portrayed as a gentle movement, a unifying, convergent factor, abundance, or it can be seen as violent, rushing, and dangerous. The meaning of the water depends upon its appearance and function in the dream. Walking on water means that the dreamer has faith in a greater power to prevent drowning in overwhelming circumstances. Whereas drowning in water may mean that the dreamer is unable to sustain a buoyant perspective to overcome. The downward spiral of their weighty emotions ties them to an overpowering feeling of loss of control, which simultaneously submerges and suffocates them.

Notice carefully the appearance of the water in a dream. For instance, if it is troubled, dark, or cloudy, that is a big indicator of the dreamer's feelings. Clear water also has a cleansing or refreshing aspect to consider. Dirty water could be showing a negative behavior that the dreamer needs to change or be aware of in his or her waking life.

Snow is another form of water. This symbol can predict cold emotions or frozen feelings held in suspense. In contrast, the symbol of snow on a beautiful peaceful landscape will emit feelings of purity of heart, bliss and contentment. The context of the rest of the dream will support or conflict with the overall theme.

Weather and Natural Elements Dreams

Pleasant, positive conditions in temperature and in the sky represent peace. Unpleasant, dark, or destructive negative conditions in the temperature or sky represent adversity, trouble, difficulty, and a need for prayer. Tornadoes, hurricanes, cyclones, windstorms, tidal waves, and tsunamis represent destructive events with great force. The color white symbolically represents God bringing great changes with a positive transition. The dark, ominous shades of gray and black colors represent an enemy or negative disturbances coming into the dreamer's life or the lives of others represented in the dream. It is important to speak peace into the storms of life to successfully overcome their obstacles. Storms arise in order to cause our faith to grow and be strengthened.

Word of Knowledge Dreams

Word of knowledge or angel dreams come to deliver answers, wisdom, knowledge or information that concentrate on the dreamer's questions when they are seeking God in prayer. Before going to sleep ask God to answer your needs in a dream. Angels are God's messengers. Throughout history individuals have experienced angelic visitations in their dreams. Saint Theresa of Avila is one such person.

St. Teresa of Avila lived life by this motto, "It is love alone that gives worth to all things." She devoted her life to prayer and friendship with God. She developed different levels of prayer and meditation some of which she called "devotion of union," "devotion of ecstasy or rapture," and "mental prayer."

The *"devotion of union"* is a supernatural ecstatic state. Here one is absorbed in God's presence, only the memory and imagination are left to wander. This state is characterized by a blissful peace and sweet slumber while enraptured in God's love.

The "devotion of ecstasy or rapture," is a passive state, in which the consciousness of being in the body disappears.

> *It is doubtless not profitable for me to boast. I will come to visions and revelations of the Lord: I know a man in Christ who fourteen years ago whether in the body I do not know, or whether out of the body I do not know, God knows such a one was caught up to the third heaven. And I know such a man whether in the body or out of the body I do not know, God knows ... (2 Corinthians 12:1–4).*

Teresa described it this way, "The activity of one's senses disappear; memory and imagination are also absorbed or intoxicated in God. The body and spirit are enthralled in a sweet, happy pain. They alternate between a fearful fiery glow, a complete impotence and unconsciousness, and a feeling of strangulation, intermitted sometimes by such an ecstatic flight that the body is literally lifted into space. This after half an hour is followed by a reactionary relaxation of a few hours in a swoon-like weakness, attended by a negation of all the faculties in the union with God. From this the subject awakens in tears; it is the climax of mystical experience, productive of the trance." Indeed, St. Theresa herself was said to have been observed levitating during Mass on more than one occasion.

Yet her experience gives us wonderful descriptions of mental prayer. Teresa is one of the foremost writers on mental prayer. She said, "For mental prayer in my opinion is nothing else than an intimate sharing between friends; it means taking time frequently to be alone with him who we know loves us. The important thing is not to think much but to love much and so do that which best stirs you to love. Love is not great delight but desire to please God in everything."

God gave her spiritual delights where the angels and his presence would overwhelm her senses. God overcame her with waves of glory. Sometimes her whole body was enraptured by his presence and raised from the ground. If she felt God was going to levitate her body, she would stretch out on the floor and called the nuns to sit on her and hold her down. Far from being excited about these events, she often begged God not to give her any more favors in public.

In her books, she analyzed and dissected mystical experiences the way a scientist would conduct an experiment. She never saw these gifts as rewards from God but the way he "chastised" her. The more love she felt the harder it was to offend God. She said, "The memory of the favor God has granted does more to bring such a person back to God than all the infernal punishments imaginable."

Teresa spent a lot of time developing her friendships until God told her "No longer do I want you to converse with human beings but with angels." After that God always came first in her life.

Teresa felt that the best evidence that her spiritual visions and delights came from God was that the experiences gave her peace, inspiration and encouragement. "If these effects are not present I would greatly doubt that the raptures come from God; on the contrary I would fear lest they be caused by rabies." Sometimes, however, she couldn't avoid complaining to her closest friend, Jesus, about the hostility, jealousy, and gossip that surrounded her. When Jesus told her, "Teresa, that's how I treat my friends." Teresa responded, "No wonder you have so few friends." But since Christ has so few friends, she felt they should be good ones. To read more about her, visit www.Catholic.org/prayers

Chapter Six
Soul Scripting

God's Mark on Us

The Triune God—the Father, the Son, and the Holy Spirit spoke:

> *Let us make human beings in our image, make them reflecting our nature so they can be responsible for the fish in the sea, the birds in the air, the cattle, and, yes, Earth itself, and every animal that moves on the face of Earth (Genesis 1:26–2 MSG).*

We want relationships that bring us joy and comfort. We desire careers that enable us to use the gifts and talents we possess yet lend enough challenge to keep us from boredom. Deep within the soul of every person alive is an eternal image that God has imprinted as his mark upon his creation. We are uniquely endowed with an intentional sense of eternity deposited into each of our souls, which can only find fulfillment in knowing God and doing what he created us to do (*Ecclesiastes 3:11*).

> *Ephesians 2:10 For we are His workmanship, created in Christ Jesus for good works, which God prepared beforehand so that we would walk in them (NASU).*

The spiritual and supernatural mark of our maker can be realized in everyday life as we are guided by and obey God through the direction of the Holy Spirit. With God's enlightenment, the dreams we dream at night become the roadmaps that help direct us to his higher plans for our lives.

> *"For just as the heavens are higher than the earth, so are my ways higher than your ways and my thoughts higher than your thoughts" (Isaiah 55:9).*

131

If we will call on God, we will begin to comprehend God's ways and thoughts for us by understanding his messages to us, and his individual purpose for each of our lives will be discovered. By embracing the changes that our dreams bring, we can walk the new road that he intended for us to walk.

Behold, I will do a new thing, Now it shall spring forth; Shall you not know it? I will even make a road in the wilderness And rivers in the desert, … Because I will give waters in the wilderness, And rivers in the desert, To give drink to My people, My chosen. This people I have formed for Myself; They shall declare My praise (Isaiah 43:19–21).

This higher road may not always be easy, but it leads to maturity in character and fulfillment of the specific destiny that we were each created to fulfill.

"For the gifts and the calling of God are irrevocable" (Romans 11:29).

We choose this higher spiritual road when we decide to go with God by accepting Jesus and the leading of the Holy Spirit. Throughout our life journey, God continually increases the process of sensitizing our soul to recognize the natural ways he wants to supernaturally speak to us. This book specifically addresses hearing God's voice through our dreams. This path enables us to encounter peace, joy, and fulfillment, and it will satisfy our desire to be special, successful, and loved. Along the narrow way each person discovers a divine strategy waiting to unfold in his or her faith walk. Within every soul is a dream that calls each of us to reflect the image and nature of the God who created us. It is like a flower bud that will soon blossom if given the proper nourishment and attention. Our life dreams are calling us to emerge from the cocoon, spread our wings and catch the breath of God's Spirit, the Holy Spirit, so that we can each soar to the highest heights to become the best we were created to be.

Vision of Eagles

Recently I saw a vision of a group of bald eagles. Each one was flying in perfect precision and rank in a "V" formation (Victory) through the beautiful blue sky. They were unified on a mission to bring the harvest of souls into God's Kingdom.

Then I saw the Spirit of the Lord in the form of a huge, majestic eagle soar underneath the team of small eagles. His magnificent wingspan surpassed that of the group of flying eagles providing a platform for them to rest upon. They could take their ease upon his strong pinions as the awesome eagle carried them.

Suddenly, the mighty eagle that represented the Lord quickly accelerated and moved out from under the eagles positioning himself in front of the "V" formation. I saw Newton's first Law of Motion take place. The law states "Every object persists in its state of rest or uniform motion in a straight line unless it is compelled to change that state by forces impressed upon it."

We will continue moving in a straight line at the same level unless there is a greater force that comes to alter our path or patterns. As the breath of the Spirit came, it created a swirling updraft that lifted the whole team to a new level of anointing and breakthrough. The large eagle continued to soar high above and in front of the team of eagles drawing them higher and higher.

The Scripture *Deuteronomy 33:27* came to me:

> *The eternal God is your refuge, and underneath are the everlasting arms. He will drive out your enemy before you, saying, "Destroy him!"*

The Lord has gone out before us to destroy our enemies so we can soar through the heavenly doors and gates he is opening for us. All we have to do is learn to flow in the powerful updraft his Spirit is creating. The Holy Spirit gave me several more encouraging Scriptures that go along with this vision.

First, he spoke *Psalm 90:16–17*

*Let Your work appear to Your servants, and Your glory to their children.
And let the beauty of the LORD our God be upon us, and establish the work
of our hands for us; yes, establish the work of our hands.*

I asked the Lord when he was going to cause his works to appear again. He replied with a simple question, "When are you going to do them?"

The Lord is getting ready to release some of his "greater works" upon his friends, the bondservants who are walking with him in humility and have pure hearts. He wants us to trust him on a new level. Prepare your hearts to receive a new wave of power that will sweep over you.

He also gave me *Psalm 91:1–4*

*He who dwells in the secret place of the Most High shall abide under the
shadow of the Almighty. I will say of the LORD, 'He is my refuge and my
fortress; my God, in Him I will trust.' "Surely He shall deliver you from the
snare of the fowler and from the perilous pestilence. He shall cover you with
His feathers, and under His wings you shall take refuge; His truth shall be
your shield and buckler.*

We must learn to dwell in the secret place of his presence so that we remain covered by his wings. This huge eagle was leading the way and his wings were covering us. The Lord is going to demonstrate his intentions in this hour to bring you into alignment with your destiny and greater purpose.

*"But now ask the beasts, and let them teach you;
And the birds of the heavens, and let them tell you.
 Or speak to the earth, and let it teach you;
And let the fish of the sea declare to you.
Who among all these does not know
That the hand of the Lord has done this,
In whose hand is the life of every living thing,
And the breath of all mankind? (Job 12:7-10 NASU)*

The Lord is encouraging us to listen to the sound of the Holy Spirit's wind of change as his still small voice whispers a new direction. Anticipate the winds of change. Renew yourself in faith and rise up in victory. These God-directed changes will enable you to take a turn for the better and leave past troubles behind. You have been in a preparation process to receive the love of the Lord in a new way.

> *1 Corinthians 2:9–10 "No eye has seen, no ear has heard, no mind has conceived what God has prepared for those who love Him—but God has revealed it to us by His Spirit …"*

The Spirit of the Lord has been searching the deep things of God to reveal them to his friends in their dreams. Set your heart to see and understand. He will begin to put all the pieces of your life together so that you can see the big picture from his perspective.

Our spiritual heritage is full of people like Kathryn Kuhlman, Aimee Semple McPherson, Charles Finney, John and Charles Wesley, George Whitefield, A.A. Allen, John G. Lake, Jack Coe, William Branham, and others who preached the gospel and walked under a healing and signs and wonders mantle. It is time for us to ask the Lord to take us to higher heights to receive our own revelatory, healing, and miracle mantles. Those who pioneered the faith before us made mistakes, as we all do in our humanity but that should not preempt us from honoring them for advancing the kingdom of God. What did God say about the heroes of faith in *Hebrews 11:32–35?* Every one of God's heroes in the Bible failed in some area of his or her life. Yet when God memorializes them in Hebrews we are left with the memory of their successes to celebrate, not their failures. Only a negative, judgmental spirit of accusation and legalism focuses on people's failures and shortcomings and refuses to extend God's grace and mercy.

With God's love empowering our new mantles we will be able to overtake the plowman and expedite the harvest with an accelerated speed.

> *Amos 9:13–14 "The days are coming," declares the* LORD, *"when the reaper will be overtaken by the plowman and the planter by the one treading*

grapes. New wine will drip from the mountains and flow from all the hills. I will bring back My exiled people Israel; they will rebuild the ruined cities and live in them. They will plant vineyards and drink their wine; they will make gardens and eat their fruit."

God is moving to establish his Kingdom in our lives and he is doing it through dreams and visions.

The song between the heart of God and the human spirit and soul has many methods of expression: the Bible; a still small voice; an audible voice; visions; circumstantial confirmations; signs and wonders; and the list goes on. However, this book deals specifically with the ways that God speaks to many of us through dreams as they relate to helping us become what we are called to be—productive, responsible, successful, prosperous, loved, and fulfilled. God speaks to the human soul through dreams that influence and challenge our intellect, emotions, and will. As we grasp these challenges we are able to grow and mature in different aspects of life. The life we live here on earth is our training ground for eternity. Every day we are faced with decisions and tests we must overcome with the skills and wisdom we have been given. If any of us lack wisdom we should ask God who is willing to give us his wisdom without measure. The trials of life that we overcome form and broaden our horizons of understanding. The spirit of a person is immortal, and we are responsible for choosing where the spirit will reside for eternity. Will we choose to have our spirit return to God in heaven who gave it; or will we choose to live in the smoking section of hell? The choice belongs to each of us. The colors and symbols that appear in our dreams can help us determine if we are being led by the Holy Spirit or by our own selfish, soulish desires.

The Human Soul and Spirit

By apprehending the precious promises of God in our lives we can participate in the divine power of his nature.

His divine power has given us everything we need for life and godliness through our knowledge of him who called us by his own glory and goodness. Through these he has given us his very great and precious promises, so that through

136

them you may participate in the divine nature and escape the corruption in the world caused by evil desires (2 Peter 1:3–4).

In the Bible, the word *spirit* refers to the immortal part of us, and it includes the soul. In Scripture, the word *soul* refers to the material part of us—the part that houses the mind, will, and emotions. We each have a soul and a spirit. The spirit is the eternal living part of a person that was in God from the beginning of time and will return to God when the earthly body of a Christian dies. The spirit is able to reflect the mirror image of the Creator here on earth as our minds are renewed by receiving and applying his spoken and written word. If our spirit is immersed in the living, transforming word of God, and is prayerfully developed in its fullness by consistent times of intimate communication with God, the spirit has the potential to walk in, or be a partaker of his precious and magnificent promises obtainable through the divine power of God.

Seeing that His divine power has granted to us everything pertaining to life and godliness, through the true knowledge of Him who called us by His own glory and excellence. For by these He has granted to us His precious and magnificent promises, so that by them you may become partakers of the divine nature, having escaped the corruption that is in the world by lust (2 Peter 1:3–4 NASU).

The spirit enables us to have an intimate relationship with God, who is Spirit. The Bible teaches that our spirit only comes alive when it is inhabited by the Holy Spirit at the point of salvation through the acceptance of Jesus as the one true way, the light, and the only way to God. In other words, the spirit comes alive only through Christ and then becomes the portal of communication between God and the soul (mind, will, emotions). The Bible teaches us that only those who have the Holy Spirit living inside of us are actually spiritually alive.

1 Corinthians 2:11 For what man knows the things of man except the spirit of the man which is in him? Even so no one knows the things of God except the Spirit of God.

Hebrews 4:12 For the word of God is living and powerful, and sharper than any two-edged sword, piercing even to the division of soul and spirit, and of joints and marrow, and is a discerner of the thoughts and intents of the heart.

James 2:2 For as the body without the spirit is dead, so faith without works is dead also.

Those who do not have the Holy Spirit living on the inside are governed by the soul, which can be dangerous:

"The heart is more deceitful than all else and is desperately sick; who can understand it? I, the LORD, search the heart, I test the mind, Even to give to each man according to his ways, According to the results of his deeds" (Jeremiah 17:9–10 NASB).

When we invite the spirit of God to inhabit our human spirit, God can then begin to govern the soul. However, a soul that is not governed by God does not have the filter necessary to discern good and evil. Even before salvation, God is able to speak to man's soul through dreams. However, unless man's soul becomes enlightened by accepting Christ, the necessary discernment to interpret dreams through a God-shaped filter is missing. The soul is enlightened when a person's spirit is fed by communication with God through the Holy Spirit and Jesus, the living word. Our soul and our spirit are renewed through communion with the triune God. When the Spirit of God enters our life he releases the keys to health, welfare, prosperity, and fulfillment into our renewed spirit through the vehicle of our soul.

Most of us know who we are, where we would like to be, and what we would like to be doing. The problem is that who we are, where we are, and what we are doing now is worlds apart from the goals God has set for us. We may be happy and fulfilled in one area of life, but we are drastically lacking in the others. Once we start looking for God's answers to life in our dreams we will find that he has placed most of them within the spirit of our mind once it is renewed by the Spirit of God and his living transforming word. The Spirit of God knows everything. When his Spirit enters us at salvation we are given access to spiritual vision and knowledge.

God communicates to the soul of man through dreams in the night. As we meditate upon our beds our souls begin to dialogue with God through thoughts that our dreams will mirror in picture forms.

My eyes stay open through the watches of the night that I may meditate on your promises (Psalm 119:148).

Our dreams empower us to see the promises of God manifest before our spiritual eyes. Seeing the promises manifested enables us to believe what was previously only a thought. Dreams bring imagination into the tangible substance realm of faith. We believe what we see with the eyes of our spirit and with our natural eyes. In this sense, seeing is believing as God communicates through his Spirit to our spirit and soul by giving us dreams.

Dreams can serve as a gateway to the supernatural expressions of God. Our dreams will lead us into a closer relationship with the One who desires to redeem all of mankind. The divine light that came into the world also comes into our dreams to reveal pictures of darkness that detract from our life's calling. As true light shines in our hearts we are able to remove the things that cause us to stumble in the darkness.

Soul Scripting

The definition of *soul scripting* is this: the ability of the human mind, will, and emotions (the soul) to receive and transmit messages as a draft or screenplay, which is then acted out in our dream lives. These messages can be influenced by God, evil forces, or by our daily waking lives as interpreted by the soul—our conscience, mind, will, and emotions. The dreaming process helps us to understand what is going on inside of us and what we have allowed to influence us. Dreams are a visual depiction of what lies within the human soul. It is our job to interpret what we are being influenced by, through the biblical interpretation of the script our soul has written. Discerning the difference in what has influenced our dreams can often be difficult. However, with the guidance of the Holy Spirit, we can learn to become more and more accurate in interpreting the message of our dreams. The soul reflects what we think, want, and feel and it is influenced by more than just our own thoughts throughout the day. The script written on the tablet of our soul—either by the happenings of our daily lives or by God—indicates when we are out of balance due to sin and wrong choices and when we need a course change or adjustment. We must look at the soul's messages through dreams as a reflection of ourselves. God's creative force sheds light on a specific dream to help us adjust our methods, actions, and the avenues we stroll down. Those who invite, receive, and experience the Creator of the universe into their lives have his life source living within them. Their souls have an eternal light that shines in and through them to show the correct path.

> *You have also given me the shield of Your salvation; Your gentleness has made me great. You enlarged my path under me; so my feet did not slip (2 Samuel 22:36–37).*

However, when we surrender our souls to darkness rather than to light, we invite an impure message into the soul.

> *Your eye is a lamp for your body. A pure eye lets sunshine into your soul. But an evil eye shuts out the light and plunges you into darkness (Luke 11:34 NLT).*

Over the past twenty-eight years I have intently listened to and interpreted thousands of people's dreams from every walk of life. Each one is unique. These varied experiences revealed that each dream has a voice all its own. That still small voice of inspiration speaks to the dreamer who is often desperate to hear answers to life's questions. In dreams, our spirit and soul enjoy the opportunity to communicate and dialogue with the voice of God, inspired images, and angelic messengers. Conversations in dreams are woven amidst the voice of our Creator, the leading of our souls, and our personal desires. Some people have not developed their spiritual ears to hear, or eyes to see what the Creator is saying through dreams. Dreamers often focus on and empower the negative interpretation of their dreams and overlook or ignore the positive invitations and directives the dreams offer. Conforming to and believing the positive images that God shows about us will transform us into who he says we are and who he intended us to be from the beginning. We must embrace the wisdom dreams are giving us and not rely on our own prejudices, and desires.

Dreams are often a window into divine conversations which have the ability to enlighten our souls though colors of light, symbols, shadows, types, and images. Once we learn the symbolic language of dreams we will begin to walk in an increasing level of understanding of the wisdom being communicated to us. Then our wakened consciousness will be able to communicate with the omniscient Creator through our thoughts and prayers and by asking questions to which only he holds the answers. Our God-given dreams hold the answers to the questions we hide within; once the correct interpretation is embraced we have the courage to give the dream expression.

Creative Dreams

Creative dreams have the ability to produce positive points of reference. They also remove negative, false childhood programming and responses. Godly wisdom, course corrections, and redirection or soul re-scripting often come from God's voice in our dreams. If we are not discerning, at life's crossroads we will follow after our own voice of prejudice and selfish desire instead of making the strategic turns that lead us to success. The spirit knows and recognizes the real us. The soul will formulate dreams that will help guide us through changes and stages of growth and development. Dreams have the ability to perpetuate the difficult maturing process. The soul and spirit connect us to the Creator so they have an ability to bring forth understanding and divine knowledge as they work in harmony with the Holy Spirit.

> *Ecclesiastes 12:6 Remember your Creator before the silver cord is loosed, or the golden bowl is broken, or the pitcher shattered at the fountain, or the wheel broken at the well.*

God knows the path and the course corrections we need to take when the spirit is overwhelmed. *When my spirit was overwhelmed within me, then You knew my path (Psalm 142:3a).* Soul dreams call us to change by causing us to objectively look at our mind, will, and emotions as they relate to God, our relationships, health, well-being and prosperity.

Sanctify them by Your truth. Your word is truth (John 17:17).

Dreams Reveal Truth

Since you have purified your souls in obeying the truth through the Spirit in sincere love of the brethren, love one another fervently with a pure heart, having been born again, not of corruptible seed but incorruptible, through the word of God which lives and abides forever (1 Peter 1:22–23).

Dreams reveal the truth of where you are, where you are going, and what obstacles you need to remove to get there. Dreams unleash powerful feelings and thoughts within us. A correct interpretation enables us to open the package and apply its wisdom to our lives. Dreams reveal the keys that are necessary to unlock and derail us from harmful, destructive, repetitive life patterns. Instead of going around the mountain one more time, a new track is laid that takes us into a higher reality.

God wants to superimpose his heart and plans over ours. We each have a divine destiny and we can choose if that is what will move us forward, closer to God's wisdom and plan for our lives. The level of personal and spiritual growth we attain is dependent upon the level of truth we are willing to embrace. Dreams tell the truth, the whole truth and nothing but the truth—our prayer should be, "God please help me walk in the light of that truth!"

For we can do nothing against the truth, but for the truth (2 Corinthians 13:8).

Dreams reveal the sometimes painful changes that must be embraced if we are to live a fulfilled life and reach our destiny.

Psalm 139:3 You comprehend my path and my lying down, and are acquainted with all my ways.

142

Our souls will recognize truth as it is revealed by the Holy Spirit to our spirits. Truth will begin to search out every matter of concern we may have and confront us with the changes necessary to get our lives back into balance. The soul scripting process that brings about change can take a long or a short time depending on the dreamer's level of committed understanding of the revealed truth. Change as a response to revealed truth is a difficult and challenging process, but the fruits that grow from it produce a very rewarding life.

One Friday night at a local bookstore in Texas, a teenage girl named Katherine came to our dream interpretation stand to share her recurring dream. She saw herself standing at the top of a large carpeted stairway. Behind her was a beautiful door with a bright light shining out through the door jams. In front of her was a wide open staircase that narrowed as it led down to the marble floor of the lobby. She wanted to turn and go through the beautiful light framed door that was behind her but she didn't know what was behind it. She always chose to descend the stairs, but each time she ended up tripping and falling.

In response to Katherine's dream the Breath of the Spirit dream interpretation team communicated to her that she had a high calling on her life. God was shining his light upon a new door of opportunity that was going to bring the answers to the questions she had about her destiny. We encouraged Katherine to set her goals high and not to compromise by choosing the familiar, easy or lesser way. We assured her that she was well able to succeed as God had shone his light on her path. We explained that God's light will prevent her from stumbling or falling in darkness.

Proverbs 24:16 For a righteous man may fall seven times and rise again, but the wicked shall fall by calamity.

We told Katherine that when the door of her heart is opened she will experience the illumination and love of God. God will remove the fear of failure and the fear of the unknown future.

When destiny knocks on the door of our hearts we must answer the door. Dreams give us divine insight into problem solving, correct decision-making, relationship development and the changes of life in general.

There is often a vacuous cavern between where we are now and who God intends for us to be. Dreams help to bridge the expanse of that gap. They show us where we have been, where we are, and where our destiny is leading us. Oftentimes issues of our past try to bind us to shame or failure. They attempt to hinder us from becoming who we are called and destined to be. Through the re-scripting of the soul, dream images give a futuristic picture to help us navigate through the circumstances of life. Seeing ourselves in a new light through fresh images of success and prosperity help to erase the false images we have embraced. Through re-scripting we are often able to bridge the gap between who we are now and who we will become through the journey of life. Our connection to God also connects us to mankind, as none of us live unto ourselves alone. The choices we made in the past have formed us into who we are today. The choices we make today will determine the paths we take tomorrow. The paths we take tomorrow will determine our future and destiny.

But the path of the just is like the shining sun, that shines ever brighter unto the perfect day (Proverbs 4:18).

Dreams have the ability to lead us out of darkness and guide us into God's ever increasing light. One way to know the path to our future and destiny is to embrace the dreams God gives. Dream truth will clearly indicate the progress we have made and the work and decisions that are necessary to further our life goals.

Not that I have already attained, or am already perfected; but I press on, that I may lay hold of that for which Christ Jesus has also laid hold of me (Philippians 3:12–16).

Taking it a bit deeper, the soul longs for truth to resolve the root issues that bind or hinder our progress, growth, and success. Truth is like fertilizer. When it is applied it causes us to grow and flourish. Jesus shared this profound parable in *Luke 13:7–9:*

Finally, he said to his gardener, 'I've waited three years, and there hasn't been a single fig! Cut it down. It's just taking up space in the garden.'

"The gardener answered, 'Sir, give it one more chance. Leave it another year, and I'll give it special attention and plenty of fertilizer. If we get figs next year, fine. If not, then you can cut it down'" (NLT).

Truth will continue to confront the dreamer's soul by causing dreams to reoccur until the truth is embraced. Truth has the power to bring the necessary changes to reality, reforming the character and habits of the soul so that we are able to create the godly life we desire. Dreams only seem impossible when we view them through eyes of fear. When we behold their wisdom with eyes of faith they become a living reality of truth. Forgetting and releasing the painful failures in our past helps us move on to a healthier and happier tomorrow.

1 John 1:9–10 If we confess our sins, He is faithful and just to forgive us our sins and to cleanse us from all unrighteousness. If we say that we have not sinned, we make Him a liar, and His word is not in us.

Our soul knows the truth and recognizes the gifts, talents, and abilities that lie dormant within us and in others. Forgiveness and repentance cleanse our soul bringing new clarity, aim, purpose, and love to life. This newfound freedom will unleash these dormant assets to flourish.

Truth is foundational and critical for our growth. Unless we accurately see and accept ourselves as we really are, we have no hope of prospering or becoming the best we can be. Dreams replace the distorted pictures others have tried to paint of our lives through forced expectations. The dreams our soul paints are very different. These true pictures of destiny empower us to see ourselves becoming who we truly are. Truth enables us to bring reality into our lives as a central focus and to see ourselves clearly though the eyes of our loving Creator.

When we experience his perfect love, it casts out the fear of change, rejection, and the unknown.

1 John 4:18–19 There is no fear in love; but perfect love casts out fear, because fear involves torment. But he who fears has not been made perfect in love. We love Him because He first loved us.

We then become able to open the hidden doors of our hearts and allow his watchful inspection to remove sin, clutter, false visions, and confusion.

Not all dreams are inspired by God. But we can still benefit from the script they reveal if we learn how to decode their hidden messages, by recording our dreams with an open mind, honesty, thankfulness, and objectivity.

Habakkuk 2:2–3 "Then the Lord answered me and said: 'Write the vision and make it plain on tablets, that he may run who reads it. For the vision is yet for an appointed time; but at the end it will speak, and it will not lie. Though it tarries, wait for it; because it will surely come, it will not tarry.'"

By writing down the visual truths that we receive in a dream the varied layers of the dream will reveal more than meets the eye. Prayerfully consider the dream truths that are revealed as reality. The things that are revealed to the soul in dreams, visions, and the realm of the invisible Spirit are not tangible, but they are eternal.

2 Corinthians 4:18 While we do not look at the things which are seen, but at the things which are not seen. For the things which are seen are temporary, but the things which are not seen are eternal.

Dreams enable us to look past the present circumstances of our lives to see the endless possibilities that await our discovery in the eternal realm of the Spirit. The Kingdom of God is without end. From this eternal plane come the visions of the night which spark faith and hope for our near future and all eternity.

Chapter Seven
God's Numbers

God is the master mathematician just like he is the master of all. He is eternal and limitless, so he operates outside of time, but he designed man to operate within times and seasons. For this reason numbers are a necessary part of our waking and dream lives. The Bible provides many examples of God's consistency in the tapestry he weaves across generations and throughout the intricacies of our world. His seal of spiritual harmony rest upon everything. Just as the Bible illustrates, God has always spoken through times and seasons. He works within the mathematical order he created, an organized sequence of timing and a delicate balance of the conditions we live by. God's divine order includes days, hours, even minutes—and it involves calculations that make up gravity, inertia, and many other scientific laws. God is the same yesterday, today and forever—he does not change.

God's Mighty Works in Numbers

Isaiah encourages us to know the God who measures every drop of water, every mountain range, every speck of dust and the magnificent expanse of heaven in his loving hands.

Isaiah 40:12–15 "Who has measured the waters in the hollow of His hand, measured heaven with a span and calculated the dust of the earth in a measure? Weighed the mountains in scales and the hills in a balance? Who has directed the Spirit of the Lord, or as His counselor has taught Him? With whom did He take counsel, and who instructed Him, and taught Him in the path of justice? Who taught Him knowledge, and showed Him the way of understanding? Behold, the nations are as a drop in a bucket, and are counted as the small dust on the scales; Look, He lifts up the isles as a very little thing."

Isaiah 40:26 "Lift up your eyes on high, and see who has created these things, Who brings out their host by number; He calls them all by name, by the greatness of His might and the strength of His power; not one is missing."

We learn *God establishes the weight of the wind, and apportion*[s] *the waters by measure* from *Job 28:25* (the oldest book of the Bible).

The Bible teaches us to record or number our days that we may gain a heart of wisdom. As we journal, date our dreams and the answers to our prayers, we are called to remember the wonderful works God has performed so that we can celebrate and be thankful for his provision.

Psalm 77:11 I will remember the works of the Lord; surely I will remember Your wonders of old.

Psalm 107:24 They see the works of the Lord and His wonders in the deep.

When science studies the perfect works of God they marvel at his precision and handiwork.

Psalm 111:2 The works of the Lord are great, studied by all who have pleasure in them.

Everything that God does is done with perfect precision and timing. Nothing is done by chance—it is accomplished through his heavenly plan and dream designs.

Psalm 18:30 As for God, his way is perfect; the word of the Lord is proven; he is a shield to all who trust in him.

Hebrew Numerology

We do not agree with, nor do we practice the study of the occult meanings of numbers and of their supposed meanings or influence on human life through numerology. We do not direct our lives or make decisions based on numbers that are associated with our lives. We make decisions in life based on the Scripture and the leading of the Holy Spirit.

In Gematria, each Hebrew letter is assigned a numerical value. One calculates the numerical value or equivalence of the letter, word, or phrase to gain understanding of the word's meaning.

The science behind this art or study is the philosophy that the equivalence of each word is not a coincidence. The number zero is always discarded because it is only considered a placeholder.

Hebrew Letters

Alef = 1, yud = 10, kuf = 100 All of these have a value of 1.

Beit =2, kaf = 20, reish = 200 All of these have a value of 2.

God created the universe by releasing His breath in spoken words through Jesus, the living manifested Word. As we see illustrated in Scripture. God' words have a creative force. Because we are created in God's image, our words also have a creative ablility. Our words crate light or darkness; bring forth life or death, good or evil.

In the beginning was the Word, and the Word was with God. He was in the beginning with God. All things came into being through Him, and apart from Him nothing came into being that has come into being. In Him was life, and the life was the Light of men. The Light shines in the darkness, and the darkness did not comprehend it. John 1:1–5 NASU

What was from the beginning, what we have heard, what we have seen with our eyes, what we have looked at and touched with our hands, concerning the Word of Life—and the life was manifested, and we have seen and testify and proclaim to you the eternal life, which was with the Father and was manifested to us—what we have seen and heard we proclaim to you also, so that you too may have fellowship with us; and indeed our fellowship is with the Father, and with His Son Jesus Christ. These things we write, so that our joy may be made complete. This is the message we have heard from Him and announce to you, that God is Light, and in Him there is no darkness at all 1 John 1:1–5 NASU

Here is a Biblical example of Gematria using a phrase from the New Testament passage in John 8:12

Then Jesus again spoke to them, saying "I am the Light of the world; he who follows Me will not walk in the darkness, but will have the Light of life." John 8:12-13 NASU

The orbital path of the earth around the sun forms an elliptical or circular pattern. The earth is 93 million miles from the sun. Converting the miles into inches and dropping the zeros, the new figure would be 5,892,480 inches—the distance light travels from the sun to earth. Divide 5,892,480 by the speed of light, (186,000 miles per second), drop the zeros and we get 3,168 the number of the Lord Jesus Christ, who is the light of the world.

John the revelator tells us the number six hundred sixty-six is the gematria number for the Antichrist's name. The number 666 is connected to devil worship by ancient pagan mystery religions. The number value of the name "Jesus" is 888. Numbers are foundational to words and to works. Every number has a literal and a symbolic meaning that can be helpful for us to understand our dreams.

Every building that is designed, every instrument and machine that is produced, and even people have significant numbers that are assigned to them. Engineers, designers and all who create live in a world of numbers. Think of all the numbers we use every day. What is your social security number, your phone numbers, date of birth, address, PO Box number and passport numbers or driver's license number (just to list a few)?

Numbering our days includes keeping a dated journal to record the dreams, visions, and messages the Lord gives to us. This is especially important as God knows the intricacies of our lives, why should we not tune in to the details he communicates on an ongoing basis?

Psalm 90:12 So teach us to number our days that we may gain a heart of wisdom.

As we number our days and record the mighty things God has done for us, we will remember his great works and our faith and trust will increase. Every hair of our head is numbered and he sees every sparrow that falls from the sky.

Luke 12:7 But the very hairs of your head are all numbered. Do not fear therefore; you are of more value than many sparrows.

God's Heavens Declare the Glory of the Gospel Story

We read in the first chapter of Genesis that God created the firmament of the heavens with two great lights; the sun and the moon. He also made the stars. These two heavenly lights and star constellations are calculated to set forth important truths to give man hope of salvation and the computation of his earthly times and seasons. (The Mazzaroth mentioned in Scriptures is another name for the Constellations).

Job 38:31–33 "Can you bind the cluster of the Pleiades, or loose the belt of Orion? Can you bring out Mazzaroth in its season? Or can you guide the Great Bear with its cubs? Do you know the ordinances of the heavens? Can you set their dominion over the earth? ..."

The Patriarchs acted according to the mind and will of God and devoted themselves to the study of the gospel story concealed in the starry constellations to show forth his glory. From Genesis to Revelation Satan is symbolically represented by a serpent, Draco the Dragon, or Hydra. Messiah is represented as the seed, a lion, and the lamb. He goes forth to triumph, and to conquer. He is seen bruised, pierced, and as the lamb that is slain.

Psalm 147:4–5 "He counts the number of the stars; he calls them all by name. Great is our Lord, and mighty in power; his understanding is infinite."

Psalm 19:1–4 "The heavens declare the glory of God; and the firmament shows his handiwork. Day unto day utters speech, and night unto night reveals knowledge. There is no speech nor language where their voice is not heard. Their line has gone out through all the earth, and their words to the end of the world ..."

Before the Scriptures were written, God granted the Antediluvians a long life so they might perfect the star cycles in astronomy. This process lasted 600 years and was known as a *Grand* or *Great Year*! Once they had lived 600 years, each additional year the person lived furnished more proof that the cycles of the twelve constellations described the gospel story accurately. The signs of the heavens were originally star pictures. They were developed by God and he taught Adam, Enoch, and Seth the original meaning of each of them.

God gave the revelation of the stars to Adam. His son Seth was able to calculate the precise movements of the stars. Enoch walked with God and is reported by Josephus to have visited heaven on many occasions and he prophesied God's final victory through the stars.

Genesis 5:24 "And Enoch walked with God; and he was not, for God took him."

There are twelve brothers, who became the twelve tribes of Israel and each one is assigned to one of the twelve constellations in the heavens to tell the gospel story.

Genesis 49:1–2 And Jacob called his sons and said, "Gather together, that I may tell you what shall befall you in the last days: Gather together and hear, you sons of Jacob, and listen to Israel your father."

Twelve is the number of the apostles, the elect purposes of God and divine government or heavenly rule.

Genesis 42:32 "We were twelve brothers, sons of one father. One is no more, and the youngest is now with our father in Canaan" (NIV).

God gave us the heavenly stars, the moon and the sun for signs, seasons, and to help us keep time.

Genesis 1:14–19, "Then God said, 'Let there be lights in the firmament of the heavens to divide the day from the night; and let them be for signs and seasons, and for days and years; and let them be for lights in the firmament of the heavens to give light on the earth'; and it was so. Then God made two great lights: the greater light to rule the day, and the lesser light to rule the night. He made the stars also. God set them in the firmament of the heavens to give light on the earth, and to rule over the day and over the night, and to divide the light from the darkness. And God saw that it was good. So the evening and the morning were the fourth day."

Perfect Numbers

The perfect numbers are 3, 7, 10, and 12. Three is the number for divine perfection. Seven is the number for spiritual perfection. Ten is the number for ordinal perfection. An ordinal number is a number that indicates its position in a series or specific order as in first, second, third, … etc. The product of these four perfect numbers 3 x 7 x 10 x 12 = 2,520 which is the number of years of the time of Israel's punishment and Gentile rule over Jerusalem. Why is the number twelve so prominent in the heavens? Twelve represents governmental perfection and the rule of heaven.

Psalm 136:4–9 "To Him who alone does great wonders, for His mercy endures forever; to Him who by wisdom made the heavens, for His mercy endures forever; to Him who laid out the earth above the waters, for His mercy endures forever; to Him who made great lights, for His mercy endures forever—the sun to rule by day, for His mercy endures forever; the moon and stars to rule by night, for His mercy endures forever."

As we study the Scriptures we can find the meanings of numbers in our dreams through the different patterns we observe.

Seven

Seven is the number for God, spiritual perfection, and completeness. God rested from creating a perfect earth on the seventh day. He said the seventh day is a holy day for rest. The seventh month is for feast and festival days and the seventh year was a Sabbath rest for the land.

Jesus performed seven miracles on the Sabbath. Jesus healed the man with the withered hand *(Matthew 12:13)*. Jesus cast the unclean spirit out of a man *(Mark 1:23–26)*. Jesus healed Peter's mother-in-law's fever *(Mark 1:30–31)*. Jesus healed the woman with a spirit of infirmity *(Luke 13:11–12)*. Jesus healed the man with dropsy *(Luke 14:2–4)*. Jesus healed the crippled man by the Bethesda pool *(John 5:5–9)* and Jesus healed the man born blind by placing clay mud upon his eyes *(John 9:14)*.

Man is fearfully and wonderfully created. Our hearts beat at a consistent rate for six days. On the seventh day, our heart rate begins to beat at a slower rate of speed. Our bodies are designed for a Sabbath day of rest.

In science, there are seven divisions in the plant and animal kingdoms. For example, the rows of Indian corn or maize are always set with the even numbers of 8, 10, 12, 14 or 16, so you will never find a row of seven on a cob of Indian corn.

The length of man's life is three-score years and ten, or seventy years. It takes seven years for the structure of a baby's body to change completely. We grow through seven phases in life: infancy, childhood, youth, adolescence (young man or woman), man- or womanhood, decline (old man or woman), senility (aged man or woman).

Years ago, I earned a bachelor's of Science degree in Veterinary Health Technology. During my studies I learned in the animal kingdom that gestation periods are connected to the number seven. A mouse is formed in twenty-one days (3 x 7). A cat is formed in fifty-six days (8 x 7). The dog, man's best friend, is formed in sixty-three days (9 x 7). A lion, the "king of beasts" is formed in ninety-eight days (14 x 7). Sheep, the symbol God chose to represent Christians, are formed in one hundred and forty-seven days (21 x 7). Humans take two hundred and eighty days (40 x 7) to form.

The number seven is found in sound, light, and music. Sound is produced by vibrations in the air. Pitch is determined by the speed of the vibrations. When the vibrations are too slow, we consider them noise. There are seven notes in a scale and the eighth note is a repetition of the first. There are 264 vibrations but some are so slow the human ear cannot hear them all. The eye can see them when sand is placed on a metal sheet and a cord is vibrated. Then, the sand forms into a perfect geometrical shape. The vibration of light causes color. Color and sound are related in music. Each musical note produces a different color.

There are seven musical notes that harmonize with the seven colors. The pitch of the human voice can cause water, plants, animals or other people to be blessed, prosper or fail—*"He that hath an ear let him hear what the Spirit says unto the churches" Rev.2:7*. The mystic John the Revelator was made famous through his use of Gematria in the book of Revelation. The seven stars in the right hand of Christ, the twenty-four elders seated before the throne, the seven seals, seven trumpets, seven vials and the mark of the beast, 666.

In Scripture there are seven promises to the churches; The Seven Seals; The Seven Trumpets; The Seven Parables of Matthew; The Seven Gifts of *Romans 12:6–8*; the Seven Unities of *Ephesians 4:3–6*; and the Seven Characteristics of Wisdom in *James 3:17*.

There are Seven Gifts of Christ in John's Gospel: Jesus' flesh, his life, his example, The Comforter, his peace, his words, and his glory.

There are seven mysteries, or secrets which include: The Mystery of the Kingdom, The Blindness of Israel, The Church, the Body of Christ, The First Resurrection, The Purpose of Satan, The Purpose of God, and Mystery Babylon.

There are seven steps in the humiliation of Jesus and seven that led to his exaltation (*Philippians 2:5–11*).

There are seven messages of Jesus on the Cross:

- *"Father, forgive them, for they know not what they do."*
- *"Truly, I say to you, today you will be with Me in Paradise."*
- *"My God! My God! Why hast thou forsaken me?"*
- *"Woman, behold thy son, Son, behold thy mother."*
- *"I thirst."*
- *"Father, into Thy hand I commend My Spirit."*
- *"It is finished!"*

Enoch was the seventh man from Adam and God took him in a translation experience which can often happen in the dream realm. Enoch still resides in heaven today and may be one of the two witnesses who return in the book of Revelation as it is appointed unto every man to die, *Hebrews 9:27.*

The Seven Spirits of God are found in *Revelation 1:4; 3:1; 4:5; and 5:6,* and in *Isaiah 11:2.*

> *"The Spirit of the Lord shall rest upon Him, the Spirit of wisdom and understanding, the Spirit of counsel and might, the Spirit of knowledge and of the fear of the Lord."*

Each of the Seven Spirits of God are represented in the Menorah—seven burning lamps of fire—or the Lampstand before the throne of God, and are assigned a specific color. In dreams the Spirit of the Lord is represented by the color red. The Spirit of Wisdom is the color orange. The Spirit of Understanding is yellow. The Spirit of Counsel is green. The Spirit of Might is cyan or blue. The Spirit of Knowledge is indigo. The Spirit of the Fear of the Lord is magenta or violet.

Revelation 1:4 "Grace to you and peace from Him who is and who was and who is to come, and from the Seven Spirits who are before His throne."

Revelation 2:1 "These things says He who holds the seven stars in His right hand, who walks in the midst of the seven golden lampstands."

Revelation 4:5 "And from the throne proceeded lightnings, thunderings, and voices. Seven lamps of fire were burning before the throne, which are the Seven Spirits of God."

These powerful voices of praise and declaration of God's greatness release brilliant living colors in heaven. These same colors appear in our dreams and visions.

Eight

In Hebrew, the number eight means to "make fat, cover with fat, or to super abound, in strength, fertility, and abundance." Seven means completion and rest. Therefore, eight is above perfect and starts a new cycle or beginning and it also means resurrection.

There were eight miracles accomplished during Elijah's life. He shut up the heavens so it didn't rain for three years (*James 5:17*). He multiplied the widow and her son's meal (*1 Kings 17:14–16*). He raised the widow's son from the dead (*1 Kings 17:17–23*). He also called fire down from heaven, which killed 51 soldiers (*2 Kings 1:9–10*). He prayed rain down from heaven after the drought (*1 Kings 18:41–45*). His prayers caused fire to fall and kill another 51 soldiers *(2 Kings 1:11–12),* and He divided the Jordan River with his mantle *(2 Kings 2:8).*

Sixteen means double beginnings, or established beginnings. There were sixteen miracles accomplished during Elisha's life. Elisha divided the Jordan River with Elijah's mantle *(2 Kings 2:14).* He healed the bad waters *(2 Kings 2:19–22).* He cursed the forty-two young men who mocked him *(2 Kings 2:23–24).* He saw the filling of the ditches with water in *(2 Kings 3:15–27)*. The multiplying of the widow's oil to pay her debts *(2 Kings 4:1–7)* was also part of Elisha's many miracles. He raised the widow's son from the dead *(2 Kings 4:32–37)*. He healed the sons of the prophets' poisonous stew *(2 Kings 4:38–41)*. One hundred men were fed *(2 Kings 4:42–44)*. Naaman's leprosy was healed *(2 Kings 5:10–14)*. Gehazi was stricken with leprosy *(2 Kings 5:20–27)*. His prayers enabled the axe head to swim in the Jordan *(2 Kings 6:1–7)*. Elisha opened the eyes of his servant *(2 Kings 6:15–17)*. He struck the Syrian army with blindness *(2 Kings 6:18)*. He restored the sight of the Syrian army *(2 Kings 6:19–20)*. He arrested the King's messengers *(2 Kings 7:15–20)*. A dead man was raised to life from touching Elisha's anointed bones in the grave *(2 Kings 13:20–21)*.

Symbolic Numbers

Biblical interpretation of symbolism is a difficult subject to balance between science and hermeneutics. We see in the New Testament that the number 666 is given a symbolic meaning.

> *Revelation 13:18 "Here is wisdom. Let him who has understanding calculate the number of the beast, for it is the number of a man: his number is 666."*

There are many writers like E.W. Bullinger, the author of *Number in Scripture*, who attribute the meanings or symbols of numbers to having received revelation from God and then confirming it through scriptural studies.

We can see in Scripture types, shadows, and patterns that indicate the meanings of numbers or the symbols they represent.

The Symbolic Numbers One through Ten

- One: the eternal, omnipotent God, unity, link between heaven and earth, beginning, and independence.

- Two: Division, difference, separation, multiplication, agreement, witness and support.

- Three: Union, approval, complete divine fullness, unity, kindness and entirety of God, coordination, perfection, life and Holy Spirit Trinity.

- Four: Creation, earth, space, completion, creative works, great elements: earth, air, fire, water; regions; four directions: north, south, east, west; seasons: spring, summer, autumn, winter.

- Five: God's grace, favor, redemption, atonement, life, the divine name of God, a new song, the cross and anointing.

- Six: Number of man—God's greatest creation, the weakness of man and humanity, incompleteness of the physical world and the serpent.

- Seven: God's number, fullness, completeness, purification, consecration, rest, full development, fulfillment, spiritual perfection, weapon and self-defense.

- Eight: Man's ability to transcend limits of physical existence, teacher, new birth, resurrection, new beginnings, to make fat, super-abounding in strength.

- Nine: completion, end, conclusion, finality, fullness of blessings, evangelist, summing up, manifestation of the Spirit, judgment, serpent and tribulation.

- Ten: Perfection, complete, divine order, law, government, restoration, trail, testing, ten plagues, Ten Commandments, wilderness and pastor.

Nebuchadnezzar's dream

We can learn a great deal from the book of Daniel about the original "dream team" who interpreted Nebuchadnezzar's dream, about how God uses symbolism, about how to give an interpretation, and most important of all, the interpretation that is given by the Holy Spirit.

The first "dream team" can be found in *Daniel 2:17–19*:

"Then Daniel *went to his house, and made the decision known to* Hananiah, Mishael, *and* Azariah, *his companions, that they might seek mercies from the God of heaven concerning this secret, so that Daniel and his companions might not perish with the rest of the wise men of Babylon. Then the secret was revealed to Daniel in a night vision. So Daniel blessed the God of heaven."*

Interesting note: the Gematria of their four names equals 888, the name of Jesus Christ, and resurrection.

Daniel	95
Mishael	381
Hananiah	120
Azariah	292
Total	888

Not only did God reveal the unspoken dream, he also established Daniel as the only true dream interpreter. God also dramatically demonstrated that Daniel was the only one with the ability to receive the understanding of mysteries because he often sought the only true God for wisdom. None of King Nebuchadnezzar's magicians, conjurers, sorcerers, or the Chaldeans who were all skilled in the dark arts could discover the undisclosed dream, let alone its interpretation. The King's occult advisers protested his request by saying, *"Moreover, the thing which the king demands is difficult, and there is no one else who could declare it to the king except gods, whose dwelling place is not with mortal flesh" (Daniel 2:11 NASB).* Their challenge provoked the king's wrath. In a fit of rage he demanded the destruction of all the wise men of Babylon. Daniel replied with discretion and discernment to the king's commander, Arioch. He further petitioned the king for time to seek God for the dream and its interpretation.

> *Daniel 2:26–27 The king answered and said to Daniel, whose name was Belteshazzar, "Are you able to make known to me the dream which I have seen, and its interpretation?" Daniel answered in the presence of the king, and said, "The secret which the king has demanded, the wise men, the astrologers, the magicians and the soothsayers cannot declare to the king."*

The Dream:

> *Daniel 2:31–36 "You, O king, were watching; and behold, a great image! This great image, whose splendor was excellent, stood before you; and its form was awesome. This image's head was of fine* gold, *its chest and arms of* silver, *its belly and thighs of* **bronze,** *its legs of* **iron,** *its feet* **partly of iron and partly of clay.** *You watched while a stone was cut out without hands, which struck the image on its feet of iron and clay, and broke them in pieces.* **Then the iron, the clay, the bronze, the silver, and the gold were crushed together, and became like chaff from the summer threshing floors; the wind carried them away so that no trace of them was found. And the stone that struck the image became a great mountain and filled the whole earth.**
>
> *This is the dream ..."*

The Interpretation:

Daniel 2:36–49 "Now we will tell the interpretation of it before the king. **You, O king, are a king of kings.** *For the God of heaven has given you a kingdom, power, strength, and glory; and wherever the children of men dwell, or the beasts of the field and the birds of the heaven, He has given them into your hand, and has made you ruler over them all—* **you are this head of gold.** *But after you shall arise (silver)* **another kingdom inferior to yours***; then another, which shall rule over all the earth* **a third kingdom of bronze.** *And* **the fourth kingdom shall be as strong as iron,** *inasmuch as iron breaks in pieces and shatters everything; and like iron that crushes, that kingdom will break in pieces and crush all the others. Whereas you saw the feet and toes, partly of potter's clay and partly of iron, the kingdom shall be divided; yet the strength of the iron shall be in it, just as you saw the iron mixed with ceramic clay. And as* **the toes of the feet were partly of iron and partly of clay,** *so the kingdom shall be partly strong and partly fragile. As you saw iron mixed with ceramic clay, they will mingle with the seed of men; but they will not adhere to one another, just as iron does not mix with clay. Inasmuch as you saw that the stone was cut out of the mountain without hands* **And in the days of these kings the God of heaven will set up a kingdom which shall never be destroyed; and the kingdom shall not be left to other people; it shall break in pieces and consume all these kingdoms, and it shall stand forever.***, and that it broke in pieces the iron, the bronze, the clay, the silver, and the gold—***the great God has made known to the king what will come to pass after this. The dream is certain, and its interpretation is sure."**

Then King Nebuchadnezzar fell on his face, prostrate before Daniel, and commanded that they should present an offering and incense to him. The king answered Daniel, and said, **'Truly your God is the God of gods, the Lord of kings, and a revealer of secrets, since you could reveal this secret.'** *Then the king promoted Daniel and gave him many great gifts; and he made him ruler over the whole province of Babylon, and chief administrator over all the wise men of Babylon. Also Daniel petitioned the king, and he set Shadrach, Meshach, and Abednego over the affairs of the province of Babylon; but Daniel sat in the gate of the king."*

The Essence of the Dream is

> *Daniel 2:28–30, "But there is a God in heaven who reveals secrets, and* **He has made known to King Nebuchadnezzar what will be in the latter days**. *Your dream, and the visions of your head upon your bed, were these: As for you, O king, thoughts came to your mind while on your bed, about what would come to pass after this;* **and He who reveals secrets has made known to you what will be.** *But as for me, this secret has not been revealed to me because I have more wisdom than anyone living, but for our sakes who make known the interpretation to the king, and that you may know the thoughts of your heart.*

Another interesting note about Nebuchadnezzar's dream: we see three pure, unmixed monad elements of gold, silver and bronze. Elements of matter are arranged with God's Law of Numbers in The Periodic Table of Elements. Iron is a neutral element on the scale of atomic weights. The heaviest element is gold and it is at the top of the statue. The lightest mixture—clay and iron—which are also the most vulnerable, are at the bottom. Three of these kingdoms have already passed away and the fourth is nearing the end as God is shaking everything that can be shaken. Jesus is setting up his Kingdom that shall never be shaken as the rock, Jesus Christ grows into a great mountain.

Practical Uses of Numbers in Dreams

We have determined that numbers have significance in the Scriptures, in science, and in our daily lives. When God speaks to us in the night season through dreams, numbers often play a part of the mystical message he is relaying to us.

Upon awakening from a dream, notice and jot down the time and remember if there were any numbers present in the dream. Then go to the Scriptures to see if there is a chapter and verse with that number combination using the *"Waking Words of Ancient Wisdom"* dream card.

For example, if you awaken at 11:11 PM, ask yourself why was I awakened to see the number eleven repeating? What is happening in the circumstances of your waking life? Look up the meanings of the number eleven on the *Numbers Dream Symbols* card. The card will show eleven is the number of revelation, transition, mercy, and the prophet. But eleven is also the number of judgment and disorder. Next, reduce the numbers 11:11 to single digits and then add them together (1+1+1+1 = 4).

The number one symbolically represents the one eternal, omnipotent God, unity, beginning, and brings a link between heaven and earth to establish God's will.

Four is the number of creative works on earth, the number of seasons, tides, and directions; it also represents the weakness of man.

Look on your symbolic number dream card and on your *"Waking Words of Ancient Wisdom"* the chapter & verse dream cards. See if the current numbers in your waking time has meaning to you in relation to specific Bible chapters and verses as they relate to the context of the dream. You may read through several Scripture verses until you find the ones that add clarity to your dream.

> *Isaiah 11:11 "It shall come to pass in that day that the Lord shall set His hand again the second time to recover the remnant of His people who are left ..."*

> *Numbers 11:11 "So Moses said to the Lord, "Why have You* **afflicted (judgment)** *Your servant? And why have I not found favor in Your sight, that You have laid the burden of all these people on me?"*

> *Deuteronomy 11:11–12 "but the land which you* **cross over (transition)** *to possess is a land of hills and valleys, which drinks water from the rain of heaven, a land for which the Lord your God cares; the eyes of the Lord your God are always on it, from the beginning of the year to the very end of the year."*

Sometimes a number will represent a particular month, birth date, time, address, appointment, or phone number.

Example:

A young single man awoke from his dream with a specific sequence of numbers vividly engraved on his memory so he jotted them down. The next afternoon he met an attractive, single woman in a coffee shop. He struck up a friendly conversation with her. He found her very intriguing so he asked for her phone number. She quickly scribbled her number down and slid him the napkin. You can imagine his surprise when he realized the numbers she wrote were the exact same number sequence he had dreamed the previous night. He felt their meeting was orchestrated by God. They started dating, got engaged, and are now happily married.

Ask yourself questions to determine the significance of the number of people, buildings, or objects that appear in dreams. Pray and ask the Holy Spirit to give you insight and revelation concerning the significance of the numbers.

Dream Date and Scripture example

Title: Barbie's Angel Sword Dream

On April 12, 2007, an angel appeared in my dream carrying a sharp new two-edged sword with a beautiful ruby and sapphire jeweled handle. He handed the shiny sword to me and then departed.

The date I had the dream was significant because *Hebrews 4:12* contained the message the angel was to deliver.

> *Hebrews 4:12–13 For the word of God is living and active. Sharper than any double-edged sword, it penetrates even to dividing soul and spirit, joints and marrow; it judges the thoughts and attitudes of the heart. Nothing in all creation is hidden from God's sight everything is uncovered and laid bare before the eyes of him to whom we must give account.*

Elements or Symbols defined

The Word of the Lord is living and active. It penetrates the barriers of the soul, reaching our inner spirit to reveal the secrets in our hearts. We are laid bare and become transparent in its light.

Angels are heavenly messengers of fire, wind, light, or the breath of God's Spirit. They appear in dreams and visions or come in visitations to deliver messages to help guide us into truth. The word of God is pure truth.

A sword can represent the Word of the Lord, which has the

ability to cut, divide, and sort things in our heart and mind but it can also represent a physical or spiritual weapon being placed in our hands.

Jewels denote wealth, spiritual gifts, anointings, treasures, inheritance, rank, pleasure, and riches that are consecrated unto God as memorials.

Rubies are highly valued treasures such as a virtuous wife, wisdom, and lips full of knowledge because they are considered to be more precious than rubies.

Sapphires represent divine, true judgment; gifts of discerning of spirits; works of perfection; testing which enables a person to be chosen because of the costly changes in their character; integrity, and nature.

Interpretation of the dream

Even though we are periodically braced by trials and tests, the Word of the Lord comes to encourage and support our upward climb. The jeweled sword is a promised reward if the challenge of the trial is met and the test passed. I will be able to use God's Word more skillfully once the areas in my life have been touched by the piercing sword of the Lord. God's anointing to discern the voice and movement of his Spirit more accurately will increase once the weak joints of my armor and character have been strengthened in integrity, holiness and purity.

Dream Waking time and Scripture example

Title: Setting the Captives Free!

On April 27, a man dreamed he found himself behind prison bars. An angel commanded him to speak to the prison doors to open. He didn't believe the doors would obey his command so he hesitated. The angel commanded him again, "Speak to the prison doors and command them to open." When he obeyed and commanded the doors they opened and he was freed. In the next scene, he found himself behind bars again. This time he was with other prisoners clad in chains with heavy boulders crushing down on top of their backs. Again the angel who was training him commanded him saying, "Speak to the rocks and command them to fall off. Speak to the chains that bind them to be broken and command the prison doors to open." He hesitated again thinking he did not have enough authority but when he followed the angel's instructions the boulders fell off, the chains were broken and the prison doors flew open setting all of the prisoners free. He awoke at 6:11 a.m. He moved the colon over one digit to the right (from 6:11 to 61:1) and upon searching the Scriptures he found that Isaiah 61:1 is an exact fit for his dream. The angel awakened him at precisely the time he needed to confirm his dream with Scripture.

> *Isaiah 61:1 "The Spirit of the Lord God is upon Me, because the Lord has anointed Me To preach good tidings to the poor; He has sent Me to heal the brokenhearted, To proclaim liberty to the captives, And the opening of the prison to those who are bound."*

The message in the dream was given on April 27, that is, 4/27. Another interesting scripture in Isaiah 42:7 confirms his calling to be delivered, and to become a deliverer of others.

> *To open blind eyes, to bring out prisoners from the dungeon and those who dwell in darkness from the prison (Isaiah 42:7 NASU).*

The following is a prophetic word given to Barbie Breathitt on August 8th, 2006 (08-04-06), by Dr. Chuck Pierce, of Glory of Zion, located in Denton, Texas.

> "And the Lord would say unto you that, "I have formed you; and I have given you favor for a season. And I am beginning to cause you to see the mission of why I have positioned you in the earth at this time. I say you are going to be breathing from a seeing stand point. For I say I am opening your eyes to see into a realm where I AM and where I AM bringing in revelation of the night. (51 refers to Divine Revelation). I say from that revelation of the night you will breath out an expression of who I AM and night will become light saith the Lord. And you will cause people where they could not see; they will begin to see and not only will they see they will begin to live. And from their life they will begin to express Me saith the Lord."

I have found that when a prophetic word is given over me or someone else that the Lord will often confirm the prophetic word with a dream or vice versa. Spiritual things are confirmed with a witness of two.

Title: Barbie's White House Numbers Dream
Night of 8/20/2006

In a dream, I saw three white, wooden houses that looked exactly alike. They were located next to each other on the same street. The only differences I saw in the three white, wooden houses were that their addresses were three numbers different from each other. The address of the first one was 51. The address of the second one was 54. The address of the third house was 57.

Interpretation of the Elements or Symbols:

August is the eighth month. The number eight represents man's ability to transcend limits of physical existence. It also represents resurrection power, the teacher, new birth or new beginnings abounding in strength, circumcision, and to make fat. The dream came on the twentieth day of August. The number twenty means redemption, crowning accomplishment, divine completion for spiritual perfection and waiting with expectancy for deliverance. The three white houses were all numbered in the fifties. So I looked at the various meanings of the number fifty to help determine what God was trying to communicate to me through choosing the numbers 3, 51, 54 and 57. The number 50 means celebration, jubilee, deliverance, liberty, freedom, humble service, soul, hope, and Pentecost occurred 50 days after the resurrection. The number 51 speaks of divine revelation which was mentioned in the prophetic word that was given to me. If we add the numbers five and one together they equal the number six which is the number of man— God's greatest creation.

I could not find a specific biblical example for the meaning of the number fifty-four. So I took the number five and four by themselves and then I added them together to come up with the number nine. Five is the number of grace, favor, action, redemption, the five ministry offices, atonement, life, and the divine name of God. Four is the number of God's creative works and their completion, and man's weakness. It represents the four seasons, tides and winds that cover the world from the four corners of the earth. Nine represents the perfect movement of the Holy Spirit who brings the fullness of blessings and renewal through the nine Fruits and Gifts of the Spirit. Nine is also the number that represents the reproduction that comes through a womb thus we see it also indicates the ministry of the evangelist. Nine represents an end or completion and a conclusion. We also see that nine indicates judgment, tribulation and the serpent.

The number 57 does not have a specific significance from Scripture so again I looked at the meaning of the number five and seven and then added them together to make the number twelve. Seven is a number that represents God and his spiritual perfection, completeness, wholeness, and fullness. Seven stands for development, purification and consecration. Forgiveness is in the 7 x 70 and the days of creation. Twelve is the number of the apostles, the elect purposes of God, the twelve tribes and judges, divine government or rule and the spirit world. There were twelve baskets of bread left over and twelve sons of Jacob. Therefore, twelve represents plenty.

There were three white houses and a difference of three between 51, 54, and 57. So the number three is going to be important in this dream. Three is the number of the Holy Trinity: the Father, Son and Holy Spirit. Three is the number of the perfect witness and testimony, union, approval, completeness, fullness, kindness, entirety, divine perfection, life, the Spirit or the Godhead's mighty acts. Noah had three sons and there were three Wiseman. Jesus' ministry on earth lasted three years. There is time past, present, and time future. The resurrection of Jesus took place after three days just like Jonah was in the belly of the whale for three days.

Why were all three of the houses pure white? The color white means love, the Spirit of the Lord, and his holy power and purity without mixture. White represents God's light and blameless righteousness, innocence, reverence, peace, and the holiness of God. White means victory, cleanliness, redemption, simplicity, security, and the marriage covenant.

In order to come up with a correct interpretation I combined the revelation given in the prophetic word of August 4, 2006 with the confirming dream that followed on August 20, 2006. After looking up the meanings of the various numbers in this simple white house dream I concluded that God wanted to use me to create dream training resources to equip people to understand God's symbolic dream language. The Holy Spirit wanted me to train people to use the gifts of the Spirit through developing the nine fruits and various gifts of the Spirit in order to fill the Kingdom of God with his children.

Conclusion

Numbers are fascinating and factual. We can learn so much from understanding how God communicates and perfectly creates through the use of numbers. The very elements of the smallest particles of matter that make up the universe are all arranged according to numbers and God's laws. Numbers and their meanings often give the dreamer the keys that are needed to unlock the mystery that lay within a dream.

Recommended Reading

Heaven, by Judson Cornwall

Number in Scripture, E. W. Bullinger

The Witness of the Stars, E. W. Bullinger

Signs in the Heavens, by Marilyn Hickey

The Heavens Declare, by William D. Banks

Sounds of Heaven Symphony of Earth, Ray Hughes

God's Voice in the Stars Zodiac signs & Bible Truth, by Kenneth C. Fleming

Biblical Numerology A Basic Study of the Use of Numbers in the Bible, by John J. Davis

God's Appointed Times A Practical Guide for Understanding and Celebrating the Biblical Holidays, by Barney Kasdan

Recommended Breath of the Spirit Teaching CDs:

- *Numbers Hebrew Alphabets Meaning and Symbols*

- *Job's Original Bible Stars and Constellations*

- *Healing and the Seven Spirits of God*

- *Dressed for Success Clothed in Light*

- *Signs in the Heaven*

- *Technicolor Dreams*

Chapter Eight
God's Colors in Dreams

There is nothing like standing on a white sandy beach watching God paint a pink and orange horizon against a beautiful azure sky as the bright yellow sun melts into the distant purple depths. As colors add beauty and meaning to our world, they do the same to our dreams. Just as in a breathtaking sunset, the colors God places in each specific dream are important. Color or the lack thereof has significant meaning all its own and the colors in our dreams provide a key to unlocking their mysteries. Dreams are a pathway to the dwelling place of God's light because they bring us into his spiritual realm where we can receive revelation.

We know from Scripture that God is preparing a place for those who love him. When our spiritual eyes are opened, we see the eternal, invisible realm of the Spirit, which is full of colors, lights, sounds, angels, and heavenly beings.

1 Corinthians 2:9–16 However, as it is written: No eye has seen, no ear has heard, no mind has conceived what God has prepared for those who love Him—but God has revealed it to us by His Spirit. The Spirit searches all things, even the deep things of God. For who among men knows the thoughts of a man except the man's spirit within him? In the same way no one knows the thoughts of God except the Spirit of God. We have not received the spirit of the world but the Spirit who is from God, that we may understand what God has freely given us. This is what we speak, not in words taught us by human wisdom but in words taught by the Spirit, expressing spiritual truths in spiritual words. The man without the Spirit does not accept the things that come from the Spirit of God, for they are foolishness to him, and he cannot understand them, because they are spiritually discerned. The spiritual man makes judgments about all things, but he himself is not subject to any man's judgment: 'For who has known the mind of the Lord that he may instruct him?' But we have the mind of Christ (NIV).

This chapter on color and light is in no way able to thoroughly explain the many varied aspects of light and color. It is going to offer but a glimpse of the variety and importance of color to our dream experience. This chapter will awaken an awareness of light and its glorious presence and mystery as it envelops our entire life.

The dreams we have in the night seasons of our lives give revelation knowledge that enables us to understand the mysteries sealed in God's heart from the beginning of time. God comes into our dreams to show us who he is in all of his magnificent splendor, love, brilliance, and beauty.

Psalm 65:8–9 They who dwell in the ends of the earth stand in awe of Your signs; You make the dawn and the sunset shout for joy. You visit the earth and cause it to overflow; You greatly enrich it (NASB).

Each time we see God in our dreams for who he is we are changed and then transformed little by little into his image and nature.

The colors of God are immeasurable and limitless. Who can define or know them? There are spiritual dimensions of color that the human eye cannot see just as there are sounds our ears cannot hear. It is like comparing the ability of different species of animals that are able to see infrared colors or hear sounds and frequencies that humans cannot detect. In the heavenly realms there are colors and sounds we have never experienced here on earth. These heavenly colors and sound dimensions exist in the dream realm of the spirit. As we sleep the Lord comes and helps us transcend the natural realms of our sight, hearing and our natural minds so that we can see revelation by the Holy Spirit. We are given the knowledge and understanding of mysteries and beings that we have never thought of or imagined. The Spirit of the Lord enables us to step out of the natural realm into the boundless existence of eternity. In this realm there are no limitations in time or dimension. We can freely move from the present to the past and even look forward into the times of the future.

The Significance of Light

The renowned mathematician and scientist Sir Isaac Newton equated the seven colors of the rainbow to the seven known planets of his day and to the seven notes of the diatonic music scale. He discovered God designed and orchestrated the whole universe to work as one. Originally, Newton named only five primary colors: red, yellow, green, blue or (cyan) and violet. Only later did he introduce orange and indigo, giving the seven colors by analogy to the number of notes in the musical scale (*Rainbow*, from Wikipedia, the free online encyclopedia).

What is light? Scientifically speaking, light is an electromagnetic radiation with a wavelength that is visible to the eye (visible light). Albert Einstein said, "For the rest of my life I will reflect on what light is."

The three basic dimensions of light are:

1. Intensity (or brightness) of the light

2. Frequency (or wavelength), color of the light

3. Polarization (or angle of vibration), of the light which is barely perceptible.

Light is matter. It simultaneously exhibits properties of both waves and particles. "In imperial units, the speed of light is about 670,616,630.6 miles per hour or 983,571,056 feet per second, which is about 186,282.397 miles per second, or roughly one foot per nanosecond." (*Speed of Light*, from Wikipedia, the free online encyclopedia.)

God Created Light

Isaiah 40:26 Lift your eyes and look to the heavens: Who created all these? He who brings out the starry host one by one, and calls them each by name. Because of His great power and mighty strength, not one of them is missing.

Before we can fully understand the importance of color in dreams, we must grasp the spiritual relationship between color, light, and God. Some interpretations associated with light are: a source of fire, spiritual awareness, something that enlightens or provides information, visible light necessary for seeing and a given kind of illumination. Without light the color spectrum would not show its glory. In the same way, God's light reveals the colors of his glory which can communicate specific messages to us in dreams. According to *James 1:17–18* God is the Father of lights:

> *Every good gift and every perfect gift is from above, and comes down from the Father of lights, with whom there is no variation or shadow of turning. Of His own will he brought us forth by the word of truth, that we might be a kind of first fruits of His creatures.*

God is light. Our heavenly Father is full of colored light, brilliance, and intensity. Everything God creates is full of his love, majesty, power, splendor, and beautiful light. God is love and God is light. Out of these two united substances he is able to speak creative words that release life. God's creative words cause something to come out of nothing. Everything God creates comes from the light that is within him. His light brings insight, images, pictures, and colors into the spirit of the dreamer, often through the gateway of our dreams. The words that God breathes into our dreams set a creative force into action.

> *Job 32:8 "But there is a spirit in man, and the breath of the Almighty gives him understanding."*

> *Job 33:4 "The Spirit of God has made me, and the breath of the Almighty gives me life."*

Having a greater degree of the Holy Spirit's guiding light or divine presence helps direct our lives. The revelation that God shines into our hearts brings forth truthful answers to past, present, and future situations. In fact, not only our dreams, but everything that exists is created from the light and breath of God. Atoms and molecules of light form everything within our world.

> Genesis 1:3–5 *Then God said,* (spoken word) *"Let there be light" and there was light. And God saw the light that it was good; and God divided the light from the darkness. God called the light Day, and the darkness He called Night. So the evening and the morning were the first day.*

White light separates into seven different colors or wavelengths upon entering a raindrop because red light is refracted by a lesser angle than blue light. On leaving the raindrop, the red rays have turned through a smaller range than the blue rays, to produce a rainbow. Some light reflects twice in a raindrop before exiting to the viewer. When the incident light is very bright this can be seen as a secondary rainbow, with a brightness from 50 to 53 degrees. (*Rainbow;* Wikipedia the free online encyclopedia)

White light contains all the spectrums of color. When a triangular prism is used, concentrated white light is bent or diffused into the seven color spectrums of the rainbow. The triangular shape of a three-sided prism can be a symbolic representation of the three persons of God: Father, Son, and Holy Spirit. The white light of the sun is diffused in the water droplets of the clouds to paint a rainbow in the sky. The rainbow is the sign of the covenant promise between God and earth that he will never destroy the world again by flood. Just as the Trinity can be represented metaphorically by the three corners of a prism, the rainbow shows God's many varied and brilliant colors.

Genesis 9:12–18 And God said: "This is the sign of the covenant which I make between Me and you, and every living creature that is with you, for perpetual generations: I set My rainbow in the cloud, and it shall be for the sign of the covenant between Me and the earth. It shall be, when I bring a cloud over the earth, that the rainbow shall be seen in the cloud; and I will remember My covenant which is between Me and you and every living creature of all flesh; the waters shall never again become a flood to destroy all flesh. The rainbow shall be in the cloud, and I will look on it to remember the everlasting covenant between God and every living creature of all flesh that is on the earth." And God said to Noah, "This is the sign of the covenant which I have established between Me and all flesh that is on the earth."

These seven brilliant rainbow colors reflect the nature and other differing aspects of God's seven Spirits for the world to see. The corresponding meaning of each color is strategic for us to understand the implications of the colors that appear in our dreams as further outlined later in this chapter. The invisible realm of the Spirit has many beautiful colored lights and sounds.

175

Psalm 43:3 "Oh send out Your light and Your truth! Let them lead me; let them bring me to Your holy hill and to Your tabernacle."

Each of us determines the amount and type of light that we are able to receive in dreams. The white light of God's kingdom draws the light of the angelic realm to us so that we will shine with his light and draw others to his kingdom. Angels can be very active in our dreams—leading, guiding, and helping to direct us to the proper interpretations. The spiritual garments of light we wear are dependent upon the words we speak and the visions we believe.

God instructed Job to break out of his depression and despair by clothing himself with glory and beauty.

Deck thyself now with majesty and excellency; and array thyself with glory and beauty (Job 40:8 KJV).

The prophet Isaiah lets us know we can put on a light garment of praise when we are being assaulted by a spirit of heaviness or dark depression. The oil of joy will break grief and mourning away from us.

To console those who mourn in Zion, to give them beauty for ashes, the oil of joy for mourning, the garment of praise for the spirit of heaviness (Isaiah 61:3 NKJV).

The Psalmist David told his soul to bless the Lord for his greatness. In *Psalm 104* He acknowledged that God was clothed in the light of honor and majesty.

Psalm 104:1–4 Bless the Lord, O my soul! O Lord my God, You are very great: You are clothed with honor and majesty, Who cover Yourself with light as with a garment, Who stretch out the heavens like a curtain. He lays the beams of His upper chambers in the waters, Who makes the clouds His chariot, Who walks on the wings of the wind, Who makes His angels spirits, His ministers a flame of fire.

> *I will also clothe her priests with salvation: and her saints shall shout aloud for joy (Psalm 132:16 KJV).*

> *His enemies will I clothe with shame: but upon himself shall his crown flourish (Psalm 132:18 KJV).*

God's brilliant light gives internal (intrinsic) dreams about you, and external (extrinsic) dreams about others, as well as spiritual guidance and vision through the truth he reveals. God's light brings a balance between the spirit and the soul. The light of God also brings revelation knowledge and wisdom into the human spirit. Dreams ignite inspiration and hope. Where there is no revelatory light or vision to give life the people blindly perish.

> *Psalm 36:9 "For with You is the fountain of life; in Your light we see light." Where there is no light, there is no life.*

Light vs. Darkness

Have you ever asked yourself what color of light am I emanating and what sound frequency do I release to those around me? Just as the words God spoke brought our world into existence, so the words we speak frame our world as well. Positive, comforting, edifying words of faith release the brilliant colors of God's creative force. While negative, critical, judgmental, hurtful words of doubt and unbelief release a dark dismal light that clothes us like a thick gray fog. This lurking fog of depression blocks our light from shining. Our negative words repel and drive people away from us.

The things we view with our eyes either bring God's pure light into our hearts or a darkness that hardens our hearts and dulls or even blinds our spiritual eyes.

Matthew 6:22–23 The lamp of the body is the eye. If therefore your eye is good, your whole body will be full of light. But if your eye is bad, your whole body will be full of darkness. If therefore the light that is in you is darkness, how great is that darkness!

If our spiritual eyes were opened, what would we see? When people begin to operate in the gift of discerning of spirits they usually start seeing into the dark demonic realms first because it is closer to the soul realm. If we emit darkness we will draw the kingdom of darkness toward us. But God is able to turn our darkness into his light.

Psalm 18:28 "For You will light my lamp; the Lord my God will enlighten my darkness."

Even in the night season if we are emitting the bright light of the Kingdom of God in our lives it will draw the light of God and his angels toward us and it will intensify in our dreams. As the Holy Spirit trains us we begin to grow in our level of spiritual discernment. He will shift us into being able to see the glory realms of his majestic splendor, heavenly creatures, hosts of lights, and the angelic. The words we speak open gates and build a spiritual framework around us to form the atmosphere we breathe and exist in. We are responsible for creating a positive life by the choices we make and the words we pray and say every day.

Hebrews 11:3 "By faith we understand that the universe was formed at God's command, so that what is seen was not made out of what was visible" (NIV).

God is clothed in garments of honor, majesty, and light. The light of God radiates love, wisdom, and purity. He is living, powerful, and the all consuming eternal light of the world. This brilliant light encompasses the span of the universe. God is the light that leads us from death to eternal life and he has given a measure of his guiding light to every man on earth.

John 1:7–9 He [John the Baptist] *came as a witness to testify concerning that light* [Jesus] *so that through Him all men might believe. He himself was not the light; he came only as a witness to the light. The true light* [Jesus] *that gives light to every man was coming into the world.*

In God's eternal plan to bring salvation to mankind he deposited his divine light into each person he sent to the world. The given measure of divine light is sufficient to draw every man, woman, boy, and girl into the "Giver of Light." But each person must choose to walk in the light and allow God's light to bring salvation. Those who refuse to walk in the light continue to dwell in the darkness and never reach their full potential or God-given destiny. In our dreams and visions we may have face-to-face encounters just like Moses with the Creator of the universe. Dreams show us the goodness of the Lord's countenance upon us. Through our dreams, he places gladness and peace in our hearts as we sleep and shows us how to prosper and live in safety.

*Psalm 4:4–8 There are many who say, "Who will show us any good?" Lord, lift up the light of Your countenance upon us. You have put gladness in my heart, more than in the season that their grain and wine increased. I will both lie down in peace, and sleep; For You alone, O L*ord, *make me dwell in safety.*

Just as God supplied the children of Israel with light in their dwelling places while the Egyptians cowered in total darkness, he also leads us by his great light. When God decided to lead his children out

179

of Egypt's darkness he went before them as the pillar of cloud by day, and the pillar of fire by night. God's light was never removed from their presence during the night or day. This is why we can depend upon the light of his dreams by night, and his enlightenment by day.

Exodus 10:23 They did not see one another; (Egyptians) nor did anyone rise from his place for three days. But **all the children of Israel had light in their dwellings.**

Exodus 13:21–22 And the Lord went before them by day in a pillar of cloud to lead the way, and by night in a pillar of fire to give them light, so as to go by day and night. He did not take away the pillar of cloud by day or the pillar of fire by night from before the people.

Many stumble because there are areas of darkness in their lives they cannot navigate. These dark areas form strongholds that continually resist growth and progress. When the light of God comes into a dream, the dreamer is often able to clearly receive the truth about a situation for the first time, and the truth breaks the power of the lie that has held that person captive.

1 John 1:5–7 This is the message we have heard from Him and declare to you: God is light; in Him there is no darkness at all. If we claim to have fellowship with Him yet walk in the darkness, we lie and do not live by the truth. But if we walk in the light, as He is in the light, we have fellowship with one another, and the blood of Jesus, His Son, purifies us from all sin.

When we are in the captivity of darkness we lose our light and our hope.

Psalm 126 When the LORD *brought back the captives to Zion, we were*

180

like men who dreamed. Our mouths were filled with laughter, our tongues with songs of joy. Then it was said among the nations, "The LORD has done great things for them." The LORD has done great things for us, and we are filled with joy. Restore our fortunes, O LORD, like streams in the Negev. Those who sow in tears will reap with songs of joy. He who goes out weeping, carrying seed to sow, will return with songs of joy, carrying sheaves with him.

Colors and Their Meanings in Dreams

God's white light contains all the spectrums of color. The three corners of the triangular prism represent the white light of the Trinity in the seven beautiful colors in the rainbow. Our dreams are full of variations of these seven different rainbow colors, and they enable us to understand whether our soul or spirit or a balance of both are ruling our lives.

If the white light of God is filling our lives, then the dominant colors appearing in our dreams will likely be: red, symbolizing the Spirit of the Lord; blue, for the Spirit of Might, and green, representing the Counsel of God, and their positive affects will be evident in our waking lives. If our spirit is submitted to God, then we will be led by the orange Spirit of Wisdom, and not by the self-centered desires of our souls. The red, green, and blue light color spectrums are the three predominate colors of the Spirit.

For all who are being led by the Spirit of God, these are sons of God (Romans 8:14-15 NASU).

Yellow is associated with the Spirit of Understanding, indigo represents the Spirit of Knowledge, and the violet colors represent the reverential Fear of the Lord. The three light color spectrums of yellow, indigo, and violet deal with the areas of the soul. Each person's soul is made up of the intellectual mind, thoughts, beliefs, memories, will, and emotions. *Isaiah 11:2* lists the seven Spirits of God and we can find their corresponding colors demonstrated each time the beautiful circular rainbow is displayed in the heavens.

Isaiah 11:2 "The Spirit of the LORD shall rest upon Him, The Spirit of wisdom and understanding, The Spirit of counsel and might, The Spirit of knowledge and of the fear of the LORD."

Revelation 1:4 and Revelation 4:5 "And from the throne proceeded lightnings, thunderings, and voices. Seven lamps of fire were burning before the throne, which are the seven Spirits of God."

In the first chapter of Ezekiel, the prophet Ezekiel has an open vision of a raging fire-filled whirlwind from the north. This passage contains colored stones, rainbows, and four supernatural winged creatures that sparkled like the color of burnished bronze. The likeness of the living creatures' appearance was like burning coals of fire, like the appearance of torches going back and forth among the living creatures; the fire was bright, and out of the fire went lightning. The living creatures had the faces of a man, lion, ox, and eagle on each side. They ran back and forth, in appearance like a flash of lightning. The appearance of the wheels and their workings was like the color of beryl, and all four had the same likeness …

"The likeness of the firmament above the heads of the living creatures was like the color of an awesome crystal, stretched out over their heads. And under the firmament their wings spread out straight, one toward another. Each one had two which covered one side, and each one had two which covered the other side of the body. When they went, I heard the noise of their wings, like the noise of many waters, like the voice of the Almighty, a tumult like the noise of an army; and when they stood still, they let down their wings. A voice came from above the firmament that was over their heads; whenever they stood, they let down their wings. And above the firmament over

*their heads was the likeness of a throne, in appearance like a sapphire stone;
on the likeness of the throne was a likeness with the appearance of a man
high above it. Also from the appearance of His waist and upward I saw,
as it were, the color of amber with the appearance of fire all around within
it; and from the appearance of His waist and downward I saw, as it were,
the appearance of fire with brightness all around. Like the appearance of a
rainbow in a cloud on a rainy day, so was the appearance of the brightness
all around it. This was the appearance of the likeness of the glory of the
Lord ..."*

Below are the meanings of the stones in Ezekiel that God often
uses to speak to us symbolically in our dreams taken from our *Jewels and
Color* dream symbol cards.

Amber: the throne; invitation from God; the Glory of God, God
is ministering; the anointing of fire; ornamentation; like a jewel is
cherished.

Beryl: gemstone (like topaz) Tribe of Zebulon, aquamarine.

Bronze: forgiveness, atonement, pride, and judgment.

Crystal: resembling smooth ice, hail, rock crystal (prism) bringing
clarity to a situation, diamonds have a high refractory power, called
"stone of fire." Less clear stones are used for drilling and grinding.

Sapphire: blue gemstone, Tribe of Dan, gem used for scratching
other substances, people that grate against us doing the work of
perfection in us, this stone is identified with heaven.

God is transforming us in our dreams from being dull, burnt
stones that have gone through the fires of testing and wilderness trials
to bring us into ever increasing clarity and perfection so we can enter our
Promised Land. We are becoming beautiful living stones with all seven
vibrant colors of his Spirit working through us.

The dry bones of Ezekiel need the spiritual water and dream

light of God's spoken word to release a sure sound to rally and connect us to the army of the Lord. When we see the beauty of a rainbow and the seven colors that radiate from it, we are reminded of the covenant promise God gave that he would never destroy the earth again by flood.

God's light is reflected through the drops of water in the atmosphere that form a perfect circle of colored light. This same emerald colored rainbow appears above his throne in heaven. We behold the seven majestic colors of the rainbow with our natural eyes in the earth's atmosphere. The colors of rainbow light and its symbolism are able to connect heaven and earth together in understanding.

The colors that God chooses for our dreams are significant and important. He does not just choose any color at random. He is communicating to us through the array of colors that are displayed in our dreams.

Some dreams that are initiated in the realm of the soul have less light. This causes the event to be viewed in a dark or cloudy atmosphere. These dark dreams can leave us with feelings of confusion, lack of clarity and a foreboding presence.

Bright and vivid dreams that are predominately red, green, and blue indicate that our spirit man is ruling in that specific dream and that we are walking in abundant light. Our understanding is enlightened and increased through the revelation and wisdom these dreams bring us.

During our school days we learned the eight basic pigments of the color wheel. However, in dreams we are not dealing with pigments but with gradients of colored light. With the language of Scripture as our basis for interpretation, here are some basic meanings of the colors we see in our dreams:

Red: love, anointing, power, passion, anger, war, bloodshed.

Yellow: mind, hope, joy, gift of God, courage, fear, coward, deceit.

Green: conscience, growth, prosperity, envy, jealousy, pride.

Blue: communion, revelation, healing, depression, anxiety.

Orange: perseverance, wisdom, powerful force, stubbornness, witchcraft.

Purple: authority, royalty, intercession, kingship, rule, false authority or Jezebel.

Black: neutral, moved with passion, sin, death, soul rule, famine.

Brown: compassion, humility, repentance, humanism, dried out.

By observing the intensity, hue, value, and tint of colors that appear in our dreams we can determine whether the dreams are coming from the spirit or the soulish realm.

a. *Intensity*: Exceptionally great concentration, energy, power, force, or measure of effectiveness.

b. *Hue:* The range, dimension, quality, or shade of color distinguishing it from other colors.

c. *Value*: The degree of darkness or lightness of a color.

d. *Tint:* A pale shade or gradation of a color made by adding white to lessen its saturation.

White is representative of the Holy Spirit or the Lord. So look at the content of the dream.

By analyzing the four definitions of intensity, hue, value, and tint, we can derive that the deeper, richer, and more intense the color, the stronger impression it is going to leave on the dream symbol. Conversely, the lighter or softer the hue or value of the color, the less impact, influence, or power the color has as a dream symbol.

Read through this dream noting the colors. What keys do they reveal?

Dream:

The dreamer sees a group of people that he wants to be associated with going into a grocery store. The leader of this group is tall and dressed in a long black overcoat and hat. The dreamer is wearing a bright green cap on his head. He knows that in order to be accepted, to associate with this peer group of people in the grocery store, he will have to remove his green cap. He takes his green cap off his head and slides it into his pocket. He gets his shopping cart and follows the group around in the store. He places various canned goods into his cart. When the group finally exits the store they poke fun and laugh at the dreamer while they pile into a car. He is left standing alone in the parking lot and his feelings are hurt.

Interpretation:

The dreamer is being drawn to a group of people who are being led by their flesh or darkened soul. They are busy feeding on the things of the world. In order for the dreamer to join this group he has to violate and remove the restrictions of his conscience. He removes his conscience by stuffing it into a small place to ignore it. He then proceeds to enter into soulish activities. When it is all said and done he is rejected by the worldly people who recognize that he has God's light in his life. His desire to be accepted by the world caused him to compromise his beliefs for a short time. He learned a valuable lesson. To avoid pain, rejection and disappointment we should always listen to our conscience, be lead by the Spirit and not the soul.

How Sound Relates to Color and Light

Sound can be defined as a vibratory disturbance in pressure, bone density, a fluid, or in the elastic strain in a solid with a frequency capable of being detected. Sound is a distinctive noise, an articulation made by a voice, a mental impression, to pronounce, signal, make known, proclaim, or to examine.

The speed of sound is affected by temperature, and density. At sea level, at a temperature of 70 °F and under normal atmospheric conditions, the speed of sound is 769 mph. Sound waves tend to travel faster at higher temperatures. There are different values for the speed of sound in different sources of water. They range from 1450 to 1498 meters per second in distilled water and 1531 m/s in sea water at 70 degree room temperatures. (*Speed of Light*, from Wikipedia, the free online encyclopedia.)

The majority of the human body is composed of water and bone. Both of these mediums are excellent sound conductors. When the breath of God's Spirit fills the human earthen body, we will release the sounds of God's knowledge in the earth.

Isaiah 11:9 They shall not hurt nor destroy in all My holy mountain, For the earth shall be full of the knowledge of the Lord as the waters cover the sea.

Worship through musical scales releases vibrant colors that are intertwined together with the release of beautiful light and color spectrums as we magnify the King of Kings with our voices and instruments. The praise and the prayers we release during the day open gateways for the angels and the Spirit of God to visit us during the night. Angels will bring the word and the songs of the Lord to our soul to sing.

Sound waves of God's voice travel faster through the medium of water than through open air. We know that the human body is 70% water. What power does the spoken word in prayer have on the water in our bodies? What happens when we speak or pray words, write or play music with positive and negative words or sounds? Positive words of blessing release faith, hope, and love, feelings of well-being. While negative words of cursing, criticism, or heavy metal music produce vibrations of fear, doubt, and depression, removing one's feelings of well-being. How does the sound of God's voice affect the body during a dream? The sound of God's creative voice in conjunction with the countenance of his light coming into our dreams will ignite positive healing benefits in our bodies. God is light and love. God's life changing eternal love remains the most powerful force, frequency, and positive vibration in the world.

Psalm 89:15 Blessed are the people who know the **joyful sound**! *They walk, O Lord, in the light of Your countenance.*

There are eerie sounds of darkness and there are healing sounds of light. Sins and sicknesses reproduce disease (dis–ease) because they are linked to the dark spirits of error, trauma, bad habits, or iniquity from the DNA of previous generations. Understanding our dreams enables us to change negative DNA patterns and sounds into positive DNA patterns and sounds that will release healing light and life. Prayers of repentance ignite a release of God's light that shatters diseased places of darkness in our lives.

The different sounds of musical notes produce various colored light that ministers healing to the seven major organs of the body (which also have colors associated with each one). Electric impulses travel through the cranial nerve in the eardrum—the first sensory organ that develops in infancy. These electrical impulses connect the cranial nerve to every organ in the body except the spleen. Our five natural and spiritual senses of sight, hearing, touch, smell, and taste are all impacted by the music, words, and sounds we hear. The right words spoken in our dreams, prayers, and declarations combined with proper musical keynotes will affect both physical and emotional healing. The prophet Jeremiah said, "*His word is like fire shut up in my bones*" (author paraphrase).

Jeremiah 20:9 "Then I said, 'I will not make mention of Him, nor speak anymore in His name.' But His word was in my heart like a burning fire shut up in my bones; I was weary of holding it back, And I could not."

Releasing a new song and melody or hearing the word of the Lord in our dreams changes the cycles in our lives and redirects us to embrace success with a new plan.

Romans 12:2 "Do not conform any longer to the pattern of this world, (cosmos) but be transformed by the renewing of your mind. Then you will be able to test and approve what God's will is—His good, pleasing and perfect will."

Breath of the Spirit Ministries was birthed out of following passage from the 37ᵗʰ chapter of Ezekiel. The Lord circumcises our ears to hear what he speaks to us in the night season through our dreams and visions. His prophetic word enters into our bones, our spirit, and the deepest parts of our being. His word becomes like water bringing healing to our disjointed, dry bones and restores us to abundant life.

> *Ezekiel 37:4–10 Then he said to me, "Prophesy to these bones and say to them, 'Dry bones, hear the word of the* LORD*! This is what the Sovereign* LORD *says to these bones: "I will make breath enter you, and you will come to life. I will attach tendons to you and make flesh come upon you and cover you with skin; I will put breath in you, and you will come to life. Then you will know that I am the* LORD.*"' So I prophesied as I was commanded.* [Prophesying releases a sound that causes a spiritual and physical response.] *And as I was prophesying, there was a noise, a rattling sound, and the bones came together, bone to bone. I looked, and tendons and flesh appeared on them and skin covered them, but there was no breath in them. Then he said to me, "Prophesy to the breath; prophesy, son of man, and say to it, 'This is what the Sovereign* LORD *says: Come from the four winds, O breath, and breathe into these slain, that they may live.'" So I prophesied as he commanded me, and breath entered them; they came to life and stood up on their feet—a vast army (TNIV).*

God-given dreams carry a creative ability because they are prophetic in nature. Prophecy is the testimony of Jesus. God-given dreams come to change us into his image. They reform or change us through activating our spiritual senses to see, hear, speak, taste, and feel his plans. These God-given dreams enable us to walk in the Spirit with a renewed vision, purpose, or plan. Dreams position us to receive the power to obtain the promises of God. Dreams are one of the vehicles God has chosen to show and tell us who we are called to be in Christ. His desire is for us to reach our full potential and to be successful.

> *Psalm 24:1* tells us *"The earth is the Lord's, and all its fullness, the world (cosmos) and those who dwell therein."*

189

So it only makes sense that God-given dreams would reveal keys to unlock the fullness of life. The closer we come to the Lord the more we will see our need to resonate with the sounds of heaven, to establish them on earth. God has tuned each person as a distinct sounding instrument that releases a specific sound or new song in the orchestra of life. When we learn to walk as sons of God, in the fullness of unity or harmony with the sounds of the Kingdom of heaven, earth will respond. God commands blessings upon us as we harmonize with the dreams he designs for our lives.

God has called us as mediators in the earthly realms. We bring heaven to earth through our dreams, shouts, prayers, prophecy, declarations, praise, and worship. God wants us to cry out to him for wisdom and understanding. He created the lights in the heavens and the earth to release his light and sound that causes his voice to resonate throughout creation.

> *Psalm 147:4–5 He determines the number of the stars and calls them each by name. Great is our Lord and mighty in power; his understanding has no limit.*

Our dreams are a gateway for God to visit us in the night season. Through our dreams God separates and dispels the darkness of sin from us and replaces it with the many colors of his glorious light. He rearranges the chaos in our lives to bring it into perfect order to unlock our destiny by painting a brilliant new life story.

Additional Breath of the Spirit Resources:

Dressed for Success Clothed in Light CD

God's Colors and Light CD

God's Colors in Dreams CD

Color Dream Symbols Card

Color and Music Healing Card

Chapter Nine
God's Dream Symbols

Dream Symbols as Language

Symbols are often used in comparison to counterparts. They represent something else by association, convention, or resemblance. Usually symbols depict a material object that is used to represent something more abstract. Corporations design a symbol or a logo that characterizes their company. When that trademark is seen the public automatically associates a product or company with the symbol it embodies. It represents or symbolizes an operation, an element, or quantity or quality of service.

Similarly, dreams are God's symbolic parables of the night. They are a part of his parabolic language that he uses to speak to us in our sleep. These same symbols may also appear to us as an answer to our prayers. He makes us aware of our true selves, as well as others' true identities, through the symbols he interjects into our dreams. The color, shape, size, and number of symbols will all give us needed information about the message our dream was meant to reveal. The more dream symbols and their corresponding meanings we know, the more clearly God can speak to us in dream pictures that we will understand. It is always beneficial to encourage people to record, track, and categorize their own dream symbols. This will enable them to recall the dream's meanings, which are integral to our growth and development. This picture language has been given to us so that we might understand the mysteries or their symbolic representations in our dreams.

Hosea 12:10 says, "I have also spoken by the prophets, and have multiplied visions; I have given symbols through the witness of the prophets" (KJV).

Dream symbols can be defined as things or objects that represent something or someone else in a dream or vision of the night. These symbols can also be material objects representing something subjective or abstract.

We must always rely on the Holy Spirit to give us the correct interpretation for the symbols that appear in our dreams. In one dream a symbol may represent something, but it may indicate something else entirely in another dream because the colors, characters, context, or setting of the dream is totally different. We cannot insist that one symbol is always going to mean the same thing every time, because if we did, we would be putting God in a stagnant box and trying to wall him into our limited understanding. God is a Spirit who flows like a progressive, changing river that is always new. We must learn to flow and change with him.

Matthew 13:10–11 depicts a time when Jesus walked the earth training his twelve disciples. Like us, they often had many questions.

> *And the disciples came and said to Him, "Why do You speak to them in parables?" He answered and said to them, "Because it has been given to you to know the mysteries of the kingdom of heaven, but to them it has not been given.*

This powerful Scripture illustrates to us that we have been given the ability to know the mysteries of parables and dreams in the kingdom of heaven. In a sense, to understand dreams is to learn and understand a symbolic, metaphoric language. To do this each person will develop a different dream vocabulary and understanding of the symbols' meanings.

In dreams and visions, symbols that are chosen are not usually literal. But they are the representation of a person, place, or thing.

> *Zechariah 5:5–9 Then the angel who talked with me came out and said to me, "Lift your eyes now, and see what this is that goes forth." So I asked, "What is it?" And he said, "It is a basket that is going forth." He also said, "This is their resemblance throughout the earth: Here is a lead disc lifted up, and this is a woman sitting inside the basket"; then he said, "This is wickedness!" And he thrust her down into the basket, and threw the lead cover over its mouth. Then I raised my eyes and looked, and there were two*

women, coming with the wind in their wings; for they had wings like the wings of a stork, and they lifted up the basket between earth and heaven.

There is dialogue between the angel and the prophet Zechariah. He is being trained to understand the symbolic pictures shown to him in the vision. Like the prophet we learn to ask questions in our dreams, "What is it?" "What does this symbol represent?" "What does it mean?"

The dreamer needs to be completely honest with him- or herself and think of what that particular symbol means or represents on a personal level. Symbols that appear in our dreams are spiritual indicators of our current level of godly intimacy and relationship, as well our natural state of affairs. If we see ourselves in a house and it is full of dust and spider webs, the paint is peeling, the roof is leaking, the stairs are broken down and everything is in disarray, it indicates our present personal condition.

The type of vehicle we see ourselves operating or traveling in will let us know how much power, influence, human, or spiritual effort we are exerting. A pogo stick, skateboard, or bicycle requires much physical effort and has very little influence since each can carry only one person. A motorcycle has more power than a bicycle and can carry two people on or off the road. A car, van, truck, or limo is powered by gasoline which represents the anointing and can carry a group of people depending on the size of the vehicle. There is little physical effort needed to be exerted to travel in the comfort of an air-conditioned vehicle. Airplanes, jets, and rocket ships are propelled with a different type of high-octane fuel and each of these vehicles packs a powerful, forceful thrust. They are able to carry the person out of an earthbound atmosphere into viewing things from a heavenly perspective.

Symbol Details Tell a Story in Metaphor

Why did the Holy Spirit choose this symbol and color instead of another symbol to represent this or that specific meaning in a dream? What is the function that is assigned to a particular symbol in our dream? What is the significance of the size of the dream symbol being larger or smaller than usual? Is something being magnified so that my attention is being drawn to it? Why is my nose two feet long? Could it be I am being shown that my nose is in someone else's business where it does not belong? Or am I in need of more discernment?

Peter testifies of what the Prophet Joel had seen happening in the future in *Acts 2:16–17*

> But **this is that** *which was spoken by the prophet Joel; and it shall come to pass in the last days, saith God, I will pour out of my Spirit upon all flesh: and your sons and your daughters shall prophesy, and your young men shall see visions, and your old men shall dream dreams (KJV) (author's emphasis).*

The Old Testament passage in *Joel 2:28–29* prophesies about the "this is that" which is happening in New Testament times:

> *And afterward, I will pour out my Spirit on all people. Your sons and daughters will prophesy, your old men will dream dreams, your young men will see visions. Even on my servants, both men and women, I will pour out my Spirit in those days (NIV).*

Joel saw this happening in the future and Peter announced its fulfillment in his day.

Symbol Interpretation Exercise

This exercise can be done by focusing on any object and asking the Holy Spirit questions about its function. Focus on various everyday objects and ask questions about their size, color, shape, and function. This simple activity will help develop our metaphoric thinking and symbol interpretation skills. We begin to train ourselves to ask who, what, why, when, where, and how, so that just like a detective we are able to crack the mysterious case. Why is the marker yellow and not red or some other color? Why is the cap off? What will happen to the ink if the cap remains off? Is it off because things need to be highlighted? Am I allowing my creative, artistic abilities to dry up? Seeing a water bottle half full may mean there is a need for an infilling because the dreamer has been through a season of being poured out. If it were empty that could mean that due to a dry season, the dreamer needs to be filled up again. Water represents the word of God, anointing, refreshing, cleansing, and spiritual teachings. The bottle could be a representation of our person and the level of our ability to contain the water. Does a tube of lipstick or makeup enhance or detract from the person's features in the dream? When these objects appear in our dreams we need to have a working vocabulary of their meanings and symbolic representations. If fingernails are highlighted in a manicure, is the color of the nail polish important or is it a word play that the person in the dream needs to be healed from a painful relationship with a man through the process of a "man-a-cure?"

Dream symbols communicate to the dreamer through the emotional feelings they provoke or ideas and activities they inspire. Some people are epic dreamers while others dream short narratives. Oftentimes the length of the dream is not as important as the secrets it reveals.

Discover the Buried Treasure

To understand the symbolic language of dreams, we must look past the surface to find the buried treasures. *John 20* tells us that some believe only when they are able to clearly see, firmly touch and feel their surroundings. Jesus said, *"It is the person who believes without clearly seeing that is blessed."*

> *John 20:25–29 The other disciples therefore said to him, "We have seen the Lord." So he said to them, "Unless I see in His hands the print of the nails, and put my finger into the print of the nails, and put my hand into His side, I will not believe." And after eight days His disciples were again inside, and Thomas with them. Jesus came, the doors being shut, and stood in the midst, and said, "Peace to you!" Then He said to Thomas, "Reach*

your finger here, and look at My hands; and reach your hand here, and put it into My side. Do not be unbelieving, but believing." And Thomas answered and said to Him, "My Lord and my God!" Jesus said to him, "Thomas, because you have seen Me, you have believed. Blessed are those who have not seen and yet have believed."

It is important to spend time in God's presence asking the Holy Spirit to reveal to us the meanings of the dreams he has given. Ask him for the Spirit of revelation and understanding. What is the function assigned to the symbol? What feelings, emotions, or activities does it provoke? Look past the surface and find the buried treasure. The process of searching out and discovering the answers to the meanings of our dreams enables us to retain more clarity about the symbolic vocabulary God uses.

The symbolic language of dreams requires us to be totally dependent upon the Holy Spirit for the understanding and meaning of the symbols that appear in our dreams. In addition we must also seek out and rely on God's history of symbol usage modeled throughout Scripture. Everything in our lives should be totally dependent upon him. David always prayerfully inquired of the Lord and it was said of him that he was a man after God's heart.

Helpful Dream Symbol Resources and Tools

- Bible
- Prayer
- Dictionaries
- Encyclopedias
- Dream Book Glossaries
- Google online searches
- Biblical Imagery Dictionary
- Name Book with Scripture references
- Dream Encounter Workshops and courses

- Breath of the Spirit's Dream Encounter Symbol Cards or excel spread sheet
- Personal dream journal, notebook, or online journal for recording dreams and dream symbols

Some useful tools that will help in the process of discovering symbolic meanings are the Bible, encyclopedias, Biblical Imagery Dictionaries, Christian dream books, dream symbol cards, and of course Internet Google searches. We live in the time Daniel foretold when knowledge is increasing daily. This knowledge also deals with the knowledge of the ways of the Lord. God is using dreams to cause us to seek his face for understanding. He is not a respecter of persons. Therefore each of us can have a Damascus road experience like Saul, a burning bush encounter like Moses, a smoking oven like Daniel's friends, or a flaming torch just like Abram as we encounter God like they did. One of the many benefits of dreaming is that it prepares us to change by causing us to die to ourselves. This allows us to live for Christ more fully and wholeheartedly.

The Creatures in Our Dreams

Understanding the meanings of the symbols that appear in our dreams is essential to deriving the correct interpretation. Without gathering the keys and clues that the symbols give us, we will never unlock the sealed mysteries that lie within each dream. However, a proper application and understanding of the symbols and what they represent will lead us to an inner knowing that we have found the meaning of the dream. When we are interpreting someone else's dream their spirit will bear witness with a true interpretation of the dream.

The question we must continually ask ourselves when interpreting dream symbols is, "Why did God choose this symbol and not that symbol?"

Animals frequently appear in our dreams. Some animal symbols invoke warm feelings of love and tenderness while other animal symbols thrust fear and panic upon us. If we found a little white fluffy dog in our dream, it might invoke warm feelings of love. But if we found a rhinoceros stomping through our dream we may experience fear and dread because of the devastation.

Questions to ask about the animals in your dreams

- Is the animal in my dream domesticated or undomesticated?

- Am I afraid of, or threatened by, this animal?

- What action or role did the animal play in my dream?

- What are the characteristics of the animal? For example, a fox is cunning and sly.

- Is the animal in my dream my pet?

- Does the animal appear to be my friend, protector or adversary?

Domesticated Animals

Birds

- Birds: represent messengers; blessing, gifts or curses; the Holy Spirit appears as a dove; "thoughts taking flight;" leaders either good or evil depending on the colors they display and their nature or characteristics. (See the color card.) Birds may also represent visions or strategic insights for future success.

- "Birds of a feather flock together;" warning to watch the company you are keeping; *1 Corinthians 15:33 "Do not be deceived or misled: "Evil or bad company corrupts good habits and character."*

- Birds' vision is the most highly developed of any animal.

- Birds singing, chirping, or flying: represent the Fruit of the Spirit especially joy, peace, and love. Harmony, unity, and balance will bring a bright outlook on life. Receive the message of new liberty and spiritual freedom. Remove burdens and weights you are carrying; cast your cares on Jesus.

- Dead or dying birds: difficulties, disappointments, gloom, sorrow, sadness, sickness, despair, worries that trouble your mind; curses.

- Bird eggs: new beginnings coming, fresh start, time of incubation for new ideas, prosperous results, money; nurturing, caring for or protecting young.

- Birds hatching: represents new friends, successful beginnings that will require time, effort, and work to grow an enterprise.

- Bird nest: with eggs symbolizes security, refuge to rely on or home, a prosperous endeavor or opportunity to develop a fortune. An empty nest represents loneliness, independence, or a new chapter beginning with great possibilities.

- Blackbird: is a bad omen, curse or misfortune, lack of motivation, need to utilize your full potential. Blackbird leaving or flying away represents a positive change, increase instead of lack, good fortune.

- Blue bird: represents revelation and healing news coming; spiritual joy; happy life; contentment; depression; the state birds of Missouri, Nevada; New York; Idaho.

- Rooster: alarm, time to wake up, new beginning, reproduction, faithless betrayer, boasting, bragging.

Assorted Animals

- Bull: could be wordplay for a bunch of "bull" going on or financially speaking a bull market, persecution, spiritual warfare, opposition, accusation, economic increase, bullheaded, forcefulness, reproduction, antichrist spirit that resists and fights the anointing, false prophecy.

- Cat: independent thinking, unclean spirit, crafty, something dear.

- Cow: slow laborious labor, change and progress, rumination of ideas, dairy cows offer milk, beef cows provide meat, sacrifice, sacred cow, great sin.

- Dog: loyal, friend, companion, guide, protector, unconditional love, warning of an evil attack, spirit of retaliation.

- Horse: ministry of power, authority, strength, swiftness, spiritual support.

- Lamb: baby or new Christian, follow the leader even into danger or harm, offering, gentle, Jesus as our sacrifice, true believers, innocence.

- Pig: unclean, unsaved, legalistic, false teachers, detestable things, unbeliever, gluttonous, vicious and stuck in the mire.

Undomesticated Animals

- Alligator: large powerful destructive mouth, a person in authority or influence using slander, gossip, verbal and spiritual abuse, moving below the surface, behind the scenes to bring destruction.
- Bear: evil man, bad temper, danger, Russia, bear market, judgment, anger.
- Deer: seeking water, ability to leap, graceful, surefooted, agile, timid (Jezebel's eyes that allure).
- Eagle: prophet, person with keen vision, United States.
- Giraffe: their neck is usually the focus, pride, overly developed self-esteem, high-minded, clear spiritual vision or oversight.
- Gorilla: direct, blatant, exposed, open, rebellion, guerilla warfare.
- Leopard: dangerous, powerful, dishonest enemy or rival.
- Lion: King of Beasts, Lion of the Tribe of Judah, Jesus, conqueror, overcoming bold saint, warrior, Satan.
- Monkey: foolishness, clinging, mischief, dishonesty, addiction, bad habit, mocking.
- Panther: high-level witchcraft, powerful adverse influence or

force trying to dishonor or discredit your reputation.

- Rat: disease, deceiver, desensitizes you with a numbing effect while they steal from you, feeds on garbage, wrong thinking.
- Rhinoceros: intimidation, person forcefully horning their way in, power of tradition.
- Snake: lies, tales being told, venomous words that bite, confusion if a rattler, Jesus the healer and wisdom.
- Squirrel: industrious, stores up food for the winter, pest, tormentor.
- Tiger: powerful person or minister good or evil, dangerous, rules over others with persistence because of the orange color.
- Wolf: deceiver, false person, seeks to destroy.

Insects and Bugs

These represent a small irritation, complications, or annoyances; an evil spiritual influence that is plaguing you; an unclean atmosphere or environment; illness, disease, skin rashes and infections; any area where healing or deliverance is needed. Insects represent a distasteful, loathsome, or disgusting person with stinging words that gnaws or chews on your well-being. Notice their size, color, (refer to color card) actions, whether they are flying or crawling, their location and characteristics. For extensive lists of our dream symbols refer to the dream symbol cards online at www.MyOnar.com or www.BarbieBreathitt.com

- Ant: industrious, hard worker, annoying, marching in line, share, don't vie for position, team players, pest.
- Bee: honey, cross-pollinate, stinging words, community.
- Butterfly: transformation, change brings beauty, progressing, process, freedom, connectors, cross-pollinate.
- Fly: Lord of the flies, lies, spoils anointing, defilement, pollute.
- Mosquito: blood-sucker, disease carrier, pest.
- Spider: occult, builds a web of entrapment, looks are deceiving, caught in a trap having the life sucked out.
- Wasp: witchcraft or stinging words.

Sea Creatures

- Crab: hard-shelled person, difficult to be around, pinchers, moves sideways, transformation.

- Fish: men, reaching souls, newly saved, provision, fishing for something.

- Octopus: Jezebel, controlling devourer.

- Porpoise: wordplay for purpose.

- Shark: judgmental spirit, covert, devourer, spiritual rebellion, oppression, attacks blood.

- Shrimp: seeing ourselves as small and insignificant, vacuum cleaners, filters water.

- Whale: ability to go into the deep things of the Lord, great hunger for spiritual food.

The People in Our Dreams

People that we know and love often play leading roles in our dreams. Oftentimes, we may be surprised to see the faces of those who have died when they "revisit" us in our dreams. People who we vaguely recognize, who we don't know, fear, or admire may also appear in our dreams to bring us messages or insights into ourselves. God often uses other people in our dreams to help us see strongholds or blind spots that are in our own lives. If the fear of man or peer pressure exists or if the dreamer tends to be a follower instead of a leader, that person's dreams may reflect concerns for popular public opinion. In a case like this, it is important to check the motivation of our actions and remember that we should always try to please God in everything we do.

Questions to ask yourself about the people in your dreams

- Do I know this person? How well?
- What is the person's name? What does the person's name mean? What is the person's life (favorite) Scripture?
- Is this person in authority over me? What type of influence does this person exhibit over me?
- Am I in authority over this person? What type of influence do I exhibit toward him or her?
- What does this person represent or symbolize to me? Love, success, failure?
- How would I describe this person? Use several adjectives.
- What kind of a feeling or emotion does seeing this person in my dream create in me? Positive or negative or neutral?
- What type of relationship do I have or desire to have with this person?
- What characteristic or dominant trait stands out in this person?
- Is the person in my dream behaving differently than in real life?
- Does this person's countenance glow or appear to be supernatural?

People Symbols

- Angel: messenger of God, healing spirits, sent to help us, angel of light, deceiver.
- Baby: new beginning or chapter in life, dependent.
- Boss: authority.
- Brother: Jesus, brother.
- Child: innocence, spiritual fruit, your gifts, e.g., children are a gift from God.
- Demon: messenger of Satan.
- Famous person: usually what he or she represents to you.
- Father: God, wisdom, provider, father.

- Friend: Jesus, personal friend.
- Mother: church, Holy Spirit, nurturer, mother.
- Old person: wisdom, Holy Spirit, weakness, carnal.
- Pastor: spiritual caregiver, compassion.
- Sister: friend, sister, Christian friend.

Body Parts in Dreams

In dreams, our attention can be drawn to certain parts of the body that are being highlighted or focused upon. These body parts may be exaggerated, appearing bigger than life or be so small they are barely visible. By learning what the various parts of the anatomy represent symbolically and/or literally depending on their function, we can arrive at the proper interpretation of our dream.

Parts of the Anatomy

- Breast: comfort, nurture, Shekinah Glory, many-breasted one.
- Eyes: window to soul, sight, insight, foresight, prophetic, knowledge, understanding, vision, flirt, seduction, occult third eye.
- Feet: natural spiritual walk, bring good news, gospel, Evangelist, walking on or over people, tread on scorpions & serpents.
- Hands: relationship, helping, serving, reaching out, surrenders, striking, hurting, fighting.
- Knees: prayer, intercession, humility, servant.
- Legs: walk, pillar, support, strength, (lame), seduction.
- Shoulder: government, beauty, ruler, strength, burden bearer.
- Teeth: understanding, wisdom, indecision, backbiting, biting off more than you can chew, devourer, concerned over losing your appearance.
- Thigh: faith, promise of kindness, faithfulness, strength.
- Naked: vulnerable, stripped, unprepared, no covering, no guile, reproductive, baring yourself, transparent, sexual.

- Neck: self-determination, stiff-necked, martyr, disbelief, will, beauty, strength.
- Nose: discerning, interfering, intruding, meddling, nosey, strife, smelling.
- Reproductive Organs: multiplication, blessings, increase, spiritual fruitfulness, seductive.

Buildings in Dreams

Buildings play a large part in placing us in the proper timeframe or contextual setting of a dream. Is the building a house, church, school, or office building that is in our present, past, or does it look futuristic? Buildings can often represent the dreamer's life that may be in perfect order, under construction, in disarray or in need of repair.

Questions to Ask About Rooms and Buildings

- What is the function or use of the room or building?
- Have you ever seen, visited, traveled to, worked in, or lived in that building? If so, when? In the past? Or presently? Was it in a future setting?
- On what floor did the dream take place?
- Were there stairs or an elevator leading up to or down from the room or building?
- Do you own the building?
- Were you given a street number and address?

The reader will recognize the following dream from an example in a previous chapter. The duplication of the dream is intentional. It is hoped that the same familiar dream will enable you to notice the emphasis on the buildings and how the discussion of buildings augments the concept of numbers we have already discussed.

Example: Barbie's Three White Houses Dream

- In a dream I saw 3 **white, wooden houses** in a row.
- The address of the **first house** was 51.
- The address of the **second house** was 54.
- The address of the **third house** was 57.

During this same time period Dr. Chuck Pierce gave me the following prophetic word:

> "And the Lord would say unto you that I have formed you. And I have given you favor for a season. And I am beginning to cause you to see the mission of why I have positioned you in the earth at this time. I say you are going to be breathing from a seeing standpoint. For I say I am opening your eyes to see into a realm where I AM and where I AM bringing in revelation of the night (51 refers to Divine Revelation). I say from that revelation of the night you will breath out an expression of who I AM and night will become light saith the Lord. And you will cause people where they could not see; they will begin to see, and not only will they see they will begin to live. And from their life they will begin to express Me saith the Lord.

Interpretation

This building dream focuses on three white wooden houses. They appeared exactly the same in structure, color, and size. The buildings were evenly spaced and perfectly aligned on the same side of the street. The only discernible difference in the three white houses was the repeated increase in increments of the number three, which is God's number. Three symbolizes the complete fullness, kindness, and entirety of the Holy Trinity in the Godhead. The three houses were all white which is symbolic of God's color, representing God's house or the church. The color white means the Spirit of the Lord who is holy, powerful, and pure, without mixture. White light contains all seven colors of the rainbow representing the Spirit of the Lord, his wisdom, understanding, counsel and might, knowledge, and the reverential fear he desires his church to move in. White is the color of righteousness and innocence that comes from being cleansed, purified, and being blameless because of Christ's work in our lives.

The number 50 means celebration, jubilee, liberty, hope, and humble service. In this dream there were three simple, white, wood framed buildings that displayed the numbers 51, 54, and 57 as their addresses.

- The number 51 means divine revelation. If we add the $5+1=$ (6) it equals 6 which is the number of man. God's heart is to pour out divine revelation to man, the pinnacle of his creation.

- By adding the number four to 50 we get 54. Four means God's creative works that enable earthly man to overcome his weaknesses. During the different seasons of our lives God leads us in different directions to carry out his plans and purposes. By adding the $5+4$ we get the number 9 which means God is bringing one season in life to an end or conclusion so he can release the fullness of blessing through introducing people to Christ.

- By adding seven to the number 50 we come up with the meaning of 57. Seven is God's number. It means completeness and spiritual perfection that is achieved through a purification process that leads to a consecrated life of service. $5+7=12$ which is the number for divine government and apostolic fullness.

This very simple dream with three white wooden houses and three consecutive numbers indicates God wants to pour out his Spirit on mankind to release divine revelation knowledge so that we can further his kingdom. Dreams and dream interpretation is one of the tools God has given to believers to introduce unbelievers to a living powerful God. He wants to pour out his fullness and blessings upon this world. *John 3:16–21* makes it clear that God loves the whole world. He came to save and not condemn the world through his infinite love.

> *For God so loved the world that he gave his one and only Son, that whoever believes in him shall not perish but have eternal life. For God did not send his Son into the world to condemn the world, but to save the world through him. Whoever believes in him is not condemned, but whoever does not believe stands condemned already because he has not believed in the name of God's one and only Son. This is the verdict: Light has come into the world, but men loved darkness instead of light because their deeds were evil. Everyone who does evil hates the light, and will not come into the light for fear that his deeds will be exposed. But whoever lives by the truth comes into the light, so that it may be seen plainly that what he has done has been done through God (NIV).*

Dreams allow God to come into our darkest night and bring his love and saving light.

Money and Finance

- Bank: empty bank, no one making deposits: slow business season; lack of favor represents losses;
- long lines with people making deposits represents increase, prosperity
- profitable business ventures indicate much favor; accumulating banknotes or mortgages: increased fortune and honor.
- Bankruptcy: warning; more information needs to be gathered before decisions are made; lack of strategy and proper planning will end in loss or failure.
- Cash: exchange; settling one's account; to take advantage of, "cash in on" an opportunity; slang: to "cash out" means to die.
- Checks: to receive one means increase; to pay out means loss; to write a "bad check" means deception and poverty; ability to write your own "ticket;" checks and balances; need to check on

your business, a friend or family member.

- Coins, golden: great prosperity from hidden resources; silver: slavery; rejection; relationship will or will not be redeemed depending on the context of the dream.
- Credit Card: being "given credit where credit is due;" major increase in available income; stored up favor; enhanced personal value or financial status; a loan of strength to enable the accomplishment of a task; living above your means; debt.
- Dime: silver: redemption; double grace in life; a common drug term; "a dime a dozen;" repentance: "turn on a dime" change directions instantly; ten cents: oak branch, olive leaf and torch: light, strength or peace; a tenth; favor; lacking much value.
- Dollar: currency; current favor is determined by the numbers and value of the bill of money (see the number dream symbol card); monetary unit used to measure savings, investments, inheritance, and dowry; to dream of an increase means success, promotion, and prosperity; a decrease means loss and poverty.
- Gold: taste heavenly; malleable; getting into the vein; a good spiritual conductor; high standard; glorious riches; vessel of honor; *Rev. 3:18 "buy from Me gold tried in the fire and found to be true*; first place record holder.
- Money: favor; power; prestige; wealth; medium of exchange; measures value; property and assets; precise—"on the money;" finding money: small troubles will result in happiness and change; to steal: danger of lack and deceit; roll of dollars: guard against overspending on wants and desires.

Other Dream Symbols

Building Symbols

- Barn: storage place: protection, supplies, blessings, increase.
- Business: business, calling, vocation, provision.
- Church: fellowship, transformation through learning about Jesus, Body of Christ.
- College: higher spiritual learning.

- Gymnasium: competition, game of life.
- House: you or your life, a specific location, house of God, church.
- Mall: ego, needs met, marketplace.
- Restaurant: spiritual food, fellowship.
- School: learning, training, preparation, testing.
- Warehouse: supplies in abundance.
- **Rooms**
- Attic: mind, wrong thinking, stored gifts not being used.
- Back porch: past history.
- Basement: foundational issues.
- Bathroom: cleansing.
- Bedroom: intimacy, rest.
- Dining room: eating spiritual food.
- Family room: fellowship.
- Front porch: future.
- Kitchen: place to prepare spiritual food.
- Library: research, studying to show yourself approved, history, higher learning, supplies.
- Living room: families, commune.
- Shower: washing of the word, cleansing, purification, communication.
- Study: personal.

Objects in Dreams

Different objects will appear in different dreams but their goal is to communicate a message to the dreamer.

Questions to ask about Objects

- What does this object reveal to me through its meaning, operation or function?
- How is this object used? In the usual or an unusual way?
- Is there importance to its color, size, or shape?

Object Symbols

- Book: history, knowledge, life, Bible, wisdom.
- Brick: man's efforts and labor, conformity, fitting into a mold.
- Clothes: anointing, mantles, covering, calling, creative fashions, seasonal clothes.
- Cultural clothes: represent an invitation to travel to that country to impact people.
- Computer: information, facts, resource, knowledge expanding.
- Crops: seasons, harvest.
- Dart: fiery darts, enemy, hurtful words used as a form of amusement.
- Flowers: favor, fragrance, gifts, beauty, grace, blessing.
- Flying: revelatory or prophetic gift, freedom.
- Gold: tried in the fire, purity, great value.
- Gun: powerful words come from a long distance.
- Jewels: spiritual truths, building stones, woman, spiritual inheritance or gifts.
- Knife: cutting, hurtful words.
- Lamp: light to your path, knowledge, understanding.
- Mirror: image, reflection of God, or negative influence.
- Money: favor, greed, blessings.
- Names: how you are known, titles, identity.
- Oil: anointing, power, fuel, healing.
- Silver: redemption, slavery, betrayal, knowledge.

- Stone: spiritual truths, white stone: new name.
- Sword: stabbing words, gospel, sword of the Spirit, Bible.
- Table: communion, fellowship, table it: sharing openly.
- Telephone: communication, gossip, prayer.

Food in Dreams

We would all like to believe that we are mature enough to eat spiritual meat at every meal. The truth is most of us would rather be fed milk, because it is less costly and much easier to digest. The milk of the Word is easier to understand than the meat of the Word. We start out with the milk of the word and the milk of the Spirit. As we walk in obedience and develop our intimacy and friendship with the Lord we are then given the meat of the Word and the meat of the Spirit to sustain us. We have to continually chew meat in order to properly digest the deeper meaning, understanding and application it brings to our lives.

Food Symbols

- Banana: gentleness.
- Bread: Word of God.
- Cake: something sweet and delicate to eat.
- Corn: increase, multiplication, dying to self.
- Grapes: faithfulness, wrath.
- Grapefruit: self-control.
- Leaven: doctrines of man, causes issues to rise.
- Lemon: sour thoughts, actions or attitudes.
- Manna: heavenly revelation.
- Meat: strong revelatory teachings.
- Milk: elementary, simple teachings.

- Oil: anointing, lubricating a difficult situation of friction.
- Orange: love.
- Peach: peace.
- Pear: patience.
- Strawberry: goodness, healing of the flesh.
- Tomato: kindness.
- Water: Holy Spirit, anointing, Word, refreshing, cleansing.
- Wheat: increase, multiplication, harvest, dying to self.
- Wine: joy, something new, or something old and very costly, sweet teaching, and drunkenness, to whine: murmur or complain.

Nutrition

Food in dreams usually represents new creative ideas, belief systems and contemplation or "food for thought," mentally digesting ideas, or feeding your spiritual hunger by repeatedly communing with the goodness of God.

- Apples: good health, a tranquil, peaceful spirit, sin of temptation, word, appreciation, breath of the Spirit bringing freedom, applesauce: nonsense.
- Alcohol: consumed in social settings and celebrations, relaxation, medicating pain, if abused: healing or deliverance may be needed, foreign spirits, addictive behaviors, if drunk: the person is totally out of control they will bring heartbreak, embarrassment, and disappointment to those around them.
- Bakery: good things to eat formed from pleasant words, righteousness being established, the furnace of affliction, persecution followed by promotion, fiery test trials and pitfalls, poverty, *Genesis 40:1–22*, Chief baker hung on a tree, lost his head and birds ate his flesh, *Hosea 7:4 adulterers, an oven whose fire a baker need not stir from the kneading of the dough.*

- Banquet: great preparations and planning will bring success and happiness, *Esther 2:18* to celebrate one's loyal friends and associates; invitation to a wedding is coming; *Matthew 22:1* the Kingdom of Heaven is like a banquet; *Luke 14:13* to be blessed; invited the poor, crippled, lame and blind.
- Cake: self indulgence in lighthearted interests.
- Chocolate: signifies self-reward or indulgence in too many excesses, need to practice some restraint, pain killer, abundant provision, romance, sweet spirit, courtship, gifts, peace offering, you need comforting, craving affection or love.
- Dessert: represents pleasure, immoderation, celebration, repayment, justice, temptation, enjoying the luxuries in life.
- Famine: loss in business revenues, lack of favor or connections, lean times, low to no productivity, starving for attention in relationships, if your enemy is in famine you will prevail and be successful, do not rejoice in his sorrow and misfortune, but extinguish any selfish ambitions.
- Feast: to honor guest, companionship, celebration with friends and associates, to take your designated place, abundance or surplus, reveling in pleasures, laughter *Ecclesiastes 10:19*, return of a prodigal, Feast[s] of: Dedication, Passover, Unleavened Bread, Harvest, First Fruits, Weeks, Ingathering, Tabernacles.

Plants and Flowers

Plants represent life, growth, increase, fruitfulness, abundance, commerce, and prosperity if green and healthy; decay, decline, barrenness, poverty or death if dry, brown, or scorched. Pay attention to the times of planting and harvest and the fruit it produces. Pruning means great increase is coming. The color of the flowers, fruit, or vegetables is important (refer to color dream symbol card).

- Aloe: healing balm of comfort from being burned in relationships; wisdom and integrity.
- Almond: virginity, hope, watchfulness, and fruitfulness.
- Allspice: compassion.

- Apple blossom/tree: promise, good health is blooming, pleasing prosperity, tranquil spirit, show approval and appreciation, temptation is coming; *Song of Solomon 2:3* lover; *Song of Solomon 7:8* breath; *Song of Solomon 8:5* roused; awaken, become active; perpetual concord, Arkansas, Michigan.
- Blue bonnet: revelation, insight, protection or healing is covering your mind; Spring in Texas; blue woolen cap in Scotland.
- Bouquet: collection of talents and spiritual gifts coming together to bring forth a legacy; fragrance of the Lord; gentleness, favor, grace, wealth, pleasant celebration, admirers, to catch: expect good things, if withered: rejected love.
- Flowers: people flourishing *Psalm 103:15,* beauty, reproductive, blossom, fertility: male and female organs, heavenly realm, blessings, favor, love, expand, growth, increase, pleasure, withered: *Isaiah 28:4, Psalm 102:4, 11,* and *1 Peter1:24;* or dying: doubt, disappointments, negative situation, terror, *James 1:11,* lack, dry spirit in need of water and refreshing.
- Forest: surrounded by many people or leaders, feeling lost like Hansel or Gretel, claims lives *2 Samuel 18:18,* stately beauty and tranquility; palace, sing for joy, prosperity, influence, journey, obstacles, shelter for animals, fuel.
- Garden: comfort, tranquility, wealth leading to independence; "King's Garden," surrounded by a hedge of thorns; walls of stone, "watchtowers," "lodges," places of secret prayer and communion with God, *Genesis 24:63; Matthew 26:30–36; John 1:48;* self-cultivation, growth, change, feelings of inner peace, fertile work, fruitful, Eden, perfection, original state of man, prospering, flowering, field of labor, planting of the Lord, Paradise, New Jersey, if overgrown: entanglements, worldly traps, religious traditions.
- Gardener: *John 15:1,* the Father, God, *John 20:15,* Jesus.
- Leaves: healing of the nations: *Revelation 22:2,* joy, health, vitality, dry or withered: hope deferred, loss, illness, loneliness, to go away from or out of, to remain unmoved in a given condition, give over after death into another's control, forsake, abandon, deposit information.

- Oak: righteousness, prosperous life, enlarge, promotion, burial place, meeting place for angels, Absalom's head got stuck in, young prophet sat under, sacred, burn offerings under, acorns: increased fruitfulness, *Isaiah 1:29,* shame, and disgrace will bring an end to your work.
- Roses: Jesus' sweetheart, romance, Rose of Sharon, favor, (pink: love, grace, gentility, You're so lovely, perfect happiness, please believe me; friendship, dark pink: thank you; light pink: admiration); (pink and white: I love you still, and always will); (rosebud: beauty and youth, a heart innocent of love, red: pure and lovely; white: innocent girlhood, moss: confession of love); (red: passionate love, I love you, desire, respect, courage, job well done, unconscious beauty); (red and yellow: congratulations); (red and white: unity); (white: purity, spiritual love, charm, secrecy, silence, You're heavenly, reverence, humility, youthfulness, innocence, I am worthy of you); (white-dried: death is preferable to loss of virtue); (white on red: unity, flower emblem of England); (Yellow: infidelity, decrease of love; joy, gladness, friendship, jealousy, welcome back, remember me, try to care, zealous, rose of Texas); (yellow and orange: passionate thoughts); (bridal: happy love); (musk: capricious beauty); (pale: friendship); (peach: lets get together, closing a deal); (Carolina: love is dangerous); (Christmas: peace and tranquility); (coral or orange: perseverance, flamboyance, enthusiasm, desire, fascinated); (dark crimson: mourning); (tea: I'll remember always); (thorn-less: love at first sight) faithfulness, anniversary, enjoyable occurrence, thank-you, gathering roses: marriage proposal, fulfilled hopes and desires, great happiness, Iowa, New York, June.
- Tares: weedy growth in field, bad elements that endanger the beneficial or good; false things appearing real; deception, false teaching, mental strongholds, un-renewed mind, when mixed in flour causes dizziness, intoxication and paralysis, strong soporific poison, having a form of godliness, *Isaiah 29:13; Matthew 15:8; Mark 7:6; Ezekiel 23:31*
- Thorns/Thistles: cares of the world, choking out good seed, one

who is easily offended; often offensive to others; dissatisfaction, a very difficult situation to handle, enemy, *Judges 2:3* thorn in side, *Joshua 23:13* thorn in eyes, *Judges 8:16* punishment, overrun, entangled, twisted, *Luke 8:7* choked.

Transportation in Dreams

Each of us would like to believe that we are always flying high with the Lord in heavenly places in a fast moving rocket ship or powerful jet. But dreams always reveal the truth of where we are in our relationship and spiritual levels with God. Sometimes we may be soaring high above all our problems with wings as eagles, and the next thing we know we are on a pogo stick stuck in the mud. The vehicle that appears in our dream represents our current level of impact and ability or is revealing our future ministry or life potential. The positions we find ourselves in regarding vehicles indicates who or what is in control of our lives.

Questions to Ask About Transportation

- Am I in the driver's seat, passenger's seat, or back seat of the vehicle?

- Am I in or out of the vehicle, under or over the vehicle? Have I ever been in the trunk locked away?

- How many people can travel in this vehicle?

- What powers this vehicle? Gasoline, wind, or man's efforts and power?

- How fast does this vehicle travel?

- Does the vehicle go on land and sea?

- Does the vehicle fly?

- Does the vehicle exist?

- Is the vehicle currently used today, in the past, or in the future?

- Am I or is someone else in control or driving the vehicle?

Transportation Symbols

- Airplane: ministry soaring in spiritual or heavenly places, high-powered church, vocation, or business.

- Boat: individual ministry.

- Car: ministry or vocation.

- Covered Wagon: pioneering, trailblazing, path finding, exploring new frontier.

- Hang glider: faith ministry carried on the winds or wings of the Spirit.

- Helicopter: home group, small mobile ministry, flexible, great spiritual warfare, fellowship group, church.

- Horseback: powerful individual ministry, pioneering, trail blazing.

- Jet: fast moving powerful intercessor, church or ministry, able to navigate the spiritual realms, fast growing corporation or business.

- Pogo stick: lots of ups and downs with no forward progress.

- Sailboat: individual ministry powered by the Holy Spirit.

- Semi-truck: bringing large but partial shipments of blessing or judgment.

- Ship: large spiritual influence, complicated, flowing ministry or church, large business, or corporation.

- Skate: individual ministry that requires a lot of physical strength and effort.

- Skateboard: individual ministry with a lot of ups and downs requires physical effort, skill, balance and strength to maintain.

- Spaceship: ministry called to the outer limits of spiritual visitations, encounters, and experiences with God.

- Submarine: operates in the deep out of the view of others; undercover prayer ministry.

- Subway: moving below the foundations, behind the scenes.

- Tank: powerful ministry moving with a lot of spiritual authority and protection, spiritual warfare behind enemy's lines.

- Train: united churches, corporations or denominations, in the move of God, on the same track, unceasing work, consistent, powerful, equipping centers, training center.

- Truck: ministry or vocation able to supply others with materials.

- Unicycle: individual ministry requires balancing family, work, home, and ministry; requires a lot of effort to make progress.

- Van: group family or home group ministry or vocation able to supply others with materials; small business.

Weather in Dreams

Dreams of tornadoes, hurricanes and ominous weather conditions may leave us with foreboding feelings of fear. We may feel all of our control is taken from us as the storms of life seem to engulf our situations. For example, a dark colored storm represents the enemy's plans for destruction while a white storm represents godly winds of change coming into our lives.

Questions to Ask About the Weather

- What color was the storm? Dark and ominous, or light?
- Is this the typical time of the year for this type of weather pattern?
- Am I currently experiencing a lot of change or transition in my life?
- Is this a warning dream?
- Does the weather reflect spiritual things God is bringing into the natural?

Example: Double Rainbow, Double Anointing, Doubled

The abundance of rain in Texas has been a covenant sign of the fullness and overflow of God's anointing and spiritual teachings, refreshing, cleansing, an outpouring or shower of the Spirit or Word to be given or spread profusely. After a corporate prayer meeting on Monday, June 11, 2007, God placed a triple rainbow together in the sky that had another one resting over it. One is the number for the eternal omnipotent God, unity, beginning, and the link between heaven and earth. Three is the number of the Godhead, it also means complete, fullness, kindness and entirety. Four is the number of God's creative works. Eleven means prophet, revelation, and transition.

Weather Symbols

- Blue skies: receiving revelation, open heaven.
- Dark skies: difficulty, danger, confusion, storms approaching.
- Hurricane: winds of change coming with a powerful force.
- Rain: spiritual teachings or word.
- Sleet: danger, slippery path, storms and opposition, move with caution.
- Snow: holiness, purity, righteousness, winter season.
- Tornado: winds of change coming with a powerful force.
- Windstorm: blowing away the dross, chaff, and dry things in life.

Dream symbols communicate with a language all their own. Remember the cliché, "A picture can paint a thousand words." This is true of dreams. To cultivate the ability to interpret dreams we must study biblical symbols, types, and shadows. The parables of Jesus and their interpretations in *Matthew 13* will also provide great insights into certain symbols representing something other than the obvious. These metaphors will enhance our understanding of the language of symbols. Each person has an individualized dream vocabulary with meanings and definitions that are as specific as life experiences. A skilled dream interpreter must always rely upon the Holy Spirit to give the understanding of each dreamer's symbolic vocabulary.

Chapter Ten
Visions

Revelation from the spiritual realm often comes to us through our spiritual visual perception in visions. We can receive visions when we are awake or asleep. The vision realm connects the natural realms of reality, knowledge, and physical sensations to the spiritual realms of revelatory knowledge and spiritual sensations. We possess five natural senses of sight, touch, taste, smell, and hearing. These natural senses can be engaged with our spiritual senses to allow us to feel and experience spiritual visions. For this reason, visions are easier to remember than dreams. We can recall visions more easily because our physical body, emotions, and senses are engaged in what we see. When our emotions are involved with the learning process we more readily remember the information that is shared. Visions are imprinted on the soul; they are more literal than symbolic dreams. Most of the time visions do not require extensive interpretation because what you see often will manifest or become a reality in our waking lives.

Dreams are often like vapors. They quickly come and go and are easily forgotten. Visions, on the other hand, can be experienced over and over again just by reciting the visual experience, recalling the pictures and reliving the feelings, sensations, and emotions of the event.

Visions usually concern a time or event that is yet to come or to be experienced. Visions give us the ability to see and know things that will literally happen in the coming days or years of our lives. For this reason alone it is important to pay close attention to visions.

God often uses visions to show us the enemy's intrusive plans of destruction. This allows us the foresight and benefit of canceling the enemy's harmful plans. Then we can establish the opposite by releasing God's power and presence into a situation through prayer and intercession. We are never to come into agreement with a vision that shows any type of negative outcomes. God's plans are for us to prosper, be in good health, and to be successful, living an abundant life. The enemy's plans are always to harm, deceive, kill, steal, and destroy. He is a detractor. He leaves his victims hopeless and in despair. Knowing how Satan works versus how God operates makes it very easy to determine the source of a vision.

Visions Defined

Visions reveal images, pictures, or short dreams that are introduced into the conscious mind. Visions can also appear when the person is in a trance-like state. Visions reveal that which is not actually present at the current time or place. Visions are the expression of spiritual things to the five senses; they open the natural eyes and ears to see and hear clearly. Through visions, we see the manifestation of that which is normally invisible, inaudible, and comes from the supernatural co–existing spiritual realm. During a vision, the five natural senses are usually engaged or heightened. This allows us to physically experience what we are seeing or beholding in the realm of vision. Our body can experience many varied combinations of impartations, revelation, wisdom, and knowledge. We can experience angelic visitations, physical or emotional healing, or deliverance. We can also gain strength, feel weakness, and obtain spiritual gifts through the vision realm.

Visions can also be defined as a view, a shape, an appearance or a sequence of colorful images, symbols, vivid sounds, and strong emotions that come to us through a trance or dream.

Visions give us an unusual capability to perceive or discern through intelligent foresight. They are mental images created through the imagination, a mystical experience of seeing a supernatural reality with either the spiritual or the natural eyes.

A *vision* is defined as the faculty of sight; (good vision) something that is or has been seen; unusual capability in discernment or perception; intelligent foresight; the way in which one sees or conceives of something. Visions are mental images created by the imagination. Visions are the mystical experience of seeing as if with the supernatural eyes. Spiritual beings from the supernatural realm often appear in visions.

The terms vision and visions are mentioned over 100 times in the Bible. Visions can happen at any time. They can manifest while we are fully awake as demonstrated in *Daniel 10:7* and *Acts 9:7*; by day like Cornelius experienced in *Acts 10:3*; and Peter in *Acts 10:9*. Visions come while we are daydreaming. Visions also come by night as with Jacob in *Genesis 46:2*. God often speaks to us in vision form in prayer, during worship, and while meditating in the Word. Visions commonly occur while asleep, in a trance, or in a dream state as referenced in *Numbers 12:6, Job 4:13, and Daniel 4:9.*

Visions are produced and developed in our spirits as God releases revelation to our spiritual man. However, visions first come through the avenue of the soul, which comprises the intellectual memories of the mind, the will, and emotions. Visions are sent by God to reveal the future, release new revelation, direction, to bring comfort, encouragement, and to bring peace to the spirit.

Visions are a divine instrument of communication which are associated with spiritual revivals, as in *Ezekiel 12:21–25* and *Joel 2:28;* compare *Acts 2:17* and the nonappearance of visions with spiritual decline in *Isaiah 29:11–12, Lamentations 2:9, Ezekiel 7:26,* and *Micah 3:6.*

Visions come in many different forms and types of manifestations, but can usually be categorized in one of three groupings: open visions, external visions, and internal visions.

Open Visions

Open visions are seen with our natural or spiritual eyes—also called the eyes of your understanding.

> *That the God of our Lord Jesus Christ, the Father of glory, may give to you the spirit of wisdom and revelation in the knowledge of Him,* **the eyes of your understanding** *being enlightened; that you may know what is the hope of His calling (Ephesians 1:17–18 NKJV).*

In an open vision we may observe the spiritual or heavenly vision realm being opened and revealed. When this type of vision occurs the natural world seems to fade from reality for a short time. The person experiencing an open vision may be caught up in observing the vivid, colorful, visual pictures as if watching motion pictures of another world unfold.

The Old Testament Prophet Isaiah experienced an open vision while he was standing on the earth. His natural eyes were opened to see visions of the Lord seated on a throne in the realms of heaven. God was surrounded by flying seraphim with six wings calling out the holy acts of the Lord to one another. Isaiah's ears were opened to hear the sound of their voices echoing, *"Holy! Holy! Holy!"* He felt the shaking of the temple as it filled with the smoke of God's presence.

In this open vision Isaiah encountered a seraph that visited him with a hot coal of fire. His guilt was removed by the fiery touch, which cleansed and purged his lips. Now passionate, Isaiah was ready to be commissioned by the Lord in his prophetic calling. He heard the audible voice of the Lord speaking to him, then he clearly saw, heard, felt, and experienced the Kingdom of heaven so that he could make it known in earthly realms.

In the year that King Uzziah died, I saw the Lord seated on a throne, high and exalted, and the train of his robe filled the temple. Above him were seraphs, each with six wings: With two wings they covered their faces, with two they covered their feet, and with two they were flying. And they were calling to one another: "Holy, holy, holy is the LORD Almighty; the whole earth is full of his glory."

At the sound of their voices the doorposts and thresholds shook and the temple was filled with smoke. "Woe to me!" I cried. "I am ruined! For I am a man of unclean lips, and I live among a people of unclean lips, and my eyes have seen the King, the LORD Almighty." Then one of the seraphs flew to me with a live coal in his hand, which he had taken with tongs from the altar. With it he touched my mouth and said, "See, this has touched your lips; your guilt is taken away and your sin atoned for."

Then I heard the voice of the Lord saying, "Whom shall I send? And who will go for us?" And I said, "Here am I. Send me!" He said, "Go and tell this people: "Be ever hearing, but never understanding; be ever seeing, but never perceiving." "Make the heart of this people calloused; make their ears dull and close their eyes. Otherwise they might see with their eyes, hear with their ears, understand with their hearts, and turn and be healed."

Then I said, "For how long, O Lord?" And he answered: "Until the cities lie ruined and without inhabitant, until the houses are left deserted and the fields ruined and ravaged, until the LORD *has sent everyone far away and the land is utterly forsaken. And though a tenth remains in the land, it will again be laid waste. But as the terebinth and oak leave stumps when they are cut down, so the holy seed will be the stump in the land" (Isaiah 6:1–13 NIV).*

The New Testament also gives us another example of an open vision. Stephen was a man full of God's love, grace, and great faith. The Holy Spirit moved through him in power. He did great wonders and caused miraculous signs to appear among the people. Stephen's favor with the people provoked the religious leaders to jealousy. They began to argue their traditions with Stephen but they could not stand up against his Spirit-given wisdom. So they stirred up the people, the elders and the teachers of the law. They seized Stephen and brought him before the Sanhedrin. They produced false witnesses who testified against him. All who were sitting in the Sanhedrin looked attentively at Stephen and they saw that his face shone like the face of an angel.

But Stephen, full of the Holy Spirit, looked up to heaven and saw the glory of God, and Jesus standing at the right hand of God. "Look," he said, "I see heaven open and the Son of Man standing at the right hand of God." At this they covered their ears and, yelling at the top of their voices; they all rushed at him, dragged him out of the city and began to stone him.

Meanwhile, the witnesses laid their clothes at the feet of a young man named Saul. While they were stoning him, Stephen prayed, "Lord Jesus, receive my spirit." Then he fell on his knees and cried out, "Lord, do not hold this sin against them." When he had said this, he fell asleep (Acts 7:55–60 NIV).

Saul's Conversion to Paul

Saul had ambitiously set his sights on maliciously persecuting and destroying believers in the early church. Heaven's blinding light was sent to intervene and redirect his misguided zeal in order to properly align the course of his life. Saul's natural sight was taken from him when he encountered a divine vision as a literally blinding light invaded his dark existence.

Saul was stunned when he heard the clear, audible voice of the Lord. He had never heard God speak before even though he was a learned rabbi. Interestingly, the men traveling with him were speechless and struck with fear. They heard the sound of the Lord's voice but saw nothing.

> *As he (Saul) neared Damascus on his journey, suddenly a light from heaven flashed around him. He fell to the ground and heard a voice say to him, "Saul, Saul, why do you persecute me?" "Who are you, Lord?" Saul asked. "I am Jesus, whom you are persecuting," he replied. "Now get up and go into the city, and you will be told what you must do."*

> *The men traveling with Saul stood there speechless; they heard the sound but did not see anyone. Saul got up from the ground, but when he opened his eyes he could see nothing. So they led him by the hand into Damascus. For three days he was blind, and did not eat or drink anything (Acts 9:3–9 NIV).*

A believer named Ananias was a man of fervent prayer who knew the Lord's guiding voice. He was accustomed to the presence of the Lord in an intimate relationship. Ananias often received encouragement, love, and directions through revelation from the Lord in visions. He instantly recognized the voice of the Lord calling to him whereas Saul did not.

Jesus' words tell us:

> *I am the good shepherd; I know my sheep and my sheep know me—just as the Father knows me and I know the Father—and I lay down my life for the sheep. I have other sheep that are not of this sheep pen. I must bring them also. They too will listen to my voice, and there shall be one flock and one shepherd (John 10:14–16 NIV).*

In his vision, Ananias received specific instructions and began a dialogue with the Lord. He expressed his dreaded fears and concerns regarding Saul's murderous reputation as if the Lord were oblivious to this information. Then the Lord shared the vision he had already given to

Saul with Ananias. This let Ananias know that God had gone before him to safely prepare his way.

In the meantime, Saul's heart had been primed. He was awaiting Ananias' presence and prayers that he had already experienced in a vision. In obedience Ananias went to Straight Street. He laid hands on Saul and prayed. Instantly the blinding scales were removed from Saul's eyes and his sight was restored. When Saul opened his eyes he beheld the face of Ananias— the one he had seen in the vision days before. Then with renewed spiritual vision, Saul became the Apostle Paul, and was given natural and spiritual vision to see into the mysteries of the Kingdom of God.

> *In Damascus there was a disciple named Ananias. The Lord called to him in a vision, "Ananias!" "Yes, Lord," he answered. The Lord told him, "Go to the house of Judas on Straight Street and ask for a man from Tarsus named Saul, for he is praying. In a vision he has seen a man named Ananias come and place his hands on him to restore his sight." "Lord," Ananias answered, "I have heard many reports about this man and all the harm he has done to your saints in Jerusalem. And he has come here with authority from the chief priests to arrest all who call on your name." But the Lord said to Ananias, "Go! This man is my chosen instrument to carry my name before the Gentiles and their kings and before the people of Israel. I will show him how much he must suffer for my name." Then Ananias went to the house and entered it. Placing his hands on Saul, he said, "Brother Saul, the Lord Jesus, who appeared to you on the road as you were coming here—has sent me so that you may see again and be filled with the Holy Spirit." Immediately, something like scales fell from Saul's eyes, and he could see again. He got up and was baptized, and after taking some food, he regained his strength (Acts 9:10–19 NIV).*

Ananias prayed for Saul's sight to be restored. Then he prophesied to Saul, later known as Paul, concerning his calling. Ananias told Paul that God had chosen him to know his will by receiving visions, trances, and by hearing the voice of the Lord.

Then he (Ananias) said: 'The God of our fathers has chosen you (Paul) to know his will and to see the Righteous One and to hear words from his mouth. You will be his witness to all men of what you have seen and heard. And now what are you waiting for? Get up, be baptized and wash your sins away, calling on his name.' "When I returned to Jerusalem and was praying at the temple, I fell into a trance and saw the Lord speaking. 'Quick' he said to me. 'Leave Jerusalem immediately, because they will not accept your testimony about me' (Acts 22:14–18 NIV).

Visions have the ability to strategically lead and guide us in the way we should go. After God redirected Paul's path, he was seeking the Lord's direction in prayer as he and his ministry companions traveled throughout the region of Phrygia and Galatia. The Holy Spirit had kept them from preaching the word in the province of Asia, Mysia, and Bithynia, as there were no altars of prayer or true spiritual hunger to open missionary doors there.

And a vision appeared to Paul in the night. A man of Macedonia stood and pleaded with him, saying, "Come over to Macedonia and help us." Now after he had seen the vision, immediately we sought to go to Macedonia, concluding that the Lord had called us to preach the gospel to them (Acts 16:9–10).

This vision appears to be a possible example of a man being caught up in the coexisting spiritual realm. He may have been literally transported from one geographical location to another in order to extend an invitation to Paul in a vision to implore Paul to come help the Macedonians. This is also a good example to demonstrate that visions are not always literal. The image of a man appeared in Paul's vision but he was led to a woman named Lydia who was a seller of purple fabrics. She was a worshiper of God, was listening to Paul preach and the Lord opened her heart to respond to the things spoken. Lydia prevailed upon Paul and the other men to stay in her house in *Acts 16:14.*

Therefore, sailing from Troas, we ran a straight course to Samothrace, and the next day came to Neapolis, and from there to Philippi, which is the foremost city of that part of Macedonia, a colony. And we were staying in that city for some days. And on the Sabbath day we went out of the city to

228

the riverside, where prayer was customarily made; and we sat down and spoke to the women who met there. Now a certain woman named Lydia heard us. She was a seller of purple fabrics from the city of Thyatira, who worshiped God. The Lord opened her heart to heed the things spoken by Paul. And when she and her household were baptized, she begged us, saying, "If you have judged me to be faithful to the Lord, come to my house and stay." So she persuaded us (Acts 16:11–15).

The Baptism of Jesus

John the Baptist was sent by God to prepare the way of the Lord in the wilderness. His message was one of repentance. The Kingdom of God is always ushered in through repentant hearts. Jesus' baptism opened the heavens, ushering in a new era. John saw the Holy Spirit as a dove descending from on high to rest on Jesus. John the Baptist also heard the audible voice of God lovingly acknowledge and validate his pleasure in his son, Jesus. This took place before Jesus had done any great signs, wonders, or miracles.

Then Jesus came from Galilee to the Jordan to be baptized by John. But John tried to deter him, saying, "I need to be baptized by you, and do you come to me?" Jesus replied, "Let it be so now; it is proper for us to do this to fulfill all righteousness." Then John consented. As soon as Jesus was baptized, he went up out of the water. At that moment heaven was opened, and he saw the Spirit of God descending like a dove and lighting on him. And a voice from heaven said, "This is my Son, whom I love; with him I am well pleased" (Matthew 3:13–17 NIV).

Open visions allow us to gaze into the spiritual gates of heaven to observe what is transpiring in a higher realm while we remain here on the earth.

External Visions

External visions are seen with our spiritual and or natural eyes as they are projected from heaven into the natural realm in front of us. The Old Testament prophet Elisha prayed that the Lord would open the eyes of his servant to behold those who were for them because their numbers far outweighed those against them. He was given an external vision to see the greater number of horses and chariots driven by fiery angels surrounding their enemies on the hills. Elisha's second prayer was to strike their enemies with blindness. In this one passage we see God open eyes to the spiritual realm while blinding eyes in the natural realm.

> *When the servant of the man of God got up and went out early the next morning, an army with horses and chariots had surrounded the city. "Oh, my lord, what shall we do?" the servant asked. "Don't be afraid," the prophet answered. "Those who are with us are more than those who are with them."*

> *And Elisha prayed, "O LORD, open his eyes so he may see." Then the LORD opened the servant's eyes, and he looked and saw the hills full of horses and chariots of fire all around Elisha. As the enemy came down toward him, Elisha prayed to the LORD, "Strike these people with blindness." So he struck them with blindness, as Elisha had asked (2 Kings 6:15–18 NIV).*

The Audible Voice of the Lord

Desperate prayer caused the Lord to remember Hannah and heal her barrenness. The Lord gave her more than a son in Samuel; he gave her a prophet for a nation. The Lord stood before Samuel in the vision realm and called his name audibly. The old priestly order had grown dull of sight and the word of the Lord was rare in that day. God gives a clear vision when he releases a new order. The older generation though passing away is able to give keys of wisdom to the next generation. Eli instructed Samuel to lie down in his place of rest and wait for the coming of the Lord. Acknowledge the presence of the Lord when he comes, and declare you have ears to hear his voice.

> *(Now Samuel did not yet know the Lord, nor was the word of the Lord yet revealed to him.) And* **the Lord called Samuel again the third time.** *So he arose and went to Eli, and said, "Here I am, for you did call me." Then Eli perceived that the Lord had called the boy. Therefore Eli said to Samuel, "Go, lie down; and it shall be, if He calls you, that you must say,* **'Speak, Lord, for Your servant hears.'"** *So Samuel went and lay down in his place. Now the* **Lord came** *and* **stood** *and* **called** *as at*

other times, "Samuel! Samuel!" And Samuel answered, "Speak, for Your servant hears" (1 Samuel 3:7–10 NKJV).

The Temptation of Jesus

The Holy Spirit led Jesus into the wilderness to be tested and tried in things that were not from his Father, but that were from Satan. The devil tempted Jesus in three areas of worldly yearning: the lust of the flesh, the lust of the eyes and the pride of life *1 John 2:16.*

These difficult tests demonstrated that Jesus was able to overcome trying situations with his character and integrity still intact. The successful completion of these tests allowed Jesus to exit the wilderness carrying the unlimited power of God's love to a dying world after having been tempted in the same ways as the world he was sent to reach.

After forty days and nights of fasting Jesus was no doubt in a physically weakened condition when the tempter came to him. Satan wanted Jesus to act independently of his Father and violate the miracle realm by turning stones into bread to satisfy his own physical hunger. Jesus would have acted in disobedience by accessing the supernatural faith realm to do a miracle when his Father was not turning stones to bread. Miracles defy the natural realm. Jesus set the example by only doing miracles he saw transpiring in the realm of vision. Jesus only did what he saw his Father doing in heaven that is why he had a 100% success rate.

> *Therefore Jesus answered and was saying to them, "Truly, truly, I say to you, the Son can do nothing of Himself, unless it is something He sees the Father doing; for whatever the Father does, these things the Son also does in like manner" (John 5:19 NASU).*

Next, the devil took Jesus to the highest point of the temple in Jerusalem. He tempted Jesus to flaunt himself as if he were suddenly appearing *(Malachi 3:1)* or had come to overturn the religious systems. Whether this was a tangible, physical act or accomplished in the vision realm is difficult to determine.

231

Then the devil took Jesus to a very high mountain where he was able to show Jesus all the kingdoms of the world and their splendor at once. Adam Clarke's commentary suggests *Matthew 4:8* is a vision as he writes

> If the words, all the kingdoms of the world, be taken in a literal sense, then this must have been visionary representation, as the highest mountain on the face of the globe could not suffice to make evident even one hemisphere of the earth, and the other must of necessity be in darkness.
>
> (from Adam Clarke's Commentary, Electronic Database. Copyright © 1996, 2003, 2005, 2006 by Biblesoft, Inc. All rights reserved.)

The devil wanted to tempt Jesus to take pride in his own abilities and life instead of trusting God to provide for his needs. He wanted Jesus to take possession of the world prematurely without fulfilling his destiny by going to the cross. The Scriptures in this passage do not clearly say the temptation of Jesus took place in a vision. But because of Jesus' weakened physical condition and the presence of the ministering angels I have often wondered if the devil appeared to Jesus in a vision. The vision realm would have allowed them to journey to the temple pinnacle and mountaintop places to see the splendors of the world in a moment in time.

> *Then Jesus was led by the Spirit into the desert to be tempted by the devil. After fasting forty days and forty nights, he was hungry.* **The tempter came to him** *and said, "If you are the Son of God, tell these stones to become bread." Jesus answered, "It is written: 'Man does not live on bread alone, but on every word that comes from the mouth of God.'*
>
> *Then* **the devil took him to the holy city and had him stand on the highest point of the temple.** *"If you are the Son of God," he said, "throw yourself down. For it is written: 'He will command his angels concerning you, and they will lift you up in their hands, so that you will not strike your foot against a stone.'" Jesus answered him, "It is also written: 'Do not put the Lord your God to the test.'"*

Again, **the devil took him to a very high mountain and showed him all the kingdoms of the world and their splendor.** *"All this I will give you,"* *he said,* *"if you will bow down and worship me." Jesus said to him, "Away from me, Satan! For it is written: 'Worship the Lord your God, and serve him only.'" Then the devil left him, and angels came and attended him (Matthew 4:1–11 NIV).*

Jesus' Transfiguration

The sudden emanation of heavenly radiance from Jesus' body and clothing took place in a vision. Jesus and the disciples were overshadowed by a bright cloud. God's audible voice silenced man's as he thundered his heavenly endorsement of Jesus to earth.

Now after six days Jesus took Peter, James, and John his brother, [and] led them up on a high mountain by themselves; and He was transfigured before them. His face shone like the sun, and His clothes became as white as the light. And behold, Moses and Elijah appeared to them, talking with Him.

Then Peter answered and said to Jesus, "Lord, it is good for us to be here; if You wish, let us make here three tabernacles: one for You, one for Moses, and one for Elijah." While he was still speaking, behold, a bright cloud overshadowed them; and suddenly a voice came out of the cloud, saying, "This is My beloved Son, in whom I am well pleased. Hear Him!"

And when the disciples heard it, they fell on their faces and were greatly afraid. But Jesus came and touched them and said, "Arise, and do not be afraid." When they had lifted up their eyes, they saw no one but Jesus only. Now as they came down from the mountain, Jesus commanded them, saying, "Tell the vision to no one until the Son of Man is risen from the dead." And His disciples asked Him, saying, "Why then do the scribes say that Elijah must come first?"

Jesus answered and said to them, "Indeed, Elijah is coming first and will restore all things. But I say to you that Elijah has come already, and they did not know him but did to him whatever they wished. Likewise the Son of Man is also about to suffer at their hands." Then the disciples understood that He spoke to them of John the Baptist (Matthew 17:1–13).

Jesus took three of his disciples, Peter, James, and John with him to the mountain for an encounter with his heavenly Father. Also in attendance were two of the great cloud of witnesses *(Hebrews 12:1)* Elijah and Moses, who were sent to earth as ambassadors from heaven's counsel chambers. In their presence Jesus' countenance and appearance changed into his post-crucified state as his face and clothes shone with the brilliant radiance of the Kingdom of Heaven's light.

Assuredly, I say to you, there are some standing here who shall not taste death till they see the Son of Man coming in His kingdom (Matthew 16:28).

God's audible voice spoke out of the glory cloud that overshadowed and covered them, *"This is my beloved Son in whom I am well pleased. Hear Him!"*

The vision realm is able to connect and usher in the glorious splendor of God's magnificent heavenly kingdom on earth.

Matthew 6:10 Your kingdom come. Your will be done on earth as it is in heaven."

Internal Visions

Internal visions are viewed within the spirit by our spiritual (or mind's eye) as the pictures are displayed on the screens of our hearts' imagination or internal image center. Our conscience interacts and dialogues with the voice of the Holy Spirit as he leads, guides, and directs the course of our lives.

I, Daniel, was grieved in my spirit within my body, and the visions of my head troubled me (Daniel 7:15).

Now the Lord spoke to Paul in the night by a vision, "Do not be afraid, but speak, and do not keep silent; for I am with you, and no one will attack you to hurt you; for I have many people in this city." And he continued there a year and six months, teaching the word of God among them (Acts 18:9–11).

Revelation is foundational in the building of the Kingdom of God. In *Matthew 16*, Jesus asked his disciples to tell him who they thought he was. Peter told him that he was the Christ. Jesus confirmed that he received that fact through revelation from the Father. Jesus confirmed that the God-given revelation of Jesus being the Christ is so important, he would build his church on it and the gates of hell will not prevail against it.

> *When Jesus came into the region of Caesarea Philippi, He asked His disciples, saying, "Who do men say that I, the Son of Man, am?" So they said, "Some say John the Baptist, some Elijah, and others Jeremiah or one of the prophets." He said to them, "But who do you say that I am?" Simon Peter answered and said, "You are the Christ, the Son of the living God." Jesus answered and said to him, "Blessed are you, Simon Bar-Jonah, for flesh and blood has not revealed this to you, but My Father who is in heaven. And I also say to you that you are Peter, and on this rock I will build My church, and the gates of Hades shall not prevail against it.*
>
> *And I will give you the keys of the kingdom of heaven, and whatever you bind on earth will be bound in heaven, and whatever you loose on earth will be loosed in heaven." Then He commanded His disciples that they should tell no one that He was Jesus the Christ (Matthew 16:13–20).*

As we learn to interpret and listen to the voice of the Holy Spirit in our visions, we receive revelation that Jesus is the Christ, the Son of the living God through personal messages that pertain to his will for each of our own lives. Jesus communed with his Father in prayer to access the vision realm to see what his Father was doing in heaven.

> *Therefore Jesus answered and was saying to them, "Truly, truly, I say to you, the Son can do nothing of Himself, unless it is something He sees the Father doing; for whatever the Father does, these things the Son also does in like manner." For the Father loves the Son, and shows Him all things that He Himself is doing; and the Father will show Him greater works than these, so that you will marvel (John 5:19–20 NASU).*

These visions allowed Jesus to minister according to the perfect will and revelation knowledge of his Father. Jesus' ministry was successful here on earth because with the help of spiritual sight, through visions, he kept his eyes focused on his Father.

In Jerusalem, near the Sheep Gate, was a pool called Bethesda. It was surrounded by five covered colonnades. The disabled, blind, disfigured, lame and paralyzed gathered in large numbers to receive their healing when an angel of the Lord stirred the waters. The Father directed Jesus to pray for healing for one invalid man who had been lying by the pool for thirty-eight years. Jesus asked him one question, *"Do you want to get well?"* The cripple replied with an excuse of why he was unable to be healed. The man said, "I have no one to help me." Jesus knew it was his Father's will to heal this particular man that day. Jesus had already seen his Father heal the cripple in heaven so he responded, *"Get up! Pick up your mat and walk." At once the man was cured; he picked up his mat and walked.*

Because this miraculous event took place on the Sabbath, the religious leaders were jealous and obstinate, so they persecuted Jesus. Later they sought to kill him. In prayer, Jesus had seen his Father in a vision doing a healing work for this man out of all the multitudes waiting to be healed. The religious leaders forbade anyone from working on the Sabbath. Jesus said to them, *"My Father is always at his work to this very day, and I, too, am working."* Jesus was able to see the works his Father was doing in heaven and then demonstrate them on earth. Jesus gave them this answer:

> *I tell you the truth, whoever hears my word and believes him who sent me has eternal life and will not be condemned; he has crossed over from death to life. I tell you the truth, a time is coming and has now come when the dead will hear the voice of the Son of God and those who hear will live. For as the Father has life in himself, so he has granted the Son to have life in himself. And he has given him authority to judge because he is the Son of Man.*

> *Do not be amazed at this, for a time is coming when all who are in their graves will hear his voice and come out—those who have done good will rise to live, and those who have done evil will rise to be condemned. By myself I can do nothing; I judge only as I hear, and my judgment is just, for I seek not to please myself but him who sent me.*

If I testify about myself, my testimony is not valid. There is another who testifies in my favor, and I know that his testimony about me is valid.

You have sent to John and he has testified to the truth. Not that I accept human testimony; but I mention it that you may be saved. John was a lamp that burned and gave light, and you chose for a time to enjoy his light.

I have testimony weightier than that of John. For the very work that the Father has given me to finish, and which I am doing, testifies that the Father has sent me. And the Father who sent me has himself testified concerning me. You have never heard his voice nor seen his form, nor does his word dwell in you, for you do not believe the one he sent. You diligently study the Scriptures because you think that by them you possess eternal life. These are the Scriptures that testify about me, yet you refuse to come to me to have life (John 5:2–40 NIV).

Confess this out loud over yourself. I am the Church. Jesus is building me. The same Spirit that raised Christ from the dead lives in me. He has given me the keys of the Kingdom. As I access his heavenly presence through the vision realm, I am changed from glory to glory and my destiny is revealed as my countenance transforms through revelation. When I see him, I will be like him.

Beloved, now we are children of God, and it has not appeared as yet what we will be. We know that when He appears, we will be like Him, because we will see Him just as He is (1 John 3:2-3 NASU).

Chapter Eleven
Trances

What is a trance? A *trance* is a God-induced condition in which ordinary consciousness and the perception of natural circumstances are withheld and the soul is susceptible only to the vision imparted by God. The body and its five senses are suspended, causing time to seemingly stand still. Unable to freely move the physical body, the mind is under the control of the Holy Spirit. During a trance you may experience a total inability to function in the natural or experience a partial suspended animation. There is a heightened detachment from one's physical surroundings, as in daydreaming or contemplation. In a dream or vision state, when the soul is momentarily transported out of the body and is preoccupied or distracted from present conditions it is moved into the unseen world. Trances cause a semi- or half-conscious, ecstatic state, as between sleeping and waking. It is a daze, characterized by the absence of response to all external stimuli.

A trance can be defined as a spiritual condition of "going across; or entering into a hypnotic, cataleptic or ecstatic state; detachment from one's physical surroundings, as in contemplation or daydreaming; a dazed state, as between sleeping and waking, a stupor."

Trances occur during times of fervent prayer, intercession, fasting and meditation, reading of the Bible and ministry times of impartation when hands are laid on individuals.

Characteristics of a trance include but are not limited to falling or experiencing a sensation of falling, having a vision or a visitation, experiencing a loss of strength, seeing the Lord or an angel of the Lord.

While experiencing a trance, a person may receive a vision and or a visitation from the Lord or from his angels. The presence of the supernatural glory realm causes loss of strength. During trances, one often falls prostrate on his or her face.

Trances position us to receive visions from God the same way that sleep positions us to receive dreams of the night. Daniel fell into a trance before the angel of the Lord. When angelic heavenly beings appear, one often falls into a trance state. This is because the human spirit is not used to the higher levels of glory in which heavenly beings dwell.

> *Daniel 8:15–19 "Then it happened, when I, Daniel, had seen the vision and was seeking the meaning, that suddenly there stood before me one having the appearance of a man. And I heard a man's voice between the banks of the Ulai, who called, and said, 'Gabriel, make this man understand the vision.' So he came near where I stood, and when he came* **I was afraid and fell on my face;** *but he said to me, 'Understand, son of man, that the vision refers to the time of the end.' Now, as he was speaking with me,* **I was in a deep sleep with my face to the ground;** *but he touched me, and stood me upright. And he said, 'Look, I am making known to you what shall happen in the latter time of the indignation; for at the appointed time the end shall be.' ..."*

It is interesting that the touch of an angel strengthened Daniel enough to enable him to stand. Gabriel did not want to speak to the back of Daniel's head as he lay on the ground but preferred to communicate face to face to equip Daniel with understanding.

> *Daniel 10:8–9, Therefore I was left alone when I saw this great vision, and* **no strength remained in me; for my vigor was turned to frailty in me, and I retained no strength.** *Yet I heard the sound of his words; and while I heard the sound of his words* **I was in a deep sleep on my face, with my face to the ground.**

Ezekiel saw the rainbow glory of the seven Spirits of God and heard an audible voice in a trance.

> *Ezekiel 1:28 Like the appearance of a rainbow in a cloud on a rainy day, so was the appearance of the brightness all around it. This was the appearance of the likeness of the glory of the Lord. So when I saw it,* **I fell on my face,** *and I heard a voice of One speaking.*

The Prophet Ezekiel received revelation for the house of Israel in a scroll he was given to eat. Ezekiel's senses were engaged with the visions he saw and heard and with the scrolls he tasted.

Ezekiel 3:1—3 Moreover He said to me, "Son of man, eat what you find; eat this scroll, and go, speak to the house of Israel." So I opened my mouth, and He caused me to eat that scroll. And He said to me, "Son of man, feed your belly, and fill your stomach with this scroll that I give you." So I ate it, and it was in my mouth like honey in sweetness.

Trances take one into open doors and gates of revelation in the heavenly realms of the Spirit. Here believers receive insight into the powerful manifest presence of God as he reveals things that will take place in the future.

John the Beloved was banished to the Isle of Patmos. Instead of sinking into depression his heart rejoiced. He gladly separated himself to focus on the Lord and this positioned him to receive the revelation of Jesus Christ. All of creation expectantly waits for the light of illumination to reveal the mystery of Christ who is seated on the heavenly throne and the throne of every believer's heart.

Revelation 1:12–17 Then I turned to see the voice that spoke with me. And having turned I saw seven golden lampstands, and in the midst of the seven lampstands One like the Son of Man, clothed with a garment down to the feet and girded about the chest with a golden band. His head and hair were white like wool, as white as snow, and His eyes like a flame of fire; His feet were like fine brass, as if refined in a furnace, and His voice as the sound of many waters; He had in His right hand seven stars, out of His mouth went a sharp two-edged sword, and His countenance was like the sun shining in its strength. And when I saw Him, **I fell at His feet as dead.** *But He laid His right hand on me, saying to me, "Do not be afraid; I am the First and the Last."*

In John's revelation of God, his throne is set upon a sure foundation of righteousness and justice in the heaven. Loving-kindness and truth proceed before him, releasing the sounds of praise. Jesus is the uncreated one, all-knowing, all-powerful God, presiding on his glorious, majestic, unchanging throne ruling an everlasting Kingdom.

While John was in the Spirit he is caught up into a door into the reality of the unseen eternal Creator's realm. John the Beloved saw, heard, and felt the touch of the Son of Man's infinite love and power. He experienced the most beautiful loving light of the world in the midst of the seven lampstands.

John attempted to describe the transcendent beauty of God, the one who created all things and breathed life into existence. In John's description, The Creator had the appearance of jasper, emerald, sardis and a brilliant rainbow. His precious beauty was beyond human ability to describe. He possessed every color in the spectrum of light and the rhythms of heaven resounded from his being. John's understanding began to awaken to God's voice over the waters on the crystal sea. The sapphire blue sea of glass, like crystal, is unmoved in perfectly mirrored peace before the God of passion and power. John heard God's eternal voice and impassioned heart yearning for mankind to be redeemed as deep called unto deep from generation to generation restoring hope and life.

Divine revelation is released through the seven lamps of fire, the seven Spirits of God. They give sight and sound, wisdom, understanding, counsel, and might in the knowledge and fear of God. They never stop burning and speaking the miraculous "suddenlies" of God.

John saw the Lion of Judah and the Lamb who was slain who was given the sealed scroll. This divine love letter contains the mysteries hidden from the ages. They are the secrets of the Lord, our noble God who desires to share these things with his beloved friends. The four creatures, countless angels and the twenty-four elders form a reflective chorus who sang of the glories of God as they unfold wave upon glorious wave. They sang the songs of heaven, about things never before seen by human eyes and the awe-inspiring beauty of God, who is worthy of declaration and honor.

Though John's experience is part of the history of the Bible, the heavenly door he described is still open for those who have a desire to set themselves apart in spiritual holiness to hear, see, and receive revelation.

Peter received his call to lead the Gentiles to Christ through the spiritual progression of prayer, then entering into a trance, he saw a vision of a sheet being let down as heaven opened before his eyes.

Acts 10:10–11 Then he became very hungry and wanted to eat; but while they made ready, **he fell into a trance and saw heaven opened** …

Acts 11:5–12 I was in the city of Joppa praying; **and in a trance I saw a vision,** *an object descending like a great sheet, let down from heaven by four corners; and it came to me. When I observed it intently and considered, I saw four-footed animals of the earth, wild beasts, creeping things, and birds of the air. And I heard a voice saying to me, "Rise, Peter; kill and eat." But I said, "Not so, Lord! For nothing common or unclean has at any time entered my mouth."*

But the voice answered me again from heaven, "What God has cleansed you must not call common." Now this was done three times, and all were drawn up again into heaven. At that very moment, three men stood before the house where I was, having been sent to me from Caesarea. Then the Spirit told me to go with them, doubting nothing. Moreover these six brethren accompanied me, and we entered the man's house.

Balaam fell down in a trance with his eyes wide open. He heard the words of God and prophesied the visions of the Almighty when the Spirit of the Lord came upon him.

Numbers 24:1–5 Now when Balaam saw that it pleased the Lord to bless Israel, he did not go as at other times, to seek to use sorcery, but he set his face toward the wilderness. And Balaam raised his eyes, and saw Israel encamped according to their tribes; and the Spirit of God came upon him. Then he took up his oracle and said: "The utterance of Balaam the son of Beor, the utterance of the man whose eyes are opened, the utterance of him who hears the words of God, who sees the vision of the Almighty, **who falls down, with eyes wide open:** *'How lovely are your tents, O Jacob! Your dwellings, O Israel!' …"*

Balak's anger rose against Balaam when he would not go against the word of the Lord and blessed Balak's enemies three times instead of cursing them. Although Balaam began as a true prophet of God he was slain as a false prophet, or soothsayer.

> *Numbers 24:10—13 Then Balak's anger was aroused against Balaam, and he struck his hands together; and Balak said to Balaam, "I called you to curse my enemies, and look, you have bountifully blessed them these three times! Now therefore, flee to your place. I said I would greatly honor you, but in fact, the Lord has kept you back from honor." So Balaam said to Balak, "Did I not also speak to your messengers whom you sent to me, saying, 'If Balak were to give me his house full of silver and gold, I could not go beyond the word of the Lord, to do good or bad of my own will. What the Lord says, that I must speak?' ..."*

Conclusion

Visions and trances are more literal rather than symbolic the way dreams tend to be. Because of this they carry more weight in terms of their revelatory substance and importance. We are being transformed from glory to glory into the image of Jesus Christ every time we behold his glory. God uses the vision realm to enable us to see him, and to see what he wants us to be. Visions enable us to encounter God and his brilliant realms of glory.

Chapter Twelve
Growing Through Destiny Dreams

Traveling has allowed me to meet people from all walks of life: the energetic youth, the stayed wisdom of the old, the influential wealthy, as well as the needy poor. I have discovered that the main underlying question people have is, "What are my dreams telling me about my destiny?" Mankind is united in their quest to discover the reason they were born, and their God-given purpose in life.

Interpreting dreams requires the dreamer to develop a spiritual listening ear. Our spiritual ears must be tuned to hear the Creator's voice and the voice of our own soul that was given by God to lead and direct us back to him.

How do we develop our ability to understand a spiritual voice when we are so used to hearing the voices in the world dictate who we are and what we should be doing with our lives? There is a renewing of our minds and a changing of our hearts that must take place to allow our spirit man to take the lead in our lives.

Colossians 3:5–10 "Put to death, therefore, whatever belongs to your earthly nature: sexual immorality, impurity, lust, evil desires and greed, which is idolatry. Because of these, the wrath of God is coming. You used to walk in these ways, in the life you once lived. But now you must rid yourselves of all such things as these: anger, rage, malice, slander, and filthy language from your lips. Do not lie to each other, since you have taken off your old self with its practices and have put on the new self, which is being renewed in knowledge in the image of its Creator" (NIV).

This passage points out the negative things we need to weed out of our lives. In order to become a new person we need to change our desires and the way we walk through life. These changes will allow us to hear the voice of God in our dreams more clearly.

How do we train our spiritual eyes to see the unseen eternal realms that come to us every night in our dreams and every day in our visions?

2 Corinthians 4:16–18 "Therefore we do not lose heart. Though outwardly we are wasting away, yet inwardly we are being renewed day by day. For our light and momentary troubles are achieving for us an eternal glory that far outweighs them all. So we fix our eyes not on what is seen, but on what is unseen. For what is seen is temporary, but what is unseen is eternal" (NIV).

Dreams are like vapors that appear for a brief moment in time and then vanish away forever if they are not captured when they present themselves to us.

We often have difficulty making sense of the different aspects and components that make up our temporary, tangible lives. Who do we marry? Then once we are married, how do we maintain a successful marriage? What should we study in college? What kind of career should we pursue? How many children should we have? These and many other questions present themselves to us to resolve. How do we know we are making the correct and best decisions? What do we do if we make a wrong decision? What is my life supposed to look like? If we have difficulty interpreting the natural, earthly decisions in life, is there hope that we can forge ahead and learn to interpret the symbolic, spiritual language of our dreams?

Dreams are a gift from God to be treasured. Each dream comes in its own individually wrapped package. All we have to do is receive it, unwrap its interpretation and believe it in order to discover the answers that we so long for. Dreams are sent to us to direct us onto the proper paths in life. To discover those life paths we must learn to read and properly interpret the symbols on our dream maps. Interpreting dreams is more than being able to recall the dream's dialogue, the scenes, characters, and events that take place. It is being able to see and hear where and how to apply the wisdom that comes to us in our dreams.

God has a divine plan for us to be successful and achieve our destiny in life. God is the only one who knows the future. He reveals the paths of success in our dreams so our hope remains in him.

Jeremiah 29:11–13 reveals the Father's heart to us

"For I know the plans I have for you," declares the LORD, *"plans to prosper you and not to harm you, plans to give you hope and a future. Then you will call upon me and come and pray to me, and I will listen to you. You will seek me and find me when you seek me with all your heart. I will be found by you," declares the* LORD, *"and will bring you back from captivity."*

When our lives are diverted from God's planned path of success he sends a dream to restore our hope in a prosperous future. As we pray for understanding and seek his wisdom sincerely from our heart, we will find the answers we are looking for. God enables those who remain on the right paths to be strengthened.

Job 17:9 says, *"Nevertheless, the righteous will hold to their ways, and those with clean hands will grow stronger" (NIV).*

Dreams bring us heavenly wisdom that rains down upon those whose hearts are open to receive the saving knowledge God has created to ensure our right standing and spiritual growth. *Isaiah 45:8* explains it this way

"You heavens above, rain down righteousness; let the clouds shower it down. Let the earth open wide, let salvation spring up, let righteousness grow with it; I, the LORD, *have created it (NIV).*

The dreams God sends us from heaven come to speak the truth to us in love so we can grow up into him.

Ephesians 4:15–16 "Instead, speaking the truth in love, we will in all things grow up into him who is the Head, that is, Christ. From him the whole body, joined and held together by every supporting ligament, grows and builds itself up in love, as each part does its work" (NIV).

The building blocks that form a firm foundation for spiritual growth need to reflect Jesus who is the cornerstone. He gives us the insights we need to recognize the people who are our divine connecters. He is our source of confidence. He has created everything that is necessary for us to participate in his divine nature and godliness.

2 Peter 1:3–11 "His divine power has given us everything we need for life and godliness through our knowledge of him who called us by his own glory and goodness. Through these he has given us his very great and precious promises, so that through them you may participate in the divine nature and escape the corruption in the world caused by evil desires.

For this very reason, make every effort to add to your faith goodness; and to goodness, knowledge; and to knowledge, self-control; and to self-control, perseverance; and to perseverance, godliness; and to godliness, brotherly kindness; and to brotherly kindness, love.

For if you possess these qualities in increasing measure, they will keep you from being ineffective and unproductive in your knowledge of our Lord Jesus Christ. But if anyone does not have them, he is nearsighted and blind, and has forgotten that he has been cleansed from his past sins. Therefore, my brothers, be all the more eager to make your calling and election sure. For if you do these things, you will never fall, and you will receive a rich welcome into the eternal kingdom of our Lord and Savior Jesus Christ (NIV).

His divine power has given us every building block we need to have a prosperous life. These building blocks are faith, goodness, knowledge, self-control, perseverance, godliness, brotherly kindness, and love. These components of character are all necessary for our growth and proper spiritual development. God-given dreams continually work on bringing clarity to these areas in our lives. Dreams have a transforming ability if we will receive, believe, and act upon their messages and directives.

God has programmed every person's spirit with a specific DNA that directs us to take responsibility in reaching our destiny. Our spirit knows who we are destined to be and the paths we must take to get there. Our part is cooperating with the changes and taking the necessary risks in life. To become who we really are we must allow our life's dream to dictate our steps. Dreams reveal our inner desires and wants. If we are ever going to obtain the fullness of our abilities we must also allow our dreams to direct us to make the necessary choices for that dream to manifest in our waking lives.

Our lives, patience, and character are forged from the good, pleasant, and enjoyable experiences in life, as well as from the bad, traumatic, and hurtful ones. Each life experience has the ability to move us closer to our destiny. We must allow them to mold us by maintaining a forward momentum in our emotions and by refusing to quit. The things we suffer have an amazing ability to strengthen us by causing us to overcome. The decisions we make will ensure we don't walk on the wrong path again. It is important that we experience pain in life, because it works humility and compassion in us. But if we don't learn to forgive and move on we will continue to carry the painful poison and bitterness in our soul. Emotional pain leads to our believing destructive lies which form strongholds of isolation, addictions, avoidance, denial, and an inability to embrace true love and intimacy because of feelings of unworthiness. We were created to first have a relationship with a divine God who gives us purpose in life and secondly with man.

Our dreams contain tailor-made clarity so that we can see the areas in our lives where we have come into agreement with the enemy's destructive lies about us. As we are delivered from these lies we are able to make the proper decisions in life. We are called to rule, reign, and take dominion over worldly ways. But all too often we feel as if we are being ruled by life situations and just reacting to what life dishes out. Instead of letting our environments and life circumstances determine who we are and what we do, we are called to change the environments and influence the people around us.

Genesis 1:27–28 "So God created man in his own image, in the image of God he created him; male and female he created them. God blessed them and said to them, "Be fruitful and increase in number; fill the earth and subdue it. Rule over the fish of the sea and the birds of the air and over every living creature that moves on the ground" (NIV).

We can see in this passage that there is a process in life that makes us fruitful and causes us to increase in our skills and abilities to.

rule the situations life presents instead of allowing them to rule us. If we continually focus on and fear the problems or difficulties of life they will overtake us. But if we focus on placing our faith in God and seeking him for the answers he will supply all of our needs. Dreams are a wonderful vehicle for bringing a peaceful resolve to the problem areas of life.

The contents of our dreams help us to discern areas in our lives that are not matching up with the gallery of pictures exhibiting the "best you" in your dreams. Learning to compare and contrast our dream life with our waking life is very important to accelerate our spiritual growth process. The insights we gain from the colors, symbols, and the artistic displays in our dream gallery allow more creativity, bold confidence, and the ability to connect with others of like vision and purpose. Each dream paints a different picture on the canvas of our life. As we continue to walk through the art gallery of life we become increasingly aware of the big picture.

Dreams afford us the ability to carefully look at our lives from every angle. Dreams help us transition from playing it safe by looking at our dream life as a casual observer into becoming an active partner with what God is showing us and calling us to do. We watch to see how the dream plays out. If we are successful, we gain a new love and respect for ourselves. This infuses us with the necessary boldness and confidence to become an active participant in both our dreams and in life. We must believe in ourselves to the extent that we are willing to take risks. Our soul will help direct us over, around and through life's obstacles and challenges. Eventually we will see the exciting dreams of the night come to pass in our lives as we make the necessary changes to facilitate their existence. If we take the stance that the dreams we have are "only dreams" they will in fact remain "only a dream." If we continue to maintain this opinion we will not benefit from the wisdom or healing processes our dreams want to reveal.

Dreams have an ability to remove us from the negative influences of the wrong, painful scripts that have been written upon our hearts. Our dreams have the keys to unlock the prison doors that try to hold us as chained captives as we rehearse the hurtful betrayals of life. Studying dreams will help us understand what truths are being revealed.

Applied truths will set us free from believing false pictures or visions. Understanding dreams require prayer, a concerted, disciplined effort, and developing our skills of discernment.

The Prophet Daniel was a man of prayer. He developed his skill in understanding dreams and visions because he practiced maintaining a relationship with God. In the presence of God we will discover all we need to know about life. Even with all his effort and study he still needed angelic assistance to understand the visions of his head while on his bed. The Bible tells us that God sent the angel Gabriel to give Daniel instruction, skill, insight and understanding. All of these tools are necessary for each of us to be able to interpret our dreams as well as the dreams of others.

> *Daniel 9:21–23 "While I was still in prayer, Gabriel, the man I had seen in the earlier vision, came to me in swift flight about the time of the evening sacrifice. He instructed me and said to me, "Daniel, I have now come to give you insight and understanding. As soon as you began to pray, an answer was given, which I have come to tell you, for you are highly esteemed. Therefore, consider the message and understand the vision" (NIV).*

As Daniel considered Gabriel's message he was given the necessary keys to understanding the vision. For us to understand the visions our dreams are sending we must be able to apply dream wisdom to our lives. To discover where our dreams are leading us in the future, we need to know where we have been in the past and where we are now. Daniel wrote down the main facts of his dreams. Through mapping out the sequence of what occurred he was able to understand the rise and fall of four kingdoms once he asked for the interpretation.

> *Daniel 7:1 In the first year of Belshazzar king of Babylon, Daniel had a dream, and visions passed through his mind as he was lying on his bed. He wrote down the substance of his dream (NIV).*

To receive the full benefit from our dreams we must discern where we are in life and then take responsibility for where we are going. Negative feelings such as fear, grief, rejection, and disappointment try to remain hidden in our soul. Dreams will expose these dark issues to God's revealing, healing light. These negative feelings can then be dealt with in a way that will enable the dreamer to exchange the negative feelings for more fruitful, positive feelings of love, joy, and peace.

Prophetic dreams reveal God's intended life script, which then allows the dreamer's spirit to walk along the designated pre-described path. The dreamer's spirit was able to watch future events and experiment with possible outcomes. The Holy Spirit has already seen the success or failure of these events and now helps direct the dreamer in his waking life to align with his greatest possible destiny.

Chapter Thirteen
Dream Mapping and Diagramming

Interpreting dreams is similar to constructing a picture from the many varied shaped pieces of a puzzle. First we sort all the pieces by color then we put the straight edges of the framework together. We do this by discerning who or what is the focus of the dream. Then we begin to fill in and connect the myriad of colorful pieces. These are represented by the different symbols and the roles they play in the meaning of the dream. When the puzzle is nearing completion we are able to see and understand more about what the artist wanted us to know. As the picture becomes clearer with each added piece of the puzzle, the hidden mystery is revealed. Our soul contains the completed picture and each dream adds another clue to who we were created to become in the future.

Dream mapping is a technique that enables the skilled, mature interpreter to take a number of dreams at one time and evaluate what they are collectively telling the dreamer. These dreams can be recent dreams or dreams from the distant past. They can be dreams dreamt by the dreamer, as well as by others close to the dreamer.

A good dream interpreter will be able to give insight with understanding to help illuminate God's faith message for difficult circumstances. A series of dreams may also reveal the dreamer's strengths, weaknesses, and spiritual gifts as the group of dreams is dissected. Dream mapping is a wonderful tool that gives comfort and counsel while bringing clarity into the mystery of dreams. As each dream is correctly interpreted it unlocks the subsequent dreams until a beautiful picture is formed.

Correct dream interpretation has an ability to remove the piercing, poisonous arrows of our wrong perceptions that came from negative influences in our lives, and it can erase the painful scripts that have scarred our hearts.

Dream Mapping Example

Cooper had faithfully served his home church in many leadership capacities including serving as an elder, a deacon, and a choir and committee member since the 1950s. In 2005, after praying and considering his options, he decided not to remain in his home church, but to find another church body to serve. He found an evangelical church and had been serving for about three years in numerous ways. Cooper had been diagnosed with bladder cancer and various other aliments. In his desperation he was seeking a deeper walk and relationship with the Lord by pursuing spiritual gifts; especially the gift of healing. As he continued to cry out to the Lord in prayer he was given two amazing dreams that were both healing and restorative. The dreams were relevant to his spiritual DNA and have both intrinsic and extrinsic significance, in that the meanings contained a message to him personally as well as a message to other believers.

Dream One

Old-Time Movie Theater

About a year ago or so I had a fairly short dream. I was in the back of an old-time movie theater. The theater was the kind that had an aisle down the middle and one on each side. There was a stage across the front with curtains. It was a rather dark area. There wasn't anybody else in the theater except one person who was walking slowly down the left aisle and then crossed over to the front of the theater, turned and then said one word, "Restoration." Next, I noticed another person in the middle toward the back main entrance and that person said, "Complete Restoration."

Dream Two

Fashion Show

Early one Tuesday morning I was privileged to see a fashion show in a dream. The fashion show was held in a very ordinary room with metal folding chairs. The parade route for the fashion people was in front. It was in a different room that was separated and the curtains were removed from the stage. The ladies came in from the left and went off to the right. The first group of seven ladies were brightly dressed in red, yellow, and blue (primary colors) and they were around twenty-five years old. Then there was a break. Next, a second group of seven women came in. They were very neat, young women probably in their thirties. The colors of their clothes were more vivid and mature, with darker, business-like [tones]: dark royal blue, green, and rich purple—you know that kind of color. The material was smooth and wrinkle-free. They came in from the left and went to the right. I was puzzled about this whole thing then suddenly the word came to me "Revelation."

Initially the interpretation of the dream was a mystery, but knowing that it was special, he wrote it down, prayed and waited expectantly for God to reveal its meaning. In June, 2008 he attended our *Dream Encounters Workshop* and obtained the *Dream Encounter Symbols* book. Through these two avenues he received insight on the symbols and the meaning of his dream. After he shared his dreams with the class, the interpretation of his dream was given and he asked for and received a healing prayer. Upon returning to the doctors he was given a clean bill of health. His bladder cancer was gone, and he was completely healed. He received the "Revelation" and his "Restoration" or should I say "Complete Restoration."

Let's work through the symbols in his dream to gain understanding.

It is essential to pray. The most important thing to remember in dream interpretation is to ask the Holy Spirit to lead. His guidance will enable the choosing of the correct meanings of the symbols that are represented in the dream.

Dream Titles
Dream One: "Old Time Movie Theater"
Dream Two: "Fashion Show"

Focus: Clearly, Cooper is the focus of both of these dreams, which means the intrinsic message is first for him.

The Settings: The settings of both dreams take place in a theater with a stage and curtains.

Theater: The theater often speaks of vision being given to bring clarity. It represents the arts. The theater represents the art of moving in spiritual gifts, hearing God's voice, or the art of healing. This will give the message of the dream more of a literal meaning and application. Theaters enable the dreamer to observe how his life is playing out in thoughts, hopes, feelings, fears, and expectations. (Remember he said, "There was a rather dark area" in the theater. Darkness can represent the need for revelation, enlightenment, forgiveness of sin and/or healing.) Theaters can also represent wanting or needing public notice or assistance. A theater means a current or past situation demands that you play a certain role. For example, it could symbolize "setting the stage for," "playing the fool," "catching somebody in the act," or "getting into the act." It could also represent setting the stage for "getting one's act together," or needing to "act one's age," or even having "stage fright" or being the "stage manager." "Act the part," and an "act of God," or a need to "act on" some revelation or impression from God are common expressions as well.

Stage: A stage is a raised platform for viewing a progression of actions, an exhibit or presentations. It is a setting for an event or talent. It provides a resting place on a journey between stopping places such as accommodations or an element or a group of elements in a complex arrangement. It can also display a series during a chronological age, "All the world is but a stage …"

Curtains: Curtains are movable drapes or a screen between the stage and auditorium in a theater or hall. The ascent represents the beginning and the descent represents the ending. They can symbolize a strategic line of speech coming at the end of a play or scene, or a rampart joining two gates. Curtains can be a play on words meaning to curtail or to cut something short to ruin it or even to cause something to end in a premature death.

Curtain Call: The curtain call features the emergence of an actor, model, or the main performers at the end or grand finale of a show in acknowledgement of approval and applause.

Progression from the Left: represents past issues pending resolution while moving to the **Right:** represents the future—it is a transition or moving from the old to the new setting.

Front: represents the future and things yet to come.

Number Three: (three people) Holy Trinity, complete, fullness, kindness, entirety, Godhead.

Number Two: separation, division, witness, support and blessing.

Number Seven: (seven women) completeness, spiritual perfection, God's number, purification, consecration, weapon and self-defense. Two groups of seven women equal fourteen women in all.

Number Fourteen: means passing over into completion, restoration and revelation, deliverance, salvation and a double anointing combining the old and the new.

Number Twenty-five: forgiveness of sin, beginning of ministry training and essence of grace.

Thirty: sorrow, mourning, the Blood of Christ, consecration, maturity for ministry, and teaching.

Woman: represents the church, believers in Jesus Christ, the Holy Spirit, compassion, spiritual influences, immature or childlike to full completion and the maturity of a powerful matron.

Apparel: Apparel gives clues about whether the ventures or enterprises that are embarked on will be successful or fail—depending on the apparel's color or appearance. For example, a clean, new, or elegant garment would symbolize prosperity. However, something that is torn or soiled would represent deceit and harm to one's character or virtue. Starched clothes might symbolize the need to be flexible. Threadbare clothing could represent something or someone that is being greatly used or is a hard worker. Garments without wrinkles indicate that the dreamer has been pressed through great testing and fiery trials.

Red: The Spirit of the Lord *Isaiah 11:2*; wisdom, anointing, power, prophetic anointing, prayer, evangelist, thanksgiving, blood atonement, passion, emotion, strength, energy, fire, love, sex, excitement, enthusiasm, zeal, speed, heat, leadership, masculinity, warrior, war, sin, death, anger, rage, fighting, lust, hatred, and bloodshed.

Yellow: Spirit of understanding *Isaiah 11:2*; soul, hope, gift of God, light; marriage, teacher, family, celebration, joy, happiness, renewed mind, optimism, idealism, wealth, summer, air; courage, welcome home, honor, sunlight, fear, coward, illness, hazards, dishonesty, avarice, intellectual pride, deceitful, timidity, and weakness.

Blue: Spirit of Might *Isaiah 11:2*, faith, spiritual communion with God, prophet, word of God, grace, divine revelation, heaven, spiritual, visitation, Holy Spirit, blessings, healing, good will, life, mortal, seas, skies, peace, unity, harmony, tranquility, calmness, coolness, confidence, water, ice, loyalty, true blue, dependability, winter, depression, sorrow, anxiety, isolation, feeling blue, hopelessness, coldness and idealism.

Purple: authority, royalty, intercession, apostle, kingship, majestic, noble, prince, princess, queen, political power, spirituality, creativity, garments of the wealthy, ceremony, mystery, rule—either good or evil, arrogance, flamboyance, gaudiness, mourning, exaggeration, false authority, dishonesty, licentiousness, sensuality, and Jezebel.

Green: Spirit of Counsel *Isaiah 11:2*; growth, prosperity, wealth, health, money, provision, vigor, conscience, generosity, go, new life or beginning, tender, rest, nature, evergreen, eternal life, immortal, spring, fertility, youth, environment, aggression, inexperienced, immature, pride, envy, jealousy, flesh, carnal, mortal, and misfortune.

Revelation: something revealed not formally known or realized, manifestation of divine truth and will, expect increased wisdom, insights, skill and understanding in business, relationships, and love with a bright outlook for the future, great revelation brings jealousy and persecution.

"Restoration" and **"Complete Restoration:"** These are four passages of Scripture the Holy Spirit gave me to decree and pray over Cooper to receive his total restorative healing.

Acts 3:21
Whom heaven must receive until the times of restoration of all things, which God has spoken by the mouth of all His holy prophets since the world began.

Isaiah 38:16
O Lord, by these things men live; And in all these things is the life of my spirit; so You will restore me and make me live.

Isaiah 42:22
But this is a people robbed and plundered; all of them are snared in holes, and they are hidden in prison houses; they are for prey, and no one delivers; for plunder, and no one says, "Restore!"

Isaiah 35 was read in its entirety as a prayer over Cooper.

Cooper's dream sequence shows God bringing Cooper out of his dark season of sickness where he was unaware of how to obtain healing. In the dream God is establishing Cooper's healing and bringing his complete restoration through revelation. The first group of seven women that were clothed in the primary red, yellow, and blue colors represent his previous immature level of understanding or the church setting where the gifts of the Spirit were not embraced or practiced, *1 Corinthians 12:1; 1 Corinthians 14:12*.

The following is my spiritual insight into what Cooper's dreams were communicating to him.

Interpretation of Dream One

Old Time Movie Theater

Cooper,
Your dream, at the time it was given to you, is about you and a supernatural "act of God" that is unfolding in your life. This dream was given to you as a private screening and it reveals declarations from the Lord that he is speaking over your

life—a complete restoration beginning in the present will move backward into your past and restore anything needed to fulfill his purposes for your life. The dream suggests that something of God's purposes for your life have been delayed or put on hold, but God is completely restoring what is needed to express his purposes through you! The dream was given to show you that the Lord has a clear purpose for your life and to fill you with anticipation concerning it.

Your dream comes with a message from heaven giving you a clear picture of total restoration in your life. God set the stage for a quiet but powerful performance just for you. He is the Director and the ONLY star in the theater of your life. He is showing you that out of the darkness comes his light, beauty, and healing. He is speaking to you of complete restoration, not some restoration, but in every area you have longed for and needed. Because he lives!

On another level, your dream shows you the Lord's supernatural ability and desire to completely restore and redeem a person's life, from past to present, so that they can fulfill their destiny and Kingdom purpose.

The second group of seven ladies appeared to be in their thirties; (30 means Blood of Christ, consecration, teaching, maturity for ministry). They were clothed in smooth, wrinkle-free business-like garments of rich, dark, deep navy blue, purple, and green. These rich colors indicate that a seasoned maturity has taken place in Cooper. The seven mantles these ladies wore can also represent the church as Jesus' bride who carries a bold healing anointing, revelation, and authority to release newness of life.

Interpretation of Dream Two

Fashion Show

Cooper,

Your dream is openly unveiling for you a very deep work the Lord is doing in your life in two distinct stages until completed. The first stage is a direct experience of the Lord's supernatural power that both renews your mind and opens you up to deeper communion (intimacy) with Him. As these experiences become real and abiding for you, the Lord intends to do something much deeper that is well suited for his purposes for your life.

This second work of grace moves deeply where you experience deeper revelation and/or healing. This promises to be a season of deep spiritual growth where you experience directly his majesty and rule in areas of your life that may have been under the dominion of negative spiritual forces or the old nature—in short, the Lord intends to free you (14 means deliverance) so that you can fully serve him and live out his purposes for your life!

This dream suggests that the deeper work God does in your life may actually become a calling or purpose for you to minister to others the freeing, delivering power of the Lord! The dream is a privilege that the Lord extends to you and is intended to encourage and prepare you to make a difference for the Kingdom!

God is parading before you in a simple fashion seven beautiful influences with a powerful meaning and message for your life personally. He has given you his fundamental blessings, gifts, abilities, and knowledge for your earthly walk. You have his wisdom, revelation, hope, joy, and the mind of Christ, which gives you his anointing and the power to accomplish your destiny's purposes.

On another level, your dream says that the deeper works of God in one's life gives one credibility and supernatural power to minister the same to others!

The dream then reveals your spiritual maturing into a clearer, brighter, deeper, authority and Kingship without spot or wrinkle. The weight of your dream is on the latter seven "women." You have chosen the road less traveled and God is confirming and encouraging you that you are one of his overcomers. You have endured through a great deal and you have overcome every difficulty and trial with the power of his seven spirits.

You have taken his word and his promises with faith and followed him even in times when you had no clarity of what was behind his curtain. This dream is encompassed with your love and honor of God and his love and honor of you.

There is also a message of the simplicity of God and understanding his truth. He makes his truth known to his own in an understandable uncomplicated way.

I pray God's *"Grace and peace to you from him who is and who was and who is to come and from the seven spirits before his throne, and from Jesus Christ, who is the faithful witness, the firstborn from the dead, and the ruler of the kings of the earth"* (Revelation 1:5).

There is a message asking you to study the seven manifestations of the Spirits of God for more revelation for your heart, mind, soul, and spirit taking you to an even higher understanding of who you are in him.

The Seven Spirits of God

1. The Spirit of Justification: *"you were justified in the name of the Lord Jesus and by the Spirit of our God."* We are all justified because of God's grace and by our faith, and it is the Spirit of God who draws us and empowers us to acknowledge Jesus as our Lord and Savior *(1 Corinthians 12:3)*. This is the first work of the Spirit when one is born again.

2. The Spirit of Sanctification: *2 Thessalonians 2:13* "God from the beginning chose you for salvation through sanctification by the Spirit and belief in the truth." Sanctification is the process of God's grace by which the believer is separated from sin, and purified by life lived in the Spirit. "And the Lord would say unto you that I have formed you. And I have given you favor for a season. And I am beginning to cause you to see the mission of why I have positioned you in the earth at this time. I say you are going to be breathing from a seeing standpoint. For I say I am opening your eyes to see into a realm where I AM and where I AM bringing in revelation of the night (51 refers to Divine Revelation). I say from that revelation of the night you will breath out an expression of who I AM and night will become light saith the Lord. And you will cause people where they could not see; they will begin to see, and not only will they see they will begin to live. And from their life they will begin to express Me saith the Lord. *Galatians 5:16, 25* and *Romans 8:1–14)* The fruit of the Spirit will begin to manifest as we yield to the process of sanctification.

3. The Spirit of Life: *Romans 8:2 "For the law of the Spirit of life in Christ Jesus has made me free from the law of sin and death."* This is the Spirit of adoption *(Romans 8:15)* that makes us the sons of God *(Romans 8:16–19)*. We can now live in the resurrection power of Christ where the operation of the gifts of the Spirit cause our lives to become supernatural. The Spirit will give life to our mortal bodies. Healing and strength will come into our bodies of flesh *(Romans 8:11)* as well as giving us a glorified body in that day.

4. The Spirit of Truth: *John 14:17 "The Spirit of truth, whom the world cannot receive, because it neither sees Him nor knows Him; but you know Him, for He dwells with you and will be in you."* The truth will set us free. The truth will bring revelation knowledge as we are taught by the Holy Spirit. The Spirit of truth will reveal Jesus to us *(John 15:26)*. Vision will be given to lead us into all truth and reveal the kingdom to us. Deception will be removed, and the lies destroyed.

5. The Spirit of Wisdom: *Ephesians 1:17 "That the God of our Lord Jesus Christ, the Father of glory, may give to you the spirit of wisdom and revelation*

in the knowledge of Him." Not only will the Spirit give us knowledge of Jesus, but he will give us insight into his mind and what he is doing *(1 Corinthians 2:6–16)*. The Holy Spirit is our teacher *(John 14:26)*.

6. The Spirit of Deliverance: *Matthew 12:28 "But if I cast out demons by the Spirit of God, surely the kingdom of God has come upon you."* It is by the power of the Holy Spirit that we are delivered from sin and by that same Spirit demons are cast out and the powers of darkness are defeated.

7. The Spirit of Prayer: *Romans 8:26 "Likewise the Spirit also helps in our weaknesses. For we do not know what we should pray for as we ought, but the Spirit Himself makes intercession for us with groanings which cannot be uttered."* *Ephesians 6:18* tells us that all prayer should be done in the Spirit.

For further study

The Seven Spirits of God by Bill Burns, Faith Tabernacle, P.O. Box 1148, Kremmling, Colorado 80459

See What the Father is Doing

The New Testament passage in *John 4* speaks of the Pool of Bethesda, which is translated "outpouring." The healing angel would come and trouble the water. When the anointing began to pour, the first to step in was healed. Those who weren't able to step in became bitter, murmuring, and complaining of those who were more fortunate than they. Jesus approached a particular crippled man that his Heavenly Father had shown him in a vision. This man's crippled identity was enslaved to sickness for thirty eight years. After one supernatural encounter, strategic appointment, or divine confrontation with Jesus, his life was healed.

In the place of outpouring we will overcome the victim mentality by renewing our mind to become "victors."

> *And be renewed in the spirit of your mind, and that you put on the new man which was created according to God, in true righteousness and holiness. (Ephesians 4:23–24 NKJV)*

If we will come to Jesus for healing during this time of outpouring we won't have any more excuses for our crippled, weakened conditions.

This awesome, unparalleled move of God will usher in a new breed of leaders who will only do what they see the Father doing.

Then Jesus answered and said to them, "Most assuredly, I say to you, the Son can do nothing of Himself, but what He sees the Father do; for whatever He does, the Son also does in like manner. For the Father loves the Son, and shows Him all things that He Himself does; and He will show Him greater works than these, that you may marvel. For as the Father raises the dead and gives life to them, even so the Son gives life to whom He will. (John 5:19–21 NKJV)

The realm of vision is so powerful it ignites passion and clarity of purpose in the heart of the beholder. To walk into the greater works we must see what the Father is doing in Heaven and allow it to flow through our lives here on earth.

New Voices Will Be Heard

God is opening doors to release new voices that have only been heard on a limited level. This new breed of leadership will be full of godly wisdom, knowing the seasons, and proper timing like Issachar. The Daniel and Joseph anointings of understanding mysteries, dreams, and enigmas will also operate on a governmental level. New faces will grace the conference and media arenas with an authoritative Kingdom message of love, and the power to back it with signs, wonders, and miracles. These hidden ones will emerge out of the wilderness carrying the mantles and wisdom of past generations.

The Kingdom that is within us is expanding and beginning to flow like a river, watering the barren places. We will continue to increase and expand if we will focus on unity and God's Kingdom business and mandates of love first. Isaiah 55:11 says that every word that goes forth from his mouth shall not return to him void, but will accomplish what he pleases, and it shall prosper in the thing for which he sent it. The sound of God's voice shatters darkness. Psalm 89 tells us that we are blessed if we know the sound. The sound is God speaking. Everything he says he will do; he will accomplish everything.

Great Grace and Favor

We are in a season of supernatural endowment and great grace. Grace and favor gives us the capacity to live as an overcomer, or a victor, not as a victim who is overcome by the enemy of their soul.

The Shekinah glory descended upon the Tent of Meetings and Moses met with God face–to–face, but that glory faded. Moses died in the wilderness but Joshua continued to walk with God in the glory. He received Moses' mantle, crossed the Jordan, and entered the "Promise Land." Throughout history we see men and women who learned to walk in a "spirit of holiness with God." The Spirit of holiness is the divine nature of God manifesting in maturity with resurrection power! Enoch walked with God; and he was not, for God took him. Enoch walked in resurrection power and never experienced death.

> *Concerning His Son Jesus Christ our Lord, who was born of the seed of David according to the flesh, and declared to be the Son of God with power according to the Spirit of holiness, by the resurrection from the dead. Through Him we have received grace and apostleship for obedience to the faith among all nations for His name, among whom you also are the called of Jesus Christ. (Romans 1:3–6 NKJV)*

Enoch's anointing or mantle was to walk and talk with God in the Spirit of holiness. He displayed the divine nature of God in its fullness, walking in resurrection power!

> *So all the days of Enoch were three hundred and sixty-five years. And Enoch walked with God; and he was not, for God took him. (Genesis 5:23–24 NKJV)*

Enoch's earthly walk was the same as his walk with God in heavenly places. He was not double–minded. Enoch was renewed in the spirit of his mind. He put on the new self, in holiness, and truth in the likeness of God. Enoch was a forerunner of what we are called to be in Christ. It is the Christ in us that gives us the hope of glory. Intimacy learned in the Song of Solomon will enable the hidden ones to emerge from their wilderness wanderings with their hearts panting for the Lover of their souls. Their ears are tuned to hear the whispers of his voice as he visits them in dreams to lead them every step of the way.

Deliverers to Set the Captives Free

God is equipping deliverers to set captives free. His eyes are searching for those who will walk in his ways of truth.

> *But this is a people robbed and plundered;*
> *All of them are snared in holes,*
> *And they are hidden in prison houses;*
> *They are for prey, and no one delivers;*
> *For plunder, and no one says, "Restore!"*
> *Who among you will give ear to this?*
> *Who will listen and hear for the time to come?*
> *(Isaiah 42:22—23 NKJV)*

Kingdom revelation builds faith producing Kingdom power through which many people will be set free.

> *The LORD also will be a refuge for the oppressed, a refuge in times of trouble. And those who know Your name will put their trust in You; for You, LORD, have not forsaken those who seek You. Sing praises to the LORD, who dwells in Zion! Declare His deeds among the people. When He avenges blood, He remembers them; He does not forget the cry of the humble. Have mercy on me, O LORD! Consider my trouble from those who hate me, You who lift me up from the gates of death, That I may tell of all Your praise in the gates of the daughter of Zion. I will rejoice in Your salvation. (Psalm 9:9–14 NKJV)*

Salvation has the power to save and heal us completely in our mind, emotions, body, and spirit.

Resurrection Power to Do Miracles

On January 11, 2009, I awoke from a dream of resurrecting four men from the dead. I found myself in a room with four dead men. Several more who knew them were present, grieving for their loss. The Holy Spirit spoke to me as I entered the room and said, "Their spirits are still in the room at ceiling level." In the vision I saw myself lay hands on the stomach of one of the dead men and commanded life to enter him. His spirit manifested in the form of a transparent spirit skeleton. It lay on top of the man's dead body. As it entered his body the man's breath or spirit returned and he resurrected from the dead. When the men in the room observed what had happened their hearts were ignited with faith. They were so encouraged and immediately followed suit. The other three men were raised from the dead too. Then I was transported to another state to raise a woman from the dead in the same manner.

Leaders are to demonstrate and teach so the Body can learn to do the works of Christ. Jesus is looking for a place to lay his head. The Body of Christ must arise so his head will have a resting place. I am learning about resurrection power through the dreams God has been giving me. Resurrection power operates the best outside the four walls of the Church. Paul went down to the street to resurrect Eutychus from the dead.

> *There were many lamps in the upper room where we were gathered together. And there was a young man named Eutychus sitting on the window sill, sinking into a deep sleep; and as Paul kept on talking, he was overcome by sleep and fell down from the third floor and was picked up dead. But Paul went down and fell upon him, and after embracing him, he said, 'Do not be troubled, for his life is in him.' (Acts 20:8—10 NKJV)*

Paul left the safety of the four walls of the Church. He went into the streets to embrace the broken and the dead. He released resurrection power and brought Eutychus back to life. We are called to do the same. *Matthew 10:8* says, *"Heal the sick, raise the dead, cleanse the lepers, cast out demons. Freely you received, freely give."* When Paul stepped outside the walls of the Church, resurrection power was released. During this time of transitioning into the resurrection power, God is calling believers to pray as never before. We are to seek his face while he may be found. It is time to seek the Lord for increase.

> *Seek the Lord and His strength; seek His face continually. Remember His wonders which He has done, His marvels and the judgments uttered by His mouth. (Psalm 105:4—5 NKJV)*

A Plentiful Harvest: Gifts and Fruits

Sow for yourselves righteousness; Reap in mercy; Break up your fallow ground, For it is time to seek the Lord, Till He comes and rains righteousness on you. (Hosea 10:12 NKJV)

His rain will bring forth a plentiful harvest. This speaks of continuing to seek the Lord until breakthrough is obtained. *Isaiah 55:6* further exhorts us to *seek the Lord while he may be found and to call upon him while he is near.* Our dreams enable us to enter the presence of the Lord to access his powerful plans. A clear, clean conscience will bring forth a new level of boldness, and power to enter his presence.

I thank God, whom I serve with a clear conscience the way my forefathers did, as I constantly remember you in my prayers night and day. (2 Timothy 1:3 NASU)

We are told in *1 John 3:21–22 Beloved, if our heart does not condemn us, we have confidence toward God. And whatever we ask we receive from Him, because we keep His commandments and do those things that are pleasing in His sight."* As long as we are asking in the name and character of our Lord it shall be done for us.

Chapter Fourteen
Dream Teams in the Community

As we have seen throughout this book, God speaks to us through dreams to address many issues in our lives to bring us to greater maturity both in the soul (mind, will, and emotions) and in the spirit (wisdom, communion, and conscience). God's parabolic language communicated through dreams is right in line with the ways he has spoken to people throughout Scripture. Today, we believe God is pouring out his spirit on all flesh as Joel 2:28 states. We live in a time when Scripture says we will dream dreams, see visions and prophesy as God pours out his Spirit upon us. In response to God's calling to us through dreams that bring us closer to him, the church must adopt relevant methods of helping the world. The body of Christ has been given the ability to understand the parables God has hidden in the dreams we dream.

The church must get involved to help bring proper discernment to this means of foretold communication between God and man as prophesied for the last days. Accordingly, this chapter outlines basic guidelines and the structure necessary to implement dream interpretation teams in the church and community. Dream teams are a needed asset to bring relevance to the messages God wants to convey both to believers and non-believers about what he is doing in our lives and in the world around us. We need to understand that surviving and thriving in today's volatile world will continue to demand heightened sensitivity to the Holy Spirit. In other words, the church must lead the charge to help the world discern and learn to be fed by every word that proceeds out of the mouth of the Father in the midst of the increasing turmoil we face.

Guidelines for Dream Interpretation

1 Corinthians 14:12 "Since you are zealous for spiritual gifts, let it be for the edification of the church that you seek to excel."

When flowing in the love of Jesus, the revelatory gifts are powerful transforming tools in which believers can assist people in the church and the local community. Humble service in this way edifies and encourages love and transformation within the entire society. Synergy is imparted and true spirituality is stirred within our hearts as gifts are allowed to flow in the place of worship and more importantly in the community.

We know that prophecy is the testimony of Jesus. He continues to speak to people through dreams and visions. As the Spirit of Revelation reveals secrets and mysteries through dreams, we can use our prophetic gifts and discernment in the community to interpret dreams and visions so that understanding can be obtained. *"Worship God! For the testimony of Jesus is the spirit of prophecy" (Revelation 19:10d)*. Dreams that are not interpreted remain an obscure, sealed mystery.

Love is an essential ingredient for everyone who desires to flow in prophetic dream interpretation.

1 Corinthians 13:2 "And though I have the gift of prophecy, and understand all mysteries and all knowledge, and though I have all faith, so that I could remove mountains, but have not love, I am nothing."

Another important principle to remember is that those who desire to develop their art of dream interpretation must do so according to their level of skill, practice, and faith.

Romans 12:6 "Having then gifts differing according to the grace that is given to us, let us use them: if prophecy, let us prophesy in proportion to our faith."

We must consistently interpret dreams with compassion, encouragement, humility, and grace. We must give hope and spiritual insight to the dreamer enabling them to find their God-given destiny.

Isaiah 42:1–3 "Behold! My Servant whom I uphold, My Elect One in whom My soul delights! I have put My Spirit upon Him; He will bring forth justice to the Gentiles. He will not cry out, nor raise His voice, nor cause His voice to be heard in the street. A bruised reed He will not break, and smoking flax He will not quench; He will bring forth justice for truth."

When we practice the art of dream interpretation in any setting we should be aware of our level of skill, gifting, and we should know who is in authority. We should also make sure that we have the agreement and oversight of the senior leadership of the organization and recognize their authority before attempting to serve.

"We, however, will not boast beyond measure, but within the limits of the sphere which God appointed us—a sphere which especially includes you" (2 Corinthians 10:13).

Ways to Improve Dream Interpretation Skills

- Study the biblical parables and their interpretations.

- Study multitudes of dream symbols, colors, and numbers from a biblical perspective.

- Study the dreams and visions in the Bible.

- Maintain a consistent prayer life and stay tuned into the voice of the Holy Spirit.

- Maintain a dream journal and prayerfully consider each dream to discern the source of the dream and extract God's purpose in allowing the dream to surface.

- Practice interpreting dreams at every opportunity.

Establishing Dream Interpretation Teams

The leadership of the organization, church, or community should choose the appropriate coordinator for the dream interpretation teams.

- This person should exhibit spiritual maturity and authority, godly character, as well as leadership, integrity, and organizational skills.

- This person will be responsible for upholding the highest standards of service and communicating with team members and leadership.

- The dream team leader should be able to teach or coordinate continued training and instruction sessions.

- The leader should be able to interact with the business community and to schedule dream encounters for the teams in the marketplace.

- Dream teams should be composed of members with a variety of spiritual gifts and abilities. Those with the gifts of prophecy, healing, intercession, and the discerning of spirits make a great combination. A mixture of gifts allows the team to move in any direction as the Spirit leads.

Specific roles for dream interpretation team participants are necessary. More than one of the positions outlined below may be occupied by the same person depending upon the availability of the individuals.

Overseer

This is the person who administrates, manages, leads, organizes, coordinates, casts the vision, and directs all team leaders, team members, and dream encounter events. The overseer is responsible for answering procedural questions and adjusting team functions. Any problems, disruptions, debates or disorderly manifestations should be directed to the overseer's attention. The overseer should be mature in their spiritual gifts and people skills.

Team leader

The team leader is the person responsible for leading and maintaining the order and unity of a specific dream team. This person reports to the overseer. The team leader begins on time by opening the session with prayer and ending with prayer. The leader will notify the greeter or host when the team is ready to interpret for the next person. If no greeter is available, the leader should either assign a team member to greet the next person in line or introduce the next person in line to the dream team. The leader should assign a team member to help maintain a seven to ten minute interpreting session. The team leader's responsibility is to keep members focused and ensure they stay within the proper guidelines. Leaders must be able to teach, redirect, steward, and correct team members gently with dignity and respect. Leaders should also help members of their team by encouraging them with ideas on how to communicate with love and effectiveness.

Team member

A team member is an individual who reports to the team leader and follows the leader's instructions as part of the dream team. Each team member is responsible to arrive on time, spend time in prayer prior to each session and arrive with a ready attitude. Team members should have revelatory gifts and be able to discern God's voice clearly for themselves and others.

Intercessor

Intercessors and those who are gifted in prayer are an invaluable part of every outreach event. These individuals who watch and pray before and during dream sessions, and they continue to pray for specific needs as God directs.

Greeter or Host

The greeter or host will be the individuals with gifts of hospitality, friendly extroverts who are "people persons." They love to meet new people, express warmth and put people at ease. They will introduce the person seeking help with a dream to the team members. The host is responsible to greet the public, monitor the teams, and escort the next person to the awaiting team. The greeter explains the process so that the recipient can anticipate what will happen during the dream encounter.

Attendant/Guardian/Watcher

The attendant is the warm friendly individual who can gently but firmly intervene so that the team can complete the dream encounter within the given time-frame.

Recipient

The recipient refers to the individual who is having their dream interpreted.

After proper introductions, ask the recipient whether or not they have experienced revelatory or dream interpretation before. Explain that, "those on the team are not prophets or psychics," but will be operating under the guidelines of comfort, edification, exhortation, and encouragement to give the dreamer hope. Ask the recipient to share their dream from memory, without reading it. Team members may need to ask a few questions for clarification. The team members will tell the leader the pieces of interpretation they receive from the Holy Spirit. The team leader will determine the focus and essence of the dream's meaning. The team leader will compose a short, three sentence interpretation for the recipient. Request that all questions be held until the end of the encounter session. Answer questions with a brief explanation but avoid arguing about differences in personal beliefs. End with a brief blessing and prayer. Thank the recipient for coming. Hand the recipient their personal dream interpretation recording and evaluation form for feedback.

Team Dynamics

1. Build teams with at least two or three people; one will function as the leader.

2. Record all encounter sessions. Recording the interpretation time will insure protection for both parties. Recording also enables the recipient to write out the dream's interpretation for prayer and contemplation. Familiarize team members with the operational procedures of recording equipment.

3. Arrive early for instruction and prayer to prepare for hearing God clearly during the dream encounter time.

4. Dress should be modest, and appropriate for the setting.

5. Team members should be well groomed; breath mints should be used to ensure clean breath. If using perfume or cologne, very little should be used.

6. Each team member should bring a notepad to take notes while others are talking so that when it is his or her turn to deliver impressions and his or her interpretation to the team leader, recalling what the Holy Spirit has communicated will be easy.

7. Develop an evaluation, feedback, or comment form that will indicate the level of accuracy and impact the recipient experienced. This feedback will provide accountability for those interpreting. It will also flag any problem areas that may arise.

8. Team members and leaders should not counsel, teach, or give advice. Only the interpretation or impressions the Holy Spirit imparts to them should be shared.

9. Speak clearly using concise words and sentences.

10. Too much rambling, embellishing, exaggerating, or using redundancy is not helpful in most situations.

11. Team members and leaders should be willing to take risks by allowing the Holy Spirit to stretch them past their comfort zone or present level of faith.

12. Function as a team by supporting and preferring each other. Allow each team member the opportunity for a clarifying question and to deliver the part they have received to the leader.

13. The interpretation of the dream should be delivered with compassion, love, mercy and grace. This is not a time to expose sin, shortcomings, or to point out faults. The Holy Spirit is the one who convicts of sin. The recipient already knows their sins, weaknesses, and faults. Speak the unknown to bring encouragement to the forefront.

14. Team members should always impart faith, hope, and restoration. Form a positive response to negate the power of negative or harmful dreams, by prophesying life and blessings.

15. Use normal voice, tone and inflection.

16. Stay away from "King James English" and phrases such as "Thus saith the Lord."

17. Learn from mistakes, take correction from the team leader graciously with an open heart to learn and improve. Don't allow correction or redirection to cause discouragement or defeat.

18. Be respectful of teammates when they are speaking.

19. Volume does not indicate a greater understanding or knowledge; just speak the word with authority.

20. Preface the interpretation with "This dream is about (you, your friend, husband, boss, etc.) "I feel," "the impression I am receiving," "the picture I saw for you is," "I am sensing," "I am hearing," or "I think the dream indicates," "The essence of the message this dream is communicating is … "

21. Avoid giving an interpretation and then saying, "No, I can't tell you that," or "I have received more but I am not at liberty to share it with you now." The recipient may feel teased or provoked by these types of statements.

22. Avoid gaining insights through the natural knowledge of facts and events. In other words, don't ask casual questions that

may reveal things about the person that could influence your interpretation for them.

23. Stay away from speaking into major life changing situations such as: who to marry or date, changes in geography, employment, pregnancy and/or financial gifts or investments.

24. Ask couples if they are married, engaged, or dating and relate to them accordingly. Do not confirm engagements or dating relationships.

25. Be genuine and enjoy your time. You are an asset to the team. Ask the Holy Spirit for his peace, presence, and clarity of insight.

26. If an interpretation or impression for the recipient is not received or is not clear, don't make something up.

27. Choose words that edify, bring comfort, and provide an expectant hope for favor and success when interpreting the dream or vision of the recipient.

28. Avoid getting into political, religious, or cultural debates and discussions. Stick to dream interpretation and how it relates to the issue of having a relationship with a loving God.

Other Helpful Guidelines

Do not interpret alone or pull someone from another team. Direct the individual to an intact team.

Team members and leaders should be aware of their spiritual condition. There are times when team members may speak out of their own opinions and needs or to another's need rather than speaking the Father's heart. We need to learn to set personal issues and agendas aside so we can hear and speak only what God says: "lay aside every weight that so easily besets us and go on with the race God has set before us and lift up the name of Jesus" and draw all others to Him!

Spiritual adversity or confrontations are to be expected during our lives. In order to prepare for dream encounters, be prayed up and live a lifestyle of daily repentance and forgiveness. Remember, our level of spiritual authority is contingent upon our level of intimacy with and obedience to God.

Honor the time restraints. We want to serve and interpret as many dreams as possible with a spirit of excellence. The Holy Spirit can do a "quick work." Jesus used few words but a lot of love. One dream interpretation or prophetic word can begin an awesome work of God. This isn't a one time chance touch for them. God also desires to have a "one on one" with them. We hope their dream encounter will point them to HIM.

In lifting up the name of Jesus and loving God, it is more often our lifestyle of love, peace, and his presence that speaks louder than our words.

We're all in the process of becoming more like Jesus. God uses us, continues working within us, and keeps on changing us all at the same time! God desires to use us to love others—the second greatest commandment after loving him. Greater is he who is in us than he who is in the world. We may be the only Jesus others will ever see! Be thankful and humble for this honor to be used of God.

In conclusion, dreams are not the weird, chaotic menagerie of confusion and disjointed images you thought they were, but a mysterious message delivered to us by God in night parables. It is my hope and sincere desire that the revelation you received from reading *Dream Encounters, Seeing Your Destiny from God's Perspective* will have brought you to a new plateau of understanding. Instead of being baffled and ignoring a message from the Father, you now have the tools and wherewithal to begin to interpret your own and others' dreams. This ability will cause you to prosper and to find the narrow path of destiny God is communicating to you in the night, while you sleep. The best part is now ahead.

Sweet dreams of destiny!

MyOnar is the premiere interactive Web site that offers you access to superlative mature dream interpreters who have dedicated their lives to helping you understand the symbolic spiritual language of your dreams and visions. Our highly trained, skilled, and uniquely gifted dream coaches will help you grasp the spiritual messages in your dreams. These distinctively gifted individuals have successfully interpreted thousands of dreams for people from every walk of life, all over the world using an ancient Hebraic method. Their spiritual insights and exceptional revelatory perceptions will unlock the hidden mysteries that are concealed in the dreams you encounter during the night season.

MyOnar also offers you the opportunity to develop your own ability to hear God's voice and to ignite your dream interpretation skills. You have the freedom to determine the levels and degree of involvement, skill development, and training you would like to pursue.

MyOnar's Web store offers a large variety of resources. These various training manuals, teaching CDs, DVDs, and dream symbol cards will enable you to successfully navigate your dream journey. MyOnar will help you discover God's answers to some of the most important questions of life. Our many resources and dream symbol cards will help you in your quest to find your purpose in life, your special gifts, your destiny calling, and the plans the Creator has written on your spiritual DNA within your soul—the essence of who you are.

Through MyOnar's online dream coaching services you will learn valuable techniques from a vast well of experience and expertise. This dream site offers a variety of confidential, personal, and group training sessions through MyOnar's Web-cast. Our hope is that you will decide to enroll in MyOnar's online dream training course as the next step in becoming a gifted dream interpreter yourself.

Dream mapping is a revelatory technique that Barbie has developed and mastered through her many years of dream counseling. Dream mapping helps the dreamer discover their God-given purpose, calling, and destiny. You, the dreamer, may choose any number of your dreams to submit to your personal dream coach. These dreams will be analyzed, prayed over, and interpreted. Insights received will help you to determine what Holy Spirit is uniquely communicating to you personally. Dream mapping reveals God-given gifts, talents, strengths, and abilities, and it uncovers areas of weakness that may need development. Through dream mapping, your dream coach will help you to see yourself in a new, empowering light.

When you sign up, you will receive a free online dream journal as our gift. You always have full access to your entire dream journal and its interpretations.

"A dream is a sealed mystery waiting to be revealed."

Barbie Breathitt Enterprises is excited that so many people in God's Kingdom are exploring the understanding of dreams. We've opened an interactive Web site called MyOnar.com, impacting dreamers all over the world. Onar means "dream" in the Greek language and the book of Matthew records five unique onars (dreams). We believe it is vitally important to record God-given dreams and to search out the messages they contain. Sign up for your free online dream journal at www.MyOnar.com. From the dream journal, you can easily submit your dreams for interpretation by our superlative dream interpreters.

"Dream Encounters—Seeing Your Destiny from God's Perspective," is the "Rosetta Stone" to interpreting the illusive vapors of dreams. Uniquely inspired, and written to convince the greatest skeptics, and educate the most ardent believer, "Dream Encounters" will bring God's perspective, and understanding to the symbolic, visual, love letters, in the mysterious world of dreams. Take a journey into the sub–conscious night parables of the soul, to learn how dream truths impact your world; give direction, purpose, and destiny. Gain valuable keys to success by unlocking the mysteries of your dreams. Available as a paperback book, digital book or audio book.

The Encounter Series, a wonderful series of messages on CD's, mp3's and DVD's, is about learning, impartation, activation and encountering the realm of the Spirit where you will learn to do the work of the ministry. Our encounter training manuals and spiritual activities are designed to help you build confidence to go out and do the works of the kingdom, fulfilling your destiny and call.

The Dream Encounter CD and Manual is designed to teach, train, activate, and impart the skills to interpret and understand how God communicates to us through dreams and visions of the night. Jesus continues to teach through night parables, in other words, inspired dreams. The Bible gives us three keys that will be used in the end-time revival and outpouring of the Holy Spirit. The course topics include: Dreams, Visions, Transportations, Translations, Lucid Dreams, Colors, Numbers, Dream Symbols, Dream Interpretation, and Dream Teams and Outreaches.

The Dream Encounter Workshop 5 DVD Series Watch Barbie as she shares about God's dream language. She shows you valuable techniques to diagram your dreams, and how to follow the Holy Spirit's lead as he unlocks the secrets that reveal their hidden meanings.

Colorado Dream Encounter Workshop 10 DVD Series Topics include: Realm of the Spirit, Dream Resources and Tools, Introduction to Dreams, Biblical Foundations of Dreams, Dream Diagramming Techniques, Hindrances to Dreams, Recurring Dreams, Night Mares, Dreams & Visions, Sources and Types of Dreams, Recording and Interpreting Dreams, Impartation Prayer, Four Phases of Sleep, Purposes of Spiritual Dreams, God's Colors of Light, Power of Words, Creating Symbol Dreams, Visual Illusions, God's Symbols, Can You Read This?, and God's Numbers in Dreams.

The Revelatory Encounter CD and Manual is a prophetic course designed to teach, train, activate, and impart the ability to hear God's voice for yourself and others. This training helps you recognize and remove hindrances to hearing God's still, small voice. The course topics include: Developing Godly Character and Integrity, Old and New Testament Prophets, False Prophets, Immature Prophets, God's Friends, Knowing God's Voice, Difference between the Gift of Prophecy and the Prophetic Office, Forms of Revelation, Four Categories of Prophecy, Spirit of Prophecy, Nine Gifts of the Holy Spirit, Interpretation, Application, The Seer, The Watchmen, Intercession, Prayer, Intimacy, Spiritual Authority, and Developing Prophetic Ministry Teams.

The Angelic Encounter CD and Manual is a course that establishes a biblical foundation for the proof and ministry of angels. Topics include: What are Angels? Ministry of Angels; Types, Functions, and Characteristics of Angels; Satan and Fallen Angels; and Angels and the Death of the Saints. Barbie shares personal experiences of angelic visitations from her life.

The Kingdom Encounter 12 CD Series includes The Cycle of Life, Inheriting the Kingdom of God I and II, The Power of Peace, Entering into Rest, It's Time for a Suddenly in Your Life, It's Raining, Pure Heart, Pure Light, Ezekiel's River and Wheels, Dressed for Success, Clothed in God's Light, The Kingdom Power of Change, God's Colors and Light.

Dream Symbol Cards These artistically designed dream symbol cards enable the dreamer to tap into the hidden meanings of the symbols that appear in many dreams and visions. These cards are also useful in helping the believer decipher the symbolic language that God uses to communicate through the revelatory realm of the Spirit. *"God is speaking powerfully through dreams in this hour. So many believers are having significant dreams but do not always understand the significance of the symbols within them. Barbie Breathitt has done a marvelous job of preparing dream cards as a tremendous tool to help this process. They are very high quality and fully laminated for long-term use. I was impressed when I saw them."* Patricia King Extreme Prophetic www.extremeprophetic.com

Acquire all of Barbie's Dream Encounter Symbols Cards. They are available as single dream cards, in an excel spreadsheet or in spiral-bound collections.
- Volume I has the original 23 dream symbol cards.
- Volume II has 18 different dream symbol cards.
- Volume III has an additional 29 spiral bound dream symbol cards.
- Dream Sexology has 4 unique and informative dream symbol cards that explain the meanings of your intimate symbolic dream language.

 Healing Card is a reference card that matches illnesses and diseases with possible spiritual root causes. This Healing card is birthed from Barbie's ministry experiences and encounters of seasoned intercessors and those in healing ministries. Great for intercessors who need clear direction for their healing prayers.

 **Waking Words of Ancient Wisdom** Make it a practice to notice the time on the digital clock as you awaken from a spiritually significant dream. The numbers displayed on the digital clock are often keys to help understand the message God is giving you in your dreams. Note the time on your clock, then look up the corresponding chapter and verse in the Bible. Allow the Holy Spirit to quicken the intended "Waking Words of Ancient Wisdom" to your heart and apply them in your life. This is a wonderful way to daily explore the Bible while you seek the deeper meanings of the treasures God is revealing to you through your dreams. Visit www.BarbieBreathitt.com to obtain detailed directions for use.

"So You Want to Change the World?" is a compilation of twelve authors' perspectives on how you can make a positive difference in your world. Some key themes include: Doing the same things and expecting change. Church-as-usual isn't working. God can do amazing things with humble, broken vessels. The Secret Place is the key to hearing Heaven's heartbeat and bringing God's will to earth. Change can come through miracles, worship, and intercession. The essays reflect a variety of inspiring and exciting thought. You are encouraged and will be motivated to think and act beyond your normal routine and traditions--stretching yourself for the sake of bettering your world for His glory.

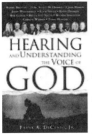

"Hearing and Understanding the Voice of God" Nine gifted and God-loving authors share their personal experiences on topics ranging from supernatural and out-of-body experiences in the third heaven to prophecy and discernment. You will quickly realize through reading these thrilling stories that hearing God happens in many different ways, and you can learn how you can tune in to Him yourself. Incredible things happen when you listen for God's voice—and when you ignore His promptings. Powerful and compelling stories challenge you into a deeper understanding about how to truly communicate with God.

For these products and additional resources by Barbie L. Breathitt please visit www.BarbieBreathitt.com, www.MyOnar.com, www.BreathoftheSpiritMinistries.com or www.BarbieBreathittEnterprises.com or call 972-253-6653. Barbie Breathitt Enterprises, L.L.C., P. O. Box 822044 North Richland Hills, Texas 76182-2044.